Performing 1
Masculinity

Crossroads in Qualitative Inquiry

Series Editors
Norman K. Denzin, University of Illinois, Urbana-Champaign
Yvonna S. Lincoln, Texas A&M University

ABOUT THE SERIES

Qualitative methods are material and interpretive practices. They do not stand outside politics and cultural criticism. This spirit of critically imagining and pursuing a more democratic society has been a guiding feature of qualitative inquiry from the very beginning. The Crossroads in Qualitative Inquiry series will take up such methodological and moral issues as the local and the global, text and context, voice, writing for the other, and the presence of the author in the text. The Crossroads series understands that the discourses of a critical, moral methodology are basic to any effort to re-engage the promise of the social sciences for democracy in the twenty-first century. This international series creates a space for the exploration of new representational forms and new critical, cultural studies.

SUBMITTING MANUSCRIPTS

Book proposals should be sent to Crossroads in Qualitative Inquiry Series, c/o Norman K. Denzin, Institute for Communication Studies, 810 S. Wright Street, University of Illinois, Champaign, IL 61820, or emailed to n-denzin @uiuc.edu.

BOOKS IN THIS SERIES

Incarceration Nation: Investigative Prison Poems of Hope and Terror, by Stephen John Hartnett (2003)

9/11 in American Culture, edited by Norman K. Denzin and Yvonna S. Lincoln (2003)

Turning Points in Qualitative Research: Tying Knots in the Handkerchief, edited by Yvonna S. Lincoln and Norman K. Denzin (2003)

Uprising of Hope: Sharing the Zapatista Journey to Alternative Development, Duncan Earle and Jeanne Simonelli (2005)

Ethnodrama: An Anthology of Reality Theatre, edited by Johnny Saldaña (2005)

Contempt of Court: A Scholar's Battle for Free Speech from Behind Bars, by Rik Scarce (2005)

The Pull of the Earth: Participatory Ethnography in the School Garden, by Laurie Thorp (2005)

Writing in the San/d: Autoethnography among Indigenous Southern Africans, edited by Keyan G. Tomaselli (2005)

Performing Black Masculinity: Race, Culture, and Queer Identity, by Bryant Alexander (2006)

Pursuing Hollywood, by Nathaniel Kohn (2006)

Performing Black Masculinity

Race, Culture, and Queer Identity

BRYANT KEITH ALEXANDER

ALTAMIRA
PRESS

A Division of
ROWMAN & LITTLEFIELD PUBLISHERS, INC.
Lanham • New York • Toronto • Plymouth, UK

ALTAMIRA PRESS

A Division of Rowman & Littlefield Publishers, Inc.
A wholly owned subsidary of The Rowman & Littlefield Publishing Group, Inc.
4501 Forbes Boulevard, Suite 200
Lanham, MD 20706
www.altamirapress.com

Estover Road, Plymouth PL6 7PY, United Kingdom

We thank Sage Publications for the right to republish the following essays in extended and
modified forms:
B. K. Alexander. 2003. "Revisioning the ethnographic site: Interpretive ethnography as a method
of pedagogical reflexivity and scholarly production." *Qualitative Inquiry* 9, no. 3:416–41.
B. K. Alexander. 2003. "Fading, twisting, and weaving: An interpretive ethnography of the black
barbershop as cultural space." *Qualitative Inquiry* 9, no. 1:101–28.
B. K. Alexander. 2004. "Passing, cultural performance, and individual agency: Performative
reflections on black masculine identity." *Cultural Studies ↔ Critical Methodologies* 4, no.
3:377–404.

British Library Cataloguing in Publication Information Available

Library of Congress Cataloging-in-Publication Data

Alexander, Bryant Keith, 1963–
    Performing Black masculinity : race, culture, and queer identity / Bryant Keith Alexander.
        p. cm.—(Crossroads in qualitative inquiry)
    Includes bibliographical references and index.
    ISBN-13: 978-0-7591-0928-5 (cloth : alk. paper)
    ISBN-10: 0-7591-0928-1 (cloth : alk. paper)
    ISBN-13: 978-0-7591-0929-2 (pbk. : alk. paper)
    ISBN-10: 0-7591-0929-X (pbk. : alk. paper)
    1. African American men—Social conditions.   2. African American men—
Intellectual life.   3. African Americans—Race identity.   4. Gay men—United
States—Identity.   5. Gender identity—United States.   6. Performance.   7.   Critical
pedagogy.   8. Alexander, Bryant Keith, 1963–   I. Title.   II. Series.
E185.86 .A3794   2006
305.38′896073—dc22

                                                                                        2006006127

Printed in the United States of America

∞ ™ The paper used in this publication meets the minimum requirements of American
National Standard for Information Sciences—Permanence of Paper for Printed Library
Materials, ANSI/NISO Z39.48-1992.

In honor of my parents Joseph Junius Alexander Sr. and Velma Ray Bell Alexander. I stand in your absent presence; loving you, still.

Your boy,
Keith

Contents

Acknowledgments

My consistent friend and colleague Judith Hamera, who has offered me a template of personal, professional, and academic sociality that has supported me in ways that have been both personal and professional. Thank you for your care and immense generosity.

Elyse Lamm Pineau, my teacher and friend, whose work continues to offer me insight, direction, and challenge.

D. Soyini Madison, your brilliance establishes high standards for us all.

Participants at the 2004 Summer Institute sponsored by The Center for Global Culture and Communication at Northwestern University hosted and organized by E. Patrick Johnson. The theme of the summer institute was "Transnational Flows of Performance: Identity in the Age of Globalization." My participation prompted the first construction of what currently appears as chapter 1 in this book. I also want to thank the brilliant scholars who attended that conference and offered me critical critique and commentary as well as their overall meaningful contribution to the occasion (Margaret Drewal, Joni Jones, Mary Weismantel, Jill Lane, Jennifer Brody, Renee Alexander, Oyku Potuglu-Cook, Brian Edwards, Katherine Hoffman, Wenshu Lee, and others). I thank Wenshu Lee and Gust Yep for continued conversation and critical insight to my cultural experience in China.

Javon Johnson, Kenneth Lee, Richie Hao, Tina McDermott, Michael Kalustian, Josh Fleming, Tony Fitzgerald, and Heidi Mueller, who were all graduate students at Cal State L.A. I have had the pleasure of working with each and have been informed by their critical scholarship. In particular, I want to give special thanks to Javon Johnson, who served as my graduate research assistant on an American Communities Program Fellowship in the research leading to chapter 2. He is a brilliant performer and scholar with a bright future.

Joseph A. Bailey II, MD, for his generous contributions in developing the American Communities Program and the Joseph A. Bailey II Endowed Chair in American Communities at California State University, Los Angeles.

Carl M. Selkin, dean of the College of Arts and Letters for his continued trust, friendship, and support, along with Betsy Davenport, Flora Saavedra-Hernandez, Rob DeChaine, and Robert Martin.

Norman K. Denzin and Yvonna S. Lincoln, editors of the *Crossroads in Qualitative Inquiry* series for their trust and support of this project, Mitch Allen my initial editor at AltaMira Press for his generosity and care in helping to shape this project into being, and Rosalie Robertson my formal editor at AltaMira for helping to shepherd this project to completion; as well as Janice Braunstein, assistant managing editor, and Sylvia Cannizzaro for their consistent care.

Sage Press for permission to reprint the following essays that appear here in extended versions: "Revisioning the ethnographic site: Interpretive ethnography as a method of pedagogical reflexivity and scholarly production." *Qualitative Inquiry* 9.3 (2003): 416–441. "Fading, twisting and weaving: An interpretive ethnography of the black barbershop as cultural space." *Qualitative Inquiry* 9.1 (2003): 101–128. "Passing, cultural performance, and individual agency: Performative reflections on black masculine identity." *Cultural Studies ↔ Critical Methodologies* 4.3 (2004): 377–404.

Special thanks to Marty Wheeler at Brentwood-Benson Music and songwriter Kyle Matthews, for the use of the song lyrics from "We Fall Down." I was particularly thrilled when on Friday April 22, 2005, Kyle Matthews called me at work both to give personal permission to use the song, and to celebrate the manner in which the song lyrics are contextualized in my father's eulogy.

Larry Schnoor, Robert Welsh, Adonis Mohtar, Randy James, and especially to my brotherman D. Nebi Hillard—thank you for your faithful friendship. Thanks Nebi for keeping me as "real" as possible, and allowing me a space in a friendship that is as much about love as it is about intellectual play.

My biological sisters and brothers—Francina, Joseph Jr., Vincent, Kateri, and Daniel—thank you for your unconditional love, support, and respect.

Those faces looking through the window from across the street in Altadena—Debra Hammond, Michelle Hooper, Charles Henderson, and Victor Parker, thanks for helping me create a sense of family in Los Angeles.

And last but not least, to my partner, Patrick H. Bailey Jr., thank you for your consistent love, friendship, support, and the sense of security and home that we have built together. Your ever-present care informs and supports my work in ways too many to count. I value my life with you and our girls.

Introduction

Exploring Modalities and Subjectivities That Shape Social Relations

If it is true, as recent performance studies researchers have argued, that culture is a set of social and political boundaries that are marked and contested in performance, then we might ask what happens to culture when the performances people give are determined, in part, by the interpretive framework . . . [of others?]

—Michael Bowman, "Performing Southern History"

In many kinds of racially fraught cultural production—novels, cultural histories, and minstrel commentaries no less than antebellum blackface performance—minstrelsy has been a ground of American racial negotiation and contradiction, based on the antebellum collision course of competing modes of production and the various historical transformations in its aftermath. From this perspective certain representative critical engagements with the minstrel tradition turn out to be little less than furtive serial positions in a debate on American racial politics.

—Eric Lott, "Blackface and Blackness"

Can we begin then to honor the difficult, to recognize the tension, accepting the process of transformation with all of its messiness and loose ends so that we can push the conversation forward, making way for the masses of previously excluded voices[,] experiences, ways of knowing and being, and dreaming? The confessional narrative, or the insertion of the autobiographical in ethnography, is not a risk-free enterprise. Behar (1996) maintained that scholars

*"stretching the limits of objectivity" run the risk of exposing
themselves in an academy that continues to feel ambivalent about
observers who forsake the mantle of omniscience.*

—George Noblit et al., *Postcritical Ethnography*

*The contingency of the subject as agent is articulated in a double
dimension, a dramatic action. The signified is distanced; the
resulting time lag opens up the space between lexical and the
grammatical, between enunciation and enounced, in-between
spatial dimension, this distancing converts itself into the
temporality of the "throw" that iteratively (re)turns the subject as
a moment of conclusion and control: a historically or contextually
specific subject. How are we to think the control or conclusion in the
context of contingency?*

—Homi K. Bhabha, *The Location of Culture*

The particularity of the preceding epigraphs helps to establish the occasion
of this book. Combined they signal three core logics: First, the performative nature of culture and the materiality of bodies are most significant in
the company of those who value and recognize that repetition, as they
both revel in the familiar and critique cultural performance for authenticity and acceptability.[1] Second, the collision or juxtapositioning of differently racialized bodies in the process of social travel, everyday mobility,
and in the referential construction of "the other," initiates a reassessment
of the real on both sides of the border. The issue becomes who gets to tell
the story—why, how, and with what consequences? Third, identity politics
are not situated on the body, but serve as a constellation of resources in
the cultural negotiation of the ideal—in the form of nostalgia, remembrance, and remorse. For me, these logics begin to illuminate the challenges, conceits, and constraints of everyday ethnography—in which the
researcher and researched (the one talking and those talked about) are
held in stasis as vulnerable subjects and agents of curiosity and cultural
critique. Their encounter is a contested performance in which each rivals
for differing goals and objectives "endowed with variable amounts of economic, cultural, and symbolic capital to pursue their interests and secure
their aims" (Fuoss 1997, 175).[2]

Performing Black Masculinity is an assortment of ethnographic explorations on race culture, and queer identity. This book does not work toward understanding what constitutes a desired version of Black masculinity, as much as it works to explore the reflexive process of being a black man in diverse social and cultural contexts, with an emphasis on the performative aspects and expectations of being and knowing (Ghoussoub and Sinclair-Webb 2000, 13). More particularly these chapters display that the social worlds that individuals move in are filled with complex boundaries. These are boundaries between domestic sites and foreign locations in tourism that cause speculation on authenticity in the confrontation between self and the other. Boundaries between the competing cultural performances of campus and community (home and work), that always necessitate negotiations, as people must cross the borders constructed even in their own identity. Boundaries between the public and private, between social constructions of normative sexuality versus personal practice, and the ways in which these are always negotiated in terms of power and propriety—ricocheting between desire and social expectations of the normal. Boundaries between teachers and students that are consequently issues relevant to the politics that mediate pedagogy and notions of the personal in the classroom. These are also the boundaries of scholarly production that always expose researchers' human vulnerabilities in opposition to the always attempted yet seldom achieved stance of objective observer.

These are a series of vulnerable chapters that in content, form, and manner begin to tease at the contested aspects of social being and at research that focuses on the cultural lives of self and others. The subjectivities in these chapters are not vulnerable because they demand empathy or sympathy from the reader. They are vulnerable because they expose that which is always being concealed in scholarly research—that being the positionality of the writer, the biases that structure ethnographic perceptions, and the moral investments that must undergird qualitative methods and interpretive practices.[3] I echo D. Soyini Madison in her important book on critical ethnography that "this 'new' or postcritical ethnography is the move to contextualize our own positionality, thereby making it more accessible, transparent, and vulnerable to judgment and evaluation" (2005, 8). These chapters question self in relation to the socializing practices that define the borders and boundaries of cultural experiences. Experiences that, while localized to specific geographic and racialized terrains, also reveal culture and ethnographic practices that seek to describe culture as both partisan and plural; partisan as an intention to foreground a particular truth and plural in that the act of performing or describing culture always implicates multiple others.[4]

Culture is socialized practice that establishes the positionality from which we all operate in relation to others and, like context, culture also establishes the contingency of the subject as agent and the agent as subject. Culture as an interpretive framework can always be contested when it comes into contact with other competing frameworks. In the process and manner of using intimate details of my social life in a self-reflexively critical manner, I attempt to provide the reader with insights to others outside the specificity of my individual experience. This while always signaling my own critical process of sense making, a process that most often shines a sanitizing light on dark places of both cultural experience and ethnographic practice. As Judith Hamera (2005) tells me in *Opening Acts*, these chapters work against "the reductive conceptions of everyday life that ignore basic communication and cultural infrastructure: bodies in/and dialogue. Such conceptions ignore the social, historical and political realities that enable and constrain communication separating the process of producing culture from those of consuming it. And reductive, decontexualized approached to everyday life eliminate the researcher, who is an integral part of the communicative and cultural context of that life" (pp. 12–14).

The chapters in this book are grounded in the aesthetic and critical traditions of performance studies and cultural studies. As a disciplinary formation, performance studies places interest on the processes of dialogic engagement with one's own and others' aesthetic communication through the lens of enacted and embodied activity as intentional. This is inclusive of the nature of everyday human activity as performance and performative, as constructive and cooperative, as instrumental and instructive.[5] For me, if "performance" as a catchall term means enacted cultural behavior, then such behavior finds the destiny and density of its purpose in place and space, and in the ways in which variables like race, gender, and sexuality are seen as habitualities used to organize social meaning through and between bodies.

The chapters in this book are also undergirded by the sometimes (de)stabilizing forces of cultural studies. Lawrence Grossberg reminds me that "cultural studies is committed to contestation, both as a fact of reality (although not necessarily in every instant) and as a strategic practice in itself." He reminds us all that "cultural studies is radically contextual" and that it is the relationship and orientation between specific cultural practices, their historical antecedents, and the current contexts in which they manifest themselves that illuminates the very nature of cultural performative contestation (1993, 90). In this sense, contestation is approached as the tensiveness that exists in the negotiation of private identities that confront each other in social and public spaces, as well as the privatized ways in which we try to process the consequences of such encounters. These chapters joined together focus on contestation as the competing forces in everyday cultural experiences that signify the self-reifying practices that maintain social and cultural relations.[6] In particular, these chapters circulate around contested constructions of blackness, masculinity, and cultural encounter. The notion of "queer" is engaged as reference to my own gender identity, but also as a destabilizing political force that establishes categories of resistance to social constructions that link race and gender identity.

In many ways this book constitutes a critique of cultural performances—as they blend and bleed the borders between the practiced positionalities of race, sex, and gender in specific spaces of cultural practice and identity location. These chapters engage in an application of Grossberg's three constructions of culture in everyday social and cultural practices. Specifically, they explore the ways in which racial, sexual, and gender identities are always and already oriented to as *texts*, texts that illuminate issues of power and propriety. These are texts that establish specific sites of contestation that are not located in/on the body, but within the psyche of the social communities who assign meaning and value to bodies and lives. These are texts that can be written and rewritten based on desire, but not really made manifest in social beings, only in social actions and in the wake of history.

These chapters explore varying modalities and subjectivities that shape social relations; modalities as in the particularity of place, space, and social practices with subjectivities as the dense materiality of race, culture, sex, and gender that do symbolic and literal battle on the fields of everyday human engagement. These are sites where bodies confront other actualities and engage performative acts of intervention for survival and remem-

brance, for recuperation and enculturation, for celebration and commitment, and for commentary and critique of self and other. The chapters
speak to performance as critical method and through performance as epi-
steme, as a way of knowing and showing the nature of human experience.
Knowing of course, that the text and context of performance is always and
already imbricated in the production of culture, in "different forms of
sense making, within various settings, in societies incessantly marked by
change and conflict" (M. Green 1996, 126).

   Each chapter in this project engages analysis from a specifically personal perspective and experience with the desire to extrapolate meaning
forward and outward. The desire is to offer worth and value to and for
others. Which I believe to be the template of sociality that all performance
and scholarship does, or should do, if it is to mean anything outside of
the experience of the ones writing it.[7] The chapters use a form of reflexivity that is not designed to reflect solely on my life, or to reductively and
romantically reveal my feelings and experiences. The chapters engage critical reflexivity as an act of knowing the self–knowing the self and how that
process of self-knowing and the results of such a process is always implicated by our relationship to others. Critical reflexivity as I am approaching
it is not a method of confusing experience with representation of that
experience.[8] It is a method that establishes a conscious level of knowing,
of reflecting and critiquing experience, and our own levels of complicity
both in the process of reflection (in/on the objects/places/spaces of reflection) and the ways in which we make sense of that reflection in public
discourse. In others words, I approach the act of writing as a contested
performance unto itself. It is an act of critical reflexivity in which I do not
divorce the experience of articulating ideas and critiquing experience from
the actuality of that experience.

   Critical reflexivity as a method is both a demonstration and a call for a
greater sense of implicating and complicating how we are always and
already complicit in the scholarly productions of our labor, and the effects
of our positions and positionalities within the diverse communities in
which we circulate. Critical reflexivity becomes especially important when
we cross cultural borders; when we enter other realms of experience that
call us to attend to the tracks that led us to that particular place, what our
presence tracks over, and what we track into other people's sacred territories. Whether under the guise of ethnography or the more blatant venue of

tourism, reflexivity makes us accountable for our positions (Haraway 1988). In this sense, critical reflexivity, like the many experimental and methodological forms that engage it (e.g., autoperformances such as auto- biography, autoethnography, and the personal narrative, as well as inter- pretive ethnography, reflexive ethnography, critical ethnography, postcrit- ical ethnography, and emotional sociology, to name but a few), takes up what are moral issues.

These are the moral issues of dealing with localized knowledge and with how it fits into and with global experience, while implicating cultural oth- ers. These are the moral and ethical issues of acknowledging that the rep- resentation of others is always a complicated and contentious undertak- ing.[9] The moral issues of how the nature of human experience deals both with text (who we are) and context (the specific and general conditions of/for living). These are the moral issues of avoiding egoism and promot- ing cultural knowledge as a mechanism for generating critical reflexive processes in/for audiences. And the moral issues of dealing with voice as an individual practice of desire and how voice always echoes communities and cultures of thought.

Critical reflexivity recognizes the necessity of negotiating the tensions in writing for the self, for the other, and for the self as other. In the proc- ess, the act of being critically reflexive recognizes the necessity to recog- nize, to be conscious of being conscious of what we write and how we write; this is a moral act. It acknowledges research, writing, and publishing as forms of political engagement that demand a clear sense of where we stand in relation to others, as well as the complications and implications of our actions.[10] I find that, within these chapters, my attempt to contrib- ute to the discourses of performance studies and the critique in cultural studies is only secondary to my primary interest of teasing through my own personal and political concerns. Which I believe always and already marks the impulse of most writing characterized as "scholarship." So within these chapters I often take myself to task for making facile reduc- tions of cultural practices or my own reactionary move in the moment of intercultural/interracial contact. I place myself as foil, less in some self- deprecating/self-hating manner than to engage in and model a critical reflexivity that I think must guide all scholarship dealing with race and culture. Both before it hits the page and in the process of writing ourselves into the text.

All the chapters in this book are framed with and through an autoethnographic lens. I employ the category of autoethnography as a centralizing methodology not just as a focus on individual and personal experience, but also as a point of entry to larger constructions of cultural experience and practice. I engage autoethnography in the double sense of the term, as does Deborah Reed-Danahay, referring both to the ethnography of personal cultural experience and to autobiographical writing that has ethnographic interests (1997, 2). Thus, autoethnography is an articulation based on the determinate memory and recall of experience via the lens of the traumatically constrained ideology that undergirds cultural encounters, but autoethnography is also a particular stratagem to describe the continuing racialization of politics in ethnographic and intercultural research. I find that, like Kenneth Mostern, I am always reflecting on why autobiography and autoethnography has been central to my work and to most African American political speech.

In these chapters, I write about cultural performance through autoethnography because of autoethnography's peculiar ability to be both specific to individual experience and to implicate cultural others in the act of telling. Like Homi Bhabha's discussion of narrative in art, my interest in autoethnography is about "the discourse of self-disclosure, the production of subjects and the positioning of spectators," within both the moment of the telling and the specter of those whom history has silenced (1996, 10). Autoethnography and autobiography signal the strained ability and the necessary critical reflection that marginalized groups must engage to find and redefine our identities. This project always takes place in relation to the historical happenings that have left not only the residue scars of experience, but also foreshadows ongoing acts of violence that still dictate human social relations.

For me, autoethnography initiates a "deliberate intervention in shaping memory and remembrance" by foregrounding the specificity of voice, who is talking and why, with a certain level of accountability from that specific racial and gendered positionality (Nero 1992, xii). In these chapters autoethnography and autobiography are used to foreground the axis of subjectivity that always governs writing and ethnographic research. They foreground the "I" that serves as the engine of the research and the origin of articulation, like the "I" in the moment of the actual experience recalled in writing to project and revision self and society.[11] In this sense, ethnography as autobiographical out-law genre, like testimonial writing, requires radical revisions of notions of individual authorship and authenticity. For the subject of ethnographic writing to circulate in transnational culture as "author," essentialist mythologies of identity and authorship must be challenged and bracketed in favor of reading [and writing] strategies that acknowledge the complexities of power in the production of life writing. (Kaplan 1998, 211)

The six chapters that make up this book are situated in particular relational, physical, social, cultural, and racial contexts that cross borders of human experience. They are both separate and interrelated. Like the work of Maurice O. Wallace these chapters might be considered a series of "generative modes" of social travel and human engagement delving into the foreign and the all together familiar (2002, 5). In chapter 1, "Crossing Borders and Changing Customs," I use the occasion of a trip to China, within a larger critical commentary on travel tourism, to focus on what intercultural theorist Donal Carbaugh has described as asynchrony, to reference the interactional dynamics that produce a wide range of detrimental intercultural outcomes manifested as misinterpretations and misunderstandings of intent. Intercultural contact in the context of tourism displays a lack of coordination in moment-to-moment interactions—discrimination among classes of people, and negative stereotyping, among others—that often intervene and may in fact characterize the very nature of tourism. Especially transnational tourism where the obvious differences in bodily materiality and cultural practices might alienate self and other.

The chapter asks to what degree these factors and variables are always and already present in tourism, where the broader humanistic concerns of intercultural communication are intervened by consumerism and consumption. In many ways this chapter is my personal reckoning with the psychic dimensions of transnationalism, in that I begin to process my own complex and contested responses to intercultural encounters in which I am complicit.[12] Hence, drawing on logics advanced by Herbert Blau but deepened and applied in this chapter, I come to understand that the subtext of the spectacle in tourism (either the identified tourist or the objectified "native") is not an intrinsic quality of embodied presence, but is inherent in the moment of intercultural encounter. A moment that is specific to time and place, but also predetermined by the cultural heritage of each involved in the moment.[13] The subtext of the spectacle in this chapter is the contestation of cultural sense-making: the way logics of sense-making circulate in the casual cultural encounters of transnational tourism.

Chapter 2, "Placement and Displacement of Black Identity," extends the discussion about the implications of border crossing, but situates the movement in a more localized and domestic practice of crossing borders between cultural/community space and academic/educational space. This chapter is most interested in the issues of situated identity politics and the ways in which Black faculty, staff-administrators, and students articulate the performative shift and the experiential difference in place and space as they move from campus to community and back again. The chapter highlights the problematic of characterizing a collective community based either in racial distinction or some presumed professional and procedural protocols that might challenge the performative sense of an assumed cultural identity.

In the chapter the metaphorical construction of the university as the "ivory tower" characterizes the institution as a place that is seemingly sheltered from the practicalities of ordinary life, set apart from (and maybe above) the surrounding community. It is constructed as a space that might be distinguished by the production of White intellectual engagements—signaling issues of class and the particularity of cultural performances. The chapter then plays this construction against some presumed notion of its opposite in a *homeplace* of "the Black community." Yet an elemental result of such a buttressing of geocultural locales is to understand that there is no endemic notion of comfortable cultural spaces. Hence culture and communities are intrinsically contested terrains where the dynamism of daily interaction requires an ongoing negotiation of self in relation to rules that both regulate behavior, as well as requires the activation of personal agency toward the transformation of social and political practices. This awareness is made evident in the narratives of Black faculty, staff, and students who migrate and negotiate the cultural borders and performative mandates between home and the university.

Chapter 3, "Passing, Cultural Performance, and Individual Agency," advances the notion of *an integrative ethnography of performance* that envelops the critique of a performance as a part of the overall textual presentation of performance. In particular, the chapter explores issues related to the contested notion of Black masculine identity, cultural authenticity, and racial performativity concretized in the trope of "passing." Passing is a reference to crossing racial identity borders as well as intra/interracial issues of identity and authenticity. The chapter uses reference to Nella Larsen's pivotal novel as an artifact to address the social tensions in racialized embodiment and cultural encounter, but then moves the discussion to focus on the performative elements of race and racial expectations as specifically linked to sex and gender (Black maleness) and how that comes in conflict with its historical foil, White femaleness.

The chapter further complicates the notion of contesting and contestatory performance by illuminating and deconstructing the performative construct of "bad man" or "the mean Black man." "Bad man" becomes both a mythical social construct of Black masculine identity, as well as a constructed performance assumed by Black men as a performative strategy to affect a particular desire; both are places of entrapment. In this way, a core element of the chapter focuses on the contestation about cultural and performative intent, as I engage a performance about interracial contact, and then attempt to respond to the critiques of that performance, highlighting the ways in which performance—both in the aestheticized construct and performance in everyday life—is about practicing a particular sociocultural agency.

Chapter 4, "(Re)Visioning the Ethnographic Site," uses and advocates interpretive ethnography as a method of pedagogical reflexivity and scholarly production. In particular, it seeks to further a discussion of the classroom as a cultural site, which places the teacher as both participant and observer in the intense cultural negotiation of lived experience, curriculum, and the politics of education. Using the constructive metaphor of *pedagogy as drag*, the chapter discusses the notion of a Black male teacher engaging feminist pedagogy and the ways in which the construct of a "feminist pedagogy," embodied by a Black male teacher, challenges stereotypical notions of a reductive Black masculinity that comes under suspicion in the particularity of pedagogical performances. Like drag in the performance of gender, drag in pedagogy is about the spectacle of the teaching body and what we as teachers reveal and what we conceal in the classroom and why. To that extent, the chapter uses a series of reflective poetic excursions on the nature and experience of viewing and discussing the performance of drag in the classroom.

Chapter 5, "Fading, Twisting, and Weaving," addresses the notion of contesting performances in a racially homogeneous cultural site. The chapter explores the tensive notions of cultural practice that establish and compete against notions of community. The chapter looks at the Black barbershop and the Black hair-care salon as a cultural site for ethnographic exploration and description, but more specifically as a site of cultural practice, where doing hair is secondary to an active process of enculturation and cultural proliferation. Within the Black barbershop and salon, issues of sex and gender become intricately interwoven in the identity construction of both proprietors and patrons, illuminating ways in which contestation is elemental to/in notions of community and demonstrating that race is not always the only abiding signifier of membership.

Chapter 6, " 'Were/Are, Fort/Da': The Eulogy as Constitutive (Auto)biography," focuses on the eulogy—and the particular situation of traveling to deliver my father's eulogy—as a contested practice filled with conflicting feelings of renewal and remorse, and of mourning and celebration. The eulogy becomes an act of private thoughts shared in public spaces, as well as the telling of a personal relationship that attempts to represent the experiences of others. In the process, the chapter argues for the eulogy as a narrative ritual of building and rebuilding relationships in time. Within this chapter auto/biography is explored once again, but in the context of exploring the eulogy, auto/biography becomes the contested act of narrating the self in relation to the other.

Crossing Borders and Changing Customs

Moments When the Spectator Becomes the Spectacle

We don't understand Chinese gestures any more than Chinese sentences.
 —G. E. M. Anscombe and G. H. von Wright, *Zettel: Ludwig Wittgenstein*[1]

In a disciplinary regime, individualization is descending. Through surveillance, constant observation, all those subject to control are individualized. . . . Not only has power now introduced individuality into the field of observation, but power fixes that objective individuality in the field of writing. A vast, meticulous documentary apparatus becomes an essential component of the growth of power. . . . This accumulation of individual documentation of overall in a systematic ordering makes "possible the measurement of overall phenomena, the description of groups, the characterization of collective facts, the calculation of gaps between individuals, their distribution in a given population" (DP 190).[2]
 —H. Dreyfus and Paul Rabinow, *Michael Foucault: Beyond Structuralism and Hermeneutics*

Positionality is vital because it forces us to acknowledge our own power, privilege, and biases just as we denounce the power structures that surround our subjects. A concern for positionality is a reflexive ethnography; it is a turning back on ourselves. We turn

back on ourselves, we examine our intentions, our methods, and
our possible effects. We are accountable for our research paradigms,
our authority, and our moral responsibility relative to
representation and interpretation.
—D. Soyini Madison, *Critical Ethnography: Method, Ethics, and Performance*

At the end of most trips, seeking evidence of enjoyment and a sort of rating of cultural excursions, family and friends often ask returning travelers a series of questions: "Did you enjoy it?" "Did you like it?" and, maybe more importantly, "Would you ever go back again?" Each question surveys its own terrain of experience: Pleasure as an assessment of preference, taste as an appraisal of worth, and the choice to return as a personal validation of culture and cultural experience. So allow me to begin with a prologue to a story, a story about a trip. A story that later becomes a twisted tale of tourism and ethnographic research; a story of intercultural encounter and countercultural experience; a story of academic reporting as confessional tale and reflexive auto/ethnography as personal sensemaking on a terrain of cultural experience. This all leads to the answers to those important questions that ultimately drive tourism and desire questions that are grounded in contestation, curiosity, consumerism, and a confluence of cultures in which the ocular politics of looking—which links the powers to see, to search, and to seize, both in tourism and in ethnography—dictates the processes of knowing and experiencing the other.[3] In this chapter I use the construct of contestation to deploy a term that signals a relational dynamic. Contestation becomes a relational confrontation between self and other, self as other, and the ways in which, through tourism and ethnographic writing, the attempt to experience the other can become a process of dominating the other.[4]

In May 2004 I traveled with my partner to China. We accompanied the marching band of the University of Southern California (USC) on their invited performance tour of three major cities: Beijing, Xian, and Shanghai. My partner serves as an assistant dean of student life at USC and was on the trip serving as a liaison to the band. I was a tagalong, as he was when I was invited as a speaker/performer/adjudicator at the All Japan Student Performance Festival several years before.[5] But that experience is another story thread that will find its way into the fabric of this larger narrative. The core of this narrative is this: From the moment that I passed through customs in Beijing I was spectacle. Chinese people of all shapes and sizes—contained within a limited range of perceived variance—stared at me, pointed fingers at me, directed the attention of their children to me, and approached me to take pictures with them. "A rather large African American man with unusual hair" (dreadlocks), as a later Chinese informant described me, I was an oddity, if not a commodity that they visually consumed. Such a performance of culture was to mark every single public minute of my eight-day experience in China.

My experiences during that trip further ignited my speculations on tourism and moments in which the tourist gaze becomes a bidirectional trajectory from the tourist and back onto the tourist. The trip that started off primarily as pleasure for me became work—work as a concerted effort of maintaining my sense of self and, more specifically, work as I began to engage a twisted auto/ethnographic venture in being and performing spectacle. The process required me to look at myself–looking at them–looking at me, to speculate on the implications of encountering racial and cultural difference in the context of transnational tourism, and to further look at tourism as performance. Particularly shifting the focus in tourism "away from the producers, marketers, framers [, actors] and providers of heritage tourism and onto tourists themselves" and more specifically on the social and intercultural encounters in tourism (Franklin 2003, 205).[6] In this way, the chapter is structured around four major divisions: expanding perspectives on tourism, exploring implications on geographical and social borders that are both breached and bridged in tourism, critical reflections on the actuality of tourist-articulated experiences, and reflections on the effects and affects of tourism.

TRYING TO GET A FOOTHOLD ON TRAVEL TOURISM

Whenever traveling across borders of place and space we risk comfort for adventure; we risk assuredness for the fulfillment of desire; we risk what we know to be real for what we would like to come to know better. This is an epistemological trap, one in which the outcomes of ethnographic inquiry is predetermined by the very problematic that informs it.[7] It is a place where an unhappy choice emerges between comfort and adventure, the familiar versus the foreign—and therein lie two more difficulties in travel and in research. First there is the shiftiness of how the conceptual objects of tourism and research vacillate between the known and the unknown, between the objectification and alienation of others, which is the dubious positionality of participant-observation research. Research that both places and displaces bodies as it seeks to offer perspective at the risk of sincere cultural experience.

The second difficulty is whether we can even get to the particularity of the moment, the modus operandi and the manner in which the gaze in tourism actually operates. In this I refer to the spectacular gaze, in which the tourist as researcher is trapped in a searing reversed gaze with the "natives," each human subject alienated as other in the tourist experience. Hence each being is objectified in an act of exoticization[8] that is as much about bleeding the borders between appreciation and deprecation as it is between marking the other as rude or ridiculous. Unlike some others, I am not interested in tourism as an instance of pleasure seeking or pleasure responding.[9] In particular I am more interested in the interlocking modes of perception and representation of tourism—both the seeing and being seen.[10] For me this is not exclusively from the perspective of economic consumerism but from the human consumption of difference. And while some have written about the *oppositional gaze*,[11] I am most interested in the *contestatorial gaze* or even the *confrontational gaze* of watching and being watched in the nexus of pleasure and dis-ease. Those moments of tourist encounters when difference is implicated in the moment of social travel fixating vision on the materiality of bodies and opening the possibility of rejecting what is seen.[12]

This chapter is really a travelogue of experiences and critical observations about cultural performance and the transnational flow of identities, set in a series of basic premises about tourism and an experience in China:

Premise one—tourism is both an act and a site of social engagement that bridges borders and boundaries of social, cultural, and political practice. Tourism is an act as it is a doing motivated by intentionality, curiosity, and desire. More specifically Adrian Franklin writes, "Tourism is an embodied experience not simply a visual experience. Consumption, identity, belonging and social order work on and through the body, as do their opposites—freedom, transgression, and disorder" (2003, 26). Tourism is a site because it takes place in the throes of elsewhere, both in traveling and in the actual destinations themselves; places far from the domestic sites of everyday experience. In this way tourism is more about the accessing of spectacle than it is about the acquisition of particular knowledge of place. Tourism is social, cultural, and political as it pivots on the spectacularization of other people's everyday and historical culture, juxtaposed against a backdrop of capitalism and cultural practices that are also actually transported in the vitreous humor of tourists. Hence tourists visit host sites and tourists as hosts are carriers of their own culture.

Tourism within the realm of discussing transnational identities and performance becomes the confluence of three encounters: social practice, individual agency, and cultural definitions of self and other.[13] In other words, the features of landscape, most often assumed to be the primary object of the tourist gaze, are really only a part of the whole cultural consumption in tourism. Bodies and governing performances of everyday life in disparate locations are made copresent in the tourist site and they are consumed. The tourist gaze is a desire expanded beyond the visuality of geographic and topographic features, toward the idea of having what tourists presume to be authentic experiences of cultures other than their own. These cultural experiences take the form of eating native foods, viewing cultural performances, and seeing bodies in place as mostly a fulfillment of pleasure, curiosity, and awe.[14] Of course these are always informed, motivated, and subsidized by competing intentions that are personal, governmental, corporate, social, economic, and always political.[15]

Premise two—tourism especially when crossing national borders works to spectacularize the materiality of raced and ethnic bodies. It becomes a confrontational moment in which marked bodies from sometimes opposing historicities regulate each other in a spectacular gaze, along an axis of difference that is both attraction and disdain with a curiosity that borders on fetishism, which seemingly is a key element in the touristic experience.[16] In writing on historicity Della Pollock states: "Historicity is, in effect, where history works itself out, in and through and sometimes against its material subjects. It is where concrete practices not only 'embody and perform differences' but also contest claims for material agency" (1998, 4). For in this sense, the material bodies that are staged in tourism are confronted with questions of the historically authentic nature of what is assumed to be true or possible, in relation to the tourist's own cloistered and particularized existence. "The authentic serves as a way to imagine and idealize the real, the traditional, and the organic in opposition to the less satisfying qualities of everyday life" (Deloria 1998, 110). In the instance of their copresence (tourist and toured), there is a question about what these bodies and historical identities do, what they perform—in place and space.

While in anthropological terms *fetishism* often refers to the worship of material objects like totems, trinkets, and talismans supposed to have inherent power,[17] I am most interested in fetishism as a performative act of looking, an unreasonable excessive attention bordering on violation of one's personal sense of comfort and place, when the confluence of difference and desirous curiosity collides. Fetishism in this case is about the borders and boundaries that we construct to define self, which are always relational—since the self is always socially constructed.[18] Maybe within that process the reasonableness of looking is relative to culture and place along with the power to look, which is authorized in the conditions of tourism that give rise to the social exchange of human commerce.

For me this is often the case, as it is in classic anthropological research, where researchers engaging the objectivist approach (as tourists do) want to visit "the natives" and see how and where they live, which in turn validates their own quality of life (or intelligence, superiority, and humanity). Pierre Bourdieu describes it this way: "Objectivism constitutes the social world as spectacle presented to an observer who takes up a 'point of view' on action, who stands back so as to observe it and, transferring into the object the principles of his relation to the object, conceives of it as a totality intended for cognition alone, in which all interactions are reduced to symbolic exchanges" (1977, 96). In particular, I am interested in the ways in which the object of the tourist gaze (or the tourist fascination) becomes that which it is expected to be and not what it is. This is also reflected in the attraction-resentment dynamic experienced and often displayed by cultural natives. Those who on one hand desire tourist money but on the other hand resent being made spectacle to the tourist gaze, as well as the arrogance of wealth and national politics that accompanies the presence of tourists (and sometimes specifically Americans). And of course, the reverse in this case of the tourist who then becomes the spectacle, as the materiality of their bodies is displaced and viewed as uncommon in the racialized terrain of tourist travel. My approach here echoes how Karl Marx (1954) addresses his theory of the fetishism of commodities, arguing that in a world of generalized commodity circulation, social relations, that being the communal and everyday activity between people, assumes the same form of relations—things to people. Tourism banks not only on the circulation of material commodities, but also on the fetishization of place, space, and people that is exchanged in the border crossing of social exchange.

Premise three—transnational tourism is a nexus where the visibility of displaced materiality—for example, a tall Black man with dreadlocks in China—rivals the spectacular visuality of the tourist site—for example, the Great Wall of China, the terra cotta warriors, Tiananmen Square, and a host of temples and palaces. I visited all these sites, but was trapped in the chasm of watching and being watched. This signals the relational variance between the spectator and the spectacle, and the organizing power of vision that stimulates wonder, pleasure, and amusement—whether inanimate objects, specific historical locations, or the ways in which human difference animates curiosity.[19]

These are the intersections in which we might further view the consequences of tourism through the theme of transnational flow of identities. But not only from a vantage point of promoting or democratizing travel but from viewing the emergent quality of performance of what happens within the confluence of bodies, time, and space; which is what I believe to be the cornerstone of tourism. Richard Bauman writes that "the concept of emergence is necessary to the study of performance [like that of culture] as a means towards comprehending the uniqueness of particular performance within the context of performance as a generalized cultural system" in any location (1977, 37). Performance is being defined here as *behavior situated in context*. In this case, travel tourism, culture, and location; the motivations of my travel; and the specificity of my being, this in relation to the specific Chinese people that I encountered in the places where I traveled in China.

Whether we are talking about touring antebellum homes in the South or traveling abroad, the tourist-traveler-researcher is knowingly and willingly displaced—in time and location. This is in order to encounter either ghosts from some eroticized past, or exoticized wonders of the world that might include both cultures (meaning people and their practices) and cultural artifacts (meaning what they make or left behind). In transnational tourism the copresence of identities between tourist and native becomes a face-off, a confrontational moment when the reality of self is challenged in the coexistence of the other.[20] In these situations, especially under the spectral investment of tourism, "visual fascination is part and parcel of this dodging effort, the rehearsal of which is actually sought in order to strengthen the illusion of impenetrability, autonomy, and coherence" of one's own material presence. Hence, "exoticization is this fetishization process at work during the confrontation with extreme cultural difference" (Strain 2003, 18). In other words, to make any subject weird is in fact to establish it as an object of the gaze, a denuded object of fascination that authorizes the privilege of looking, an assessment always in relation to the self presumption of the normal, which is relegated to the looker and not the looked upon.

BORDERS AND BOUNDARIES OF CULTURAL PRACTICE

So back to the story: My partner and I boarded a United Airlines flight from Los Angeles, California, to Tokyo, Japan, heading to Beijing, China. In planning for this trip we recalled the trip several years earlier to Japan in which I was invited as a speaker and he was the tagalong. It was an event in which Japanese students studying performance performed, in English, aspects of Japanese cultural life and American stories—using performance as a method of knowing and showing—for an all-Japanese audience and an English-speaking Black American performance studies scholar, who offered them comments and critique in English. My comments and critique were inevitably about content and form, culture and performance, language, and identity politics. These are always and already separate yet interrelated variables—whether crossing national borders or performing in already practiced places. Being in Japan just heightened my awareness of how these variables are nestled within the complex of identity politics and the shifting nature of place and space that is location and the cultural practices that socialize space. I came to a more somatic understanding that the location of culture is bodily practice and that realization is much more salient when other bodies are not performing the same practices and when the materiality of bodies is marked differently.

My partner and I thought about the ways in which the planning of that trip to Japan overestimated necessity and banalized difference. I was fixated on my performance as an academic, which necessitated the invitation and made secondary the racial and ethnic differences that might truly intervene in the social and educational endeavor. I suspect most tourists crossing national borders might also overlook these differences, though of course, as a Black man these are ever-present concerns in my personal and professional life as well as in my pedagogical practices. In the case of going to Japan, I did ask my Japanese sponsor—who had attended graduate school with me in the United States—if those attending the conference would know that I am Black. She informed me that she had not mentioned my blackness, in its particularity. But we agreed that a picture of me on the conference website would evidence the materiality of my being.

And while this seemed like an easy solution, in hindsight, I experienced angst over that choice. This was even more alarming than the reality of meeting them for the first time. I felt in some ways more vulnerable in the objectified visuality of them studying my picture. Like those anthropologists of not so long ago, who traveled the distance of space and time to take pictures of "native peoples" to promote shifting arguments for and against humanity, character, and temperament. This study of the size of the skull, the width of the nose, the distance between eyes, and the size of various and sundry body parts is considered the science of physiognomy.[21]

I felt a pressure about the moment of actual interface, a moment in which I would present my actual self as a specimen of both a Black man (and all the social and cultural constructions that go along with that) and a professor—knowing that at times some people see these as incongruent and impossibly coexistent performances. Knowing that authenticity is a trap, I still wondered what would be the standard of knowing and the measure of authenticity that my Japanese hosts would use. What media would be their source of knowledge of racial difference (of Blackness)— television and film, or news reports and sports—and in what ways does their acknowledgment always and already establish an unreasonable and untenable expectation of and for my possibility? And of course, this is also the problematic sin of which most tourists are guilty as we search for authenticity in the cultural and geographical sites that we travel.

Such speculations were also at the forefront of our thinking as we talked about our own perception and anticipation of Chinese people on this trip. More importantly, as my partner and I situated ourselves in the clutch of Chinese culture, we speculated about the condition of being the minority in the majority of what is considered a collective culture[22] and about the ways in which the "minority/majority" binary has consequences on embodied experience in location. This is separate from the problematic ways in which minority and majority are used as catchall descriptors of culture, suggesting issues of dominance and who determines social standards. It is also separate from the manner in which "minority" is often used to suggest "nonwhite," in that totalizing way that Whiteness predominates as social capital. My partner (who is White) and I were interested in the actuality of being outside the realm of the normal, the usual, and the known. In that way in which I believe transnational travel repositions identities as curiosa—that is, at the literal conjuncture of the usual and the unusual, in both cultural practices and embodied presences.

For me this is a question of borders and boundaries, as well as what is really breached in the event of tourism and internationalism travel. While crossing geographical space the self, the enculturated evidence of a particular living, is both consistently present and cautiously displaced by the features of landscape (people, place, and cultural practice) that often give it meaning. Though of course, the very nature of travel and tourism defines an amorous border of difference. The contrasting materiality of bodies clearly marks the boundaries of it based not only on location and citizenship, but also on who is looking at whom and why. The periphery of the possible between self and other is a narrow space that allows very little wiggle room for being.[23]

In writing on the construct of hybrid hyphenations, Homi Bhabha suggests that "what is at issue is the performative nature of differential identities: the regulation and negotiation of those spaces that are continually, *contingently*, 'opening out,' remaking the boundaries, exposing the limits of any claim to a singular or autonomous sign of difference—be it class, gender, or race" (1994, 219). In this way the performative nature of differential identities helps me to vision performativity in transnational tourism not only as repetitive actions plotted within grids of power relationships or as social norms within the cultural context of everyday interaction, but also as the situated act with historical meanings and as the sociocultural dynamic that gives it presence.

Here I am particularly interested in the manner in which the materiality of the body becomes performative, not in its doing but in how the body is read in relation to context and culture, both the Black male body out of context in China as well as Chinese bodies in China. In a very literal sense, I want to take Judith Butler's individual construct of cultural norms that govern the materialization of bodies and link it to the presentation of the body itself, meaning those moments, like in transnational travel, when the body is presented outside the borders of the normal, outside the borders where repetitive action and exposure have meaning situated in shared cultural knowledge. Those moments when the materiality of the foreign body becomes performatively queer for those to whom that presence operates outside of their system of knowing. In this sense being is perceived as doing, and doing something that is altogether different.[24]

Here there is a displaced or even absent citationality of the performative experience, a preexisting or shadow performativity that is disrupted or reconfigured in the displacement of the performing self. This in a location where the signification of identity is not read as normal or even commonplace; hence the notion of performativity then shifts from the active body doing and those who know what it is doing. (Here performativity is constructed in terms of audience reception.) To a cultural or racialized knowing that operates in the minds of those seeing for the first time with some prenotion of being, and their performative gestures that signal the engagement of the new and not the known. These are gestures of exposing that connect two aspects of the unacknowledged tourist experience, seeing and being seen.[25] It is unacknowledged in the sense that most tourists do not think that they will become as much a spectacle as the spectacles that they travel to see.

For me the gesture is engrained in our copresence, the directionality of our gaze at each other and the performance of both wonderment and disease. Here the assumption of knowing is really an instance of having seen. The discrepancy between object and subject is in fact for me the limits of performativity in transnational travel—not only repetitive acts, but a lack of knowledge of actions and the materiality of being or the cultural practices of knowing, being and seeing conflated in the moment of engagement.

Being without the knowledge of being within foreign cultural contexts becomes a form of doing in the absence of the known. And of course displaced presence without the lexicon of knowing becomes a cultural disruption in the everyday assumptions of social relations.[26] What I am suggesting here is that, if I do not have a full sense of Chinese cultural practices of looking, and if the Chinese people that I encountered have no history of seeing a Black man with my particularity, then we are both trapped in a moment from which neither of us can be easily rescued. In these ways tourists, and the places and people toured, truly become the subjects of cultural analysis—whether documented in written ethnographies or in those deep-seated places where cultural experience resonates with lingering impressions and the desire to make sense.

This is one of those tenuous moments in transnational travel and in reflexive ethnography[27] in which as tourist and scholar I must further reflect on my own self-implication. I need to acknowledge my own baggage here. I am speaking to the historicity of bodies and more specifically the history of race, racism, and colonialism of Black people. This is the stuff that I carry with me across borders that has given a particular historical meaning to the materiality of my body and my response to social engagements. On one hand the historical and personal experiences of racism and racial bias in the United States travels in memory, in sensate feeling, and on my body as historical markers. These realities of marginalization and oppression are in essence entries in a lifescript used to register new and yet similar experiences—they precede more in-depth analysis of new engagements both in contact and context. Hence history floods into the present, giving a particular somatic reading of the experiential moment.

In terms of the Chinese, their own history of colonialism comes to bear in ways that may translate their gaze into an act of empowerment, an empowerment of the subaltern to engage the object of the gaze. Maybe this is the revenge of the subaltern. Not revenge as malicious activity of history's compensation, but as a form of empowerment that acts on curiosity as opposed to being exclusively acted on in a need to expand its sphere of knowledge, and a territorial privilege of operating within a homeplace of their own familiarity. And maybe it is true that in everyday cultural practices we all look back. Looking back as a locational mechanism to understand self in relation to other has its own consequences, gaining knowledge or mortification.

Cultural natives always look back. The question becomes whether this is ever clearly identified in the reports of cultural workers, scholars, ethnographers, or cultural tourists—those of us who simply mark the looking back of the cultural native as rude behavior. This without a critical reflection on what occasions the encounters and how the primary objective of the tourist and the ethnographer is to look at, point at, and talk about the other. The gross assumption here that both undergirds and haunts tourism, as well as particular practices in ethnography and intercultural scholarship in general, is that the researcher/tourist is a privileged viewer and is not held to the culture-specific codes of propriety that govern human sociality in the spaces of their observation.

In such cases, the citationality of past experience contests indexical knowledge[28] that serves as both border and frame to the new experience. In this way, as Joseph Roach writes about cultural studies, what is at play might be "the Marxist idea that culture is the occasion and the instrument of struggle between contending groups with differing amounts of power or, at least, with different kinds of power" (1992, 10).[29] Hence Chinese people in this instance of tourism, like the "natives" in any geographicalized cultural context claim a territorial imperative to look back. Maybe, as E. Ann Kaplan writes, "reversing the look . . . provides a model for resisting marginalization and domination" (1997, 294). Maybe this is the everyday practice of knowing: looking to see and seeing to know, which is pathologized when the surveillance is unverifiable, uncontrolled, and no longer resides in the domain of privilege or power.[30]

Yet unlike the multiple film references that Kaplan uses to help build her argument for reversing the gaze,[31] the contestatorial gaze in tourism is experienced in the moment of the occurrence. They are not staged for the twice-removed visual gaze of the film viewer, who then processes the implications of the reconfigured gaze through the political intentionality of the filmmaker. Which in fact, might be the strategy that makes racial intersubjective looking possible,[32] thus allowing (mandating or forcing) the viewer to understand (see or appreciate) "the powerful subjectivity and agency of the non-western speaking subject [which] is made material" in the film representation—from yet a distantiated point of view that might in fact further objectify the cultural other (297). The film viewer is expected to translate what is a visual and often fictionalized experience into a politicized knowing with actualized implications. This does not lessen the impact of the gaze but mediates it—demanding the viewer to process the possible meaningfulness of particular human encounters. So there is still power in looking and learning how to look at looking, which becomes the more immediate endeavor in tourism and reflecting on touristic experiences that this chapter complicates.[33] Knowing that, being lost in translation is both about a fear of misunderstanding and for some the excitement of deciphering meaning.

Ironically *Lost in Translation*, the film directed by Sofia Coppola was the first movie selection on our flight heading to Japan and then to China. The choice of the movie seemed like an ironic commentary on our border crossing, the destination of our cultural excursion, and served as a projection or prophecy of our experience. Do you know the film? Bill Murray and Scarlett Johansson are characters lost in translation, Americans who find themselves in Tokyo. He is an aging movie star capitalizing on his continued popularity in Japan by doing a series of commercials. She is the young wife of a busy commercial photographer who spends most of her time alone. The traveler, or lead advertisement, for the film states, "when lost in translation everyone wants to be found." The two characters, who are literally and figuratively lost in the translation of Japanese language, Japanese culture, and in their own (placed and displaced) sense of being in the world, encounter each other and are able to understand and make sense of the other's predicament.

The tourist, maybe like the nonindigenous ethnographer in any cultural location, is always lost in translation. Our toolboxes and handbooks of cultural idioms offer us only facile understandings of the cultural lives and practices of those we visit—what they do, and why. Hence our moments of sense-making are undergirded and guided by systems of knowing that are inadequate. They cannot penetrate the motivations of particular cultural practices or emergent cultural performances that are situated in the unanticipated occasion of our presence.

SPECULATING ON ACTUALITIES; OR, SPECULATIVE ACTUALITIES

We are finally in China and we have traveled along literal and figurative routes of succession that lead to places of comfort and colonial opulence, in this case the summer palace of another emperor. We are standing near magnificent artifacts that signify culture and class. Yet the eyes of so many Chinese people, who are tourists themselves to this particular locale, are fixed and fixated on me. And even in the writing of these acknowledgments I am thinking about levels of my own conceit and presumption as they stared. This is not about me saying, "I was the center of attention in China." It is not about the moment when one of the White women in our tour group casually said, "Oh Bryant, I just enjoy walking behind you to see how much attention you get from Chinese people." This followed by a host of my fellow (White) travelers pointing at those who were pointing at me in some act of their own entertainment at my personal dis-ease. Which acknowledges that it was not just me who noticed the behavior as a desperate reflection on my own paranoia, at the same time as perpetrating the reality of me as a spectator. This is about me acknowledging my standpoint in social relations as tourist, researcher, and spectacle.

This was a moment, after days of being a spectacle, that I turned to one of our Chinese guides and asked the question, "Why is it that they seem to be staring at me?" In his response he attempted to assure me: "It's not because you are Black, in China we have nearly fifty-five ethnicities. It is your hair. It is very unusual and they are *just* curious. Please do not take offense."[34] And of course there is presumption in both my asking and in his answering. The presumption is in knowing whether or not his answer would provide any comfort to my experience. The presumption is also linked with subtle issues of intentionality and responsibility. The response, "Please do not take offense," acknowledges his perception of my dis-ease and the urgency in my asking the question. The response is a defense of their "harmless" intention as it is an intercultural cue for consideration against misinterpretation.

In this moment I stop and think about the materiality of bodies as the evidence of difference. I think about complications in transporting difference across borders of place and space. I think about the construction of fifty-five Chinese ethnicities as a defense against racism (or at least a response to my noticeable dis-ease). I think about the manner in which that statement claims knowledge of difference (at least in varying shades of difference within a racial sect), but still uses a degree of difference across racial borders as a defense of curiosity. This for me conflates race against the performativity of hair and the full materiality of the body as a separate motivation or excuse for agency, or what I experienced as just rude behavior.

This of course is my cultural interpretation of systems of Chinese behavior that have no common valence of action or understanding in American culture or specifically in my own lived experience as a Black American male. It is indeed a moment of conflicting, contrasting, and contesting modes of social engagement in which both the watchers and the watched are problematically constructed and both are lost in translation. Hence I am also implicated in this construction of marking and not marking difference, as my own generalizing of Chinese physical characteristics actually conflates all as the same. Hence one might say that my per-

ception of their bodily materiality is in fact evidence of my own ethno-
and geocentrism; the effects of a type of social orientation to disfamiliarity
that I must accept at the same time that my own difference is noted. This
is my painful acknowledgment as researcher, Black man, and tourist;
interrelated elements of my dense particularity in place and space.

I think about my own restricted sense of racialized and ethnic boundaries, both geographic location as well as cultural practices, and what strategies are used in examining and coming to understand difference.[35] Maybe
this is what John Urry is also referencing when he writes that "the visual
sense [of the tourist gaze] enables people to take possession of objects,"
even other people, sometimes "combining detachment and mastery" from
a distance that is as much about learning, discriminating (as in differenti-
ating difference), and pleasure seeking as it is curiosity (2002, 147). This
is how I felt whenever someone pointed at me and laughed, or those few
uncomfortable moments when I felt someone touching my hair from
behind. That moment of immediate shock and disdain of violation—
followed by the searing gaze of my anger, and the culprit then rubbing
his hand on his clothing; as if to clean something that had been soiled or
contaminated, or as an act of apology as if something had been disturbed
or desecrated.

Yet I must acknowledge that this is not just an experience that has happened in foreign places. White people in the United States have also
touched my hair or in rare cases asked to touch my hair. Throughout my
childhood growing up in the South and in the last several years—since
having dreadlocks. And in these cases what they also construct as curiosity
is experienced as more of a pathologizing and patronizing act that most
of them fail to acknowledge, given the U.S. history of racism and slavery.
Even some of the most liberal of White folk often take offense at Black
folk who are offended at such body encroachments. In particular, they do
not acknowledge the rather racist tradition of White people patting Black
people on the head, if not rubbing their heads for good luck, and the historical unrestricted White access to Black bodies. Knowing of course, that
in the reverse case—a Black man randomly touching the hair of a White
woman would still be seen as treachery, whether we are talking about the
racist South of yesterday or more modern notions of social propriety.

Here of course, I am intentionally using the most extreme (exaggerated,
eroticized, demonized, and provocative—meant to provoke) example of

the still tensive social dynamic of Black men displaying aggression toward Whites in general, and White women in particular, to make a point. The point is about the limits and sanctions of social curiosity regardless of issues of desire or disdain. And how these perceptions of privilege or these unreflexive acts of curiosity do not always translate across racial or cultural, national or international borders of difference, or even just outside of individual sense and sensibilities.

In "Spectatorial Embodiment: Anatomies of the Visible and the Female Bodyscape," Giuliana Bruno offers an analysis of *curiositas* as a desire to explore mapped on the body. It is a lust of the eyes that is also embedded in spectacle, in this case the performative spectacle to see and experience difference in tourism. In particular, Bruno places such curiosa in the context of a filmic visual focus on the female body as landscape, a territory that becomes lustful and scientific, comic and tragic, spectative and invasive.[36] A lust that I would argue sustains tourism in everyday life not just for the visceral manifestation and spectacle of otherness but also—like the pleasure in seeing an autopsy, or like the experience of those who crane their necks to look at roadside accidents—for a prioritized pleasure of knowing through seeing that competes against the propriety of privacy, the banality of being, and what might be the confused confrontation of cultural difference.

This is the type of bidirectional curiosity in tourism that objectively deconstructs live others and verges on both phobia and fetish; phobia as fear and desire of the object, and fetish as the fecundity of fixation—to both obsess and disavow the encounter and not the object.[37] I do not want to conflate the objects and subjects of the visual gaze in *curiositas* into the curiosity of people and places in my tourist experience in China, which might presumably make me or Chinese people appear to be grotesque. Yet, there are moments in all tourist experiences in which visual oddity attracts attention, and maybe it is the very nature of transnational tourism that breaches "the limits—of respect, piety, pathos—that should not be crossed" in the boundary conditions of everyday living; even to experience a sense of the other, or to write about such experiences (Behar 1996, 2). Allow me to offer another example:

"Oh No You Didn't!"—In China our tour group has just exited The Forbidden City, an imperial courtyard, an edifice built to the grandeur of emperors and the disparity between the royal court and the territories

over which it rules. While we have exited the city, as we wait for the bus, we are exposed to a menagerie of peddlers and beggars. The peddlers are selling typical trinkets (maps, information booklets, fabrics, umbrellas, purses, jewelry, etc.). The beggars are elderly men accompanying younger male performers; young men who are a/effected by what one assumes are birth defects. Some are blind, others are crippled or inflected with bodily malformations. The young men play Chinese musical instruments, while their elder companions reach out cups, drumming up donations. Most of those in our company stand back, looking with both a sense of pity and horror; this is an effect of the juxtaposition of the opulence that we have just viewed against the abject poverty with which we are now confronted. This is not unlike the types of disparity that tourists see in major U.S. cities. Our tour guide tells us not to patronize them; this is literally a commercial charge that seeks to discourage the peddlers and beggars in this area. The assumption in the charge is that they are not a part of the tour; they are not that which should be seen as a tourist attraction.

Off in the distance I (we) hear a sound. It is a sound that seems familiar; almost nostalgic, like the sound of the metal skates from my childhood scraping on the pavement. The sound is at first faint and distant but it travels quickly in intensity and suddenly it is upon us. A young man—a quadriplegic (in this case with the full absence of legs)—propelling himself through the crowd on a skateboard-type contraption is making the sound. He is a sight/site (I am a sight/site). He quickly maneuvers his way through the crowd of performers and enters an opening space near the waiting tourists. And suddenly we seem to see each other.

He approaches near where I am standing. At first he holds up a cup for a handout but his eyes are fixed (fixated) on me, as are mine on him. He then offers a snaggletoothed smile, lowers his cup, and then points his finger at me while looking to the other beggars and peddlers as if to draw attention to my presence. He seems to be laughing at me. And in this moment I almost say, "Oh no you didn't!" Meaning—"how dare you point at me as spectacle when in fact you are the spectacle!" I don't say it. But not saying it out loud does not excuse the thought or my complicity in this tensively reciprocal viewing of otherness, and the manner in which I concretize the character of that encounter in this privileged scholarly venue.[38]

Once again our joint complicity goads the question of authenticity, of

curiosity, of the criteria of spectacle in tourism, and issues of vulnerabil-
ity—I to him and he to me. Maybe in that moment our bodies were literally between colony and nation;[39] the specificity of people being in the
same circumstances and the politics of lived territories that shape knowing
and being.[40] I agree with Rosemarie Garland Thomson in "Dares to
Stares" that the beggar and I are trapped in that painful space of "the to-
be-looked-at and not-to-be-looked at further dramatizing the staring
encounter by tending to make viewers stealthy and the viewed defensive."
We are both trapped "by visually articulating the subject positions of 'disabled' and 'able-bodied'" with the racial materiality of our bodies as
added evidence of the spectacle of each to the other (2005, 31).[41]

In tourism there is a double reifying force of characterizing the other
that moves from empowerment to domination.[42] In offering this particular construction I also further question my own culpability in acts of domination as I characterize the Chinese in my tourist experience and in this
documentation of experience.[43] In particular, the issue of authenticity is
not about what is real as much as what is known. Curiosity thus serves as
the performative impulse to know, and the telling of experience becomes
an issue of representing the other; a kind of authority over the other that
is often practiced in tourism and ethnography. Hence we must continue
to question those lines of subjectification and objectification that are present both in tourism and in scholarly activities like auto/ethnography.
Strategies that seek to describe cultural experience yet always offer an
assessment of culture from a particular perspective of privilege; privilege
being constructed here as the authoritative right to tell.[44]

So in using the examples of someone touching my hair (and the specific
correlate of touching White people) along with what might be read as a
patronizing example of encountering the difference with the beggar, I
want the reader of this reflexive ethnography to be both attracted to and
disarmed by these references. I chance the shore of the reader's patience,
because I want the reader to understand issues of bodily violation and the
making of bodily spectacle as the expense of acting on curiosity. For the
construction of harm in this case is not about effect but affect, not about
damage but the felt sensation of the experience to the one being acted on.
In other words, the simplistic but altogether ignored aphorism "It's not
about you, it's about me"—is palpably felt within a liberal economy of
social interaction. Tourism is such a liberal economy that offers unregu-

lated space for social judgment within a limited confine of cultural knowing—and in this sense, I am both victim and perpetrator—I have both
constructed the space of my own victimization and I have in fact victim-
ized him.

Of course there are ways in which hair is a sensuous component of
human materiality—texture, taste, smell, and feel as an intimate contact.
The discursive and performative quality of hair as a visual communication
of culture, race, and attitude (meaning the politics of hair—color, length,
presence/absence, and configuration) attracts attention—sometimes
intentionally. The desire to touch is sometimes just the desire for a tactile
knowing. Hair, like the body, becomes if not the material evidence of
being then a politicized construct of one's being and being known. This
acknowledgment is offered neither as excuse nor apology. The same qualities that signal curiosity also establish borders between the individual and
society, culture and community, and self and other—establishing boundaries of visual access and borders of bodily limitations—which might be
culture specific but never value neutral.

I thought about the notion of visual access later that same evening
when my partner and I went out on the streets of Beijing to attend a local
market. As someone who is prone to panic attacks in crowded public
spaces and more specifically in response to the encroachment of my privacy and personal space, I obsessed about going out again. Being spectacle
gets tiresome and is often rather wearing on the nerves. In other words,
visibility can be its own place of entrapment.[45]

I obsessed about hair and the visible access of my hair. I thought about
the process of pulling my hair back in a small knot in the back of my
head and covering it with an athletic skullcap before leaving the room. I
remember my partner asking why. I hesitantly explained my intentions,
an action motivated not by some pseudo-scientific cultural experiment
but by a desire to move about the streets of Beijing without the element
of curiosity that the Chinese guide suggested. Of course in many ways, this
was a desperate act pivoted on the relationship between experimentation
and observation in social science research. It was an experiment that both
invoked and altered the environment that I sought to observe, as if a six-
foot-tall Black man could travel incognito (incognegro) on the streets of
Beijing by simply covering his hair. The strained looks continued, maybe
more intensely, as I now projected the costumed construction of pass-

ing—and passing for what I was not sure of—so once again I am implicated in my own social construction.[46]

I thought about what the Chinese guide might have meant when he
said, "Please do not take offense." Maybe it was a careful and polite construction that may have been designed to deflect larger issues of racial difference and bias (along with other material aspects of the body—such as
size and color) to the specificity and variable component of hair. I thought
about the level of personal and professional investment that the Chinese
tour guide had in potentially offering me a scripted response, both in the
sense of how culture offers particular scripts of social interaction and how
the role of tour guide is also scripted. To what degree was he selling me a
considerate and compassionate construction of socialized engagement?
One that was both designed to appease my feelings and subtly promote a
positive touristic experience.[47]

Maybe the verbal deflection of the tour guide afforded him the freedom
of dismissing the specificity of racial bias to open a space for a more communal knowing, a condoning of curiosity in the confluence of a particular
difference. Maybe racial bias in this situation is not necessarily an unfair
preference, but rather that visible marker that runs across the cultural fabric of knowing. This might suggest that in this particular tourist-gaze
dynamic, a close intersubjective relation must be achieved between tourist
and toured, like that relationship between the ethnographer and the cultural communities under ethnographic scrutiny.[48] In more concrete terms,
maybe tourism should be seen as a negotiated space of double exposures.
Mark Neumann writes:

> In a general sense, tourism is a cultural phenomenon reflecting the instabil-
> ity of modern communities, the public and private pursuits of cultural unit-
> ies and consensus, and how people, governments, and nations try to hold a
> vision of the worlds, and themselves, in place. The landscapes of tourism
> are where people are continually asked to reconcile the incongruities of
> "home" and "away," boredom and adventure, and self and other. (1999, 9)

Maybe in tourism each participant, tourist and "native," voluntarily
consents to objectification, a knowing if not anticipated objectification for
benefits that are never mutual but acknowledged as a necessary commodity in the cultural exchange of social commerce. Here I am suggesting that

the material consequences of my displaced body and the Chinese people that I encountered are already anticipated in dominant discourse long before our encounter; and we must both participate in the critical processes of both identification and disidentification that are intrinsic to the cultural exchange of tourism.[49]

This dialectic is often written in terms of negotiating language and communication as a form of communion in intercultural encounters. I am also placing this within the context of the tourist gaze and spectacle, which I argue can certainly be considered dialogical with an exchange of meaning that negotiates and regulates being. This reanimates what Frank Manning refers to as the "ambivalence about the value and efficacy of spectacle" as a potentially reflexive enterprise that allows for not only an outward viewing but also an inward reflection on the implications of being both observer and observed (1992, 293). Hence, foregrounding the recuperation and diminishment of power in the act of both looking and being known through seeing. Maybe within the frame of transnational tourism, where there may be a greater chance of differing bodily materiality, and beyond issues of actual doing or cultural practice, there has to be a joint realization of the phantasm of intercultural encounters across the chasm of geographical borders. In this way maybe "individual and group identities are being shaped in an interculture of juxtaposition and disjuncture," which is both material place and social space where we construct the other based on preconceived notions of their being (Zarilli 1992, 17).

Once again I am not excusing their behavior or my response, each is plausible in its own sphere of cultural knowing and cultural experience. Maybe there is a needed realization that cultural performances are never quite the same or not the same in meeting or mis-meeting people in the tourist gaze of social travel.[50] Maybe the fixtures and constraints of cultural performance extend beyond the borders and boundaries of observable behavior and felt experience.[51] Such performances are undergirded with logics that are both situational and historical—that which cannot be known or fully understood in momentary encounters when tourists and residents of particular locales meet and make spectacle of each other. Nor can the observances of cultural performances be attributed to the whole of cultural communities, but might reflect the emergent and situational performances of everyday life; those same spaces where tourists enter seeking some performance of cultural authenticity; which is never always and together real.

In particular, tourist sites even in transnational locations also attract those cultural natives from remote spaces within the borders of national territories but outside the realm of the everydayness of those particular sites. Meaning that I suspect that many of the Chinese people that I encountered at national tourist sites like the Great Wall of China, Tiananmen Square, and a host of temples and palaces were themselves tourists. They were domestic tourists from countryside villages or spaces outside of the tourist traffic of national commerce like folk from Des Moines, Iowa, visiting Hollywood or New York City. They too traveled to see the spectacle of the city and what it both presents and attracts. In many ways we encountered each other as evidence of some otherworldliness of possibility that exists outside of our realm of knowing and experience.

In his essay "Identifying versus Identifying with 'the Other,'" Glenn Bowman offers a perspective on this type of intercultural encounter that both confirms and defies the porous borders between cultural knowing and the culturally known:

> In this sense "culture" as a discrete entity which "thinks" its subjects dissolves; culture is here reinterpreted as a set of potential sitings of those who take up identifications within the terrain it hegemonises. However, the taking up of identifications is a labile process, dependent not only on the vagaries of individual histories but also on the global situation in which that culture exists. "Outside" influences "coming in," like "inside" persons "going out," will introduce new articulations of identity into that space. (1997, 46)

Hence we, these traveling domestic tourists and I, encountered each other knowing and not knowing whether our existence was a reflection of the real and the everyday possibility of being in other locations. Both in the city and in those assumed spaces of cultural and racial habitation that are never really true to who we are and how we experience each other. Our encounter with each other, whether in some deeply intellectualized way or in those palpable ways that leave us flush with experience— broadens our perspective and understanding of human possibility.

I wonder to what degree the effects of tourism are like those of museum exhibits; the packaging of culture to somehow exemplify the essence of lives lived. In his essay "The Fetishism of Artifacts" Peter Gathercole asks the question, "Do curators (in this context those of historical, archaeological or ethnographical collections) perceive artefacts primarily as things of themselves, rather than things beyond themselves?" (1989, 73). I find that this question is apt to the tourist experience, for, like the close/d quarters of museums, tourism creates the conditions for visually collecting humans as artifacts—either of the touristic experience itself, or some presumed notion of the cultural other. In which case, those involved become the spectacle as tourist attraction to and for each other.[52] They become double exposures of seeing and being seen with each simultaneously as insider and outsider; collecting fragments of knowing and constructing monuments of experience (Bal 1996).

In these ways tourism, like a museum, becomes a forum for intercultural learning,[53] and tour guides, like curators, exhibit and interpret their cultures/collections for outsiders.[54] Such interpretations merely prompt the exposure but never really offer deep textual knowing of the historical and everyday milieu that shaped the cultural subject/object being viewed. Maybe the actual learning happens (as is a motivational logic for tourism—cultural immersion) in the field of play, an experience in which tourists and natives become vulnerable observers of each other, and thereby come to understand the variable predicaments of the human condition (Behar 1996).

Referencing the "Pirandello effect," Ernest Gellner offers a perspective that might move from the theater of constructed aesthetic forms to the theater of tourist activity. In particular, a perspective on watching and being watched that parallels the tourist/native engagement:

> It was Luigi Pirandello who popularized the theatrical device of deliberately and systematically subverting the clean and distinct separation of audience, actors, and characters, of subject and object in effect, by making the characters speak to their author, the actors pretend to be part of the audience and interact with it, and so forth. He tried to ensure that the play was not a spectacle but a predicament. (1979, 6)

I wonder if in fact this is also an apt analogy to discuss the complicated relational roles played in the specificity of this tourist drama that I am describing. For whether through intention or happenstance, in transnational tourism the distinction between spectator and spectacle, tourist and toured is unclear; each is both actor and audience, subject and object, relating to each as the other who authorizes a particular construction of the opposing self. Hence the unidirectional effect that exists in traditional theatrical and performance venues, with an audience directing their attention to the stage and to particular actors in action. The traditionally assumed directionality of the tourist gaze now becomes bidirectionally contesting gazes that challenge while they consume.

Gellner suggests that when the Pirandello effect is achieved the border between observer and drama bleeds. Similarly in tourism—actors/audience, spectator/spectacle, tourists/natives—their copresence implicates them both, not in some out-of-the-ordinary, sacred, ritualistic, or even theatricalized cultural performative event, but in fact as a banal predicament of everyday life; when strangers through tourism encounter each other in sometimes difficult, unpleasant, or embarrassing situations from which there is no clear or easy way out and have no way of understanding the other.

But allow me to continue to develop this theatrical and narrative analogy that both describes tourism (in terms of actors, audiences, and stages) while particularly focusing on the telling of experiences in tourism (in terms of narrators and narrated; who tells and that which is told about). Here I draw on a description from Pierre Bourdieu's "A Reflecting Story" in which he uses a fictional representation to foreground a representation of history's conceit:

> The idea of [tourism], a socially instituted favorable prejudice, which is consequently endowed with all the force of the social, functions as a principle of construction of social reality that is tacitly accepted both by the narrator and his characters and by the reader. It also functions as a principle of anticipations that are ordinarily grounded in facts, since [tourism], as an essence that precedes and produces existences, opens or excludes by definition a whole range of possibles. The power of presupposition is so great, and the hypotheses of the practice induction of the habitus so robust, that they resist even what is self-evident. (1994, 371)

In this citation, I insert "tourism" in place of Bourdieu's primary discussion of "nobility" in William Faulkner's "A Rose for Emily." Such a replacement is designed both to foreground and reinsert the privilege of tourists in/as social positions to construct particular images of those they have encountered in their touristic travel. The actuality of their experience often operates under what Bourdieu calls a "principle of anticipations" that already prefigures perceptions of cultural realities that are not only about that which is foreign but alien—questioning notions of normalcy and belonging in place and space.

Of course in framing this section through the lens of speculation, I am also admitting that I do not have sufficient evidence to make final academic and intellectual assessments on Chinese culture, nor do I want to, knowing that exclusive somatic sensations of experience often serve as feeble evidence of knowing. I can only offer the description and sensemaking process of a tourist's experience in China—which really signals a threshold of consciousness between two worlds, not just embodied presences.[55] Maybe this is also partly due to (what is for me) the nuanced nomenclature of intentional actualities—like the tonal implications of Chinese language and the slippery lexicon of Chinese culture that both guides behavior and shapes knowing.[56] In relation to another rather screwed terministic screen of language through which I view those performances.[57]

China is a cultural performative landscape that has no particular linguistic term for *the gaze*, or *staring* for that matter, hence another cultural difference that both intervenes and maybe even forestalls the very nature of my commentary. For once again, one cannot assume a joint intentionality or understanding of the behaviors of others, only the frame of reference that our own culture provides. In essence this also illuminates the contestatory nature of these cultural encounters of knowing the other through tourist travel. In which case, looking is culturally determined and the relational intentionalities of looking may vacillate in a range between curiosity to domination.[58] I wonder how they, the Chinese people whom I encountered (and who encountered me), constructed the nature of their looking. In asking the Chinese tour guide, I get only one protected perspective on their intentionality. It is both protective of me as paying customer or honored guest, and of them in the multitudinous intentionalities signaled by culture and individual practice.

THE LINGERING E/AFFECTS OF TOURISM AND ETHNOGRAPHIC WRITING

I have found that published ethnographies sometimes present false endings. Closing sections of stories on cultural experience that, while contained by the constraints of space and methodological form, offer conclusions that sum up cultural lives/cultural experiences that in reality are fluid and dynamic. Culture resists a concrete knowing to both tourists and ethnographers. Curiosity lingers in the minds and bodies of those involved in intercultural contacts long after the departure from an ethnographic or touristic visit and the imminent writing of research reports or travelogues. Such ethnographic reports might also promote what Homi Bhabha refers to as a form of colonial discourse, which functions as an apparatus of power.[59] What might initiate itself as well-meaning descriptions of cultural lives might in fact turn into an act of pathologizing difference as a method of asserting power or superiority.[60]

Such a perception is of course my greatest fear for my own work. The fear is that as my discourse systematically shapes the subjects of whom I speak, the cultural lives implicated in my auto/ethnographic reports may be read as abject bodies.[61] Bodies that are linguistically splayed open and sutured together in a scholarly endeavor produced for my self-promotion as an individual academic and as a racialized citizen of particular cultural, national, and political systems; knowing of course that such dynamics are always at play both in ethnographic research and in all scholarly discourse.

My constructed method of using auto/ethnography is in fact an attempt to interrupt and bridge the processes of self-knowing and self-revealing in the company of writing about specific cultural experiences and cultural others as one of the larger issues that dictate and mediate social knowing. While such work does create a space for "subject peoples" through the production of knowledge, it does not seek to "reveal the limits of Western represenationalist discourse" by constructing a dispositive impression, in this case of China and Chinese people (Bhabha 1994, 68). My particular intention here is to focus on assumed moments of casual cultural contestation narrowly constructed in the context of tourism; when differing systems of knowing do symbolic battle with material and somatic consequences, which shall play out in different ways in the chapters that follow. Concerns of pleasure/unpleasure are invoked—yet these are in fact motivating e/affects of both tourism/ethnography and scholarly production as cultural critique.

Of course while my examples in this chapter are situated as causal encounters, they are in fact just the opposite. These are moments in which the meaningfulness of human difference has its most potent effect in shaping the perception of self and other; especially when such perceptions are translated, concretized, and publicized. My fixation on hair in this chapter (constructed as the Chinese fixation on my hair) is really a ruse. For while some Chinese people may have been curious, the quintessential nature of these exchanges could not (and can not) exclusively pivot on such a small element of materiality. What were their perceptions of race? (race, that highly contested Western construction that seems to motivate human sociality within the United States, with categories of Black and White serving as opposing poles marking gradations of difference). How did "race"—linked with the materiality of my body—play for them both within their own cosmologies and within their knowledge of other ways of knowing difference? What other politics and sensations manifest/evoke the materiality of presence? Like my own characterization of the beggar, bodies are on the line here! Bodies in their fullness as evidence of presence, of being, and of possibility are being critiqued. Bodies as signifiers of race, culture, gender, and class are being analyzed. Bodies as the encasement of the altogether real are being seen as surreal, and hence they are seen as being unreal.

I ask these questions knowing darn well that I crossed borders with preconceived and un-conceived notions of Chinese people. My own biases show very clearly as, in the opening of this chapter, I constructed Chinese people in "all shapes and sizes, yet contained within a limited range of perceived variance" as they stared at me. To what degree does that racialized and myopic construction signify my own orientation to their bodily presence, as I admonish them for noticing my difference? These are questions that I must continue to contend with (as all researchers studying culture through ethnography must contend with), for they are questions that tease at my own complicity as tourist, ethnographer, and researcher—trapped in the spectral gaze of looking and being looked at; of reading and writing about culture, as well as writing and being read through culture.

So while this is a written documentation of experience, it is also an active on-going speculation on experience. Within this closing I want to both rearticulate defining moments and prompt more detailed future lines of analysis and speculation that will further illuminate contestation in tourism, both in the specificity of my own efforts and in spurring broader developments in scholarship on tourism. In further developments I will focus on the spectacle of the USC Trojan marching band in full military-like regalia on the Great Wall of China—indeed conflicting historicities of defensive fortification, culture, class, and conquest ("conquest," which also happens to be the name of the USC fight song played on the Great Wall)—and the ways in which Chinese people gathered on the Great Wall to see the spectacle of a U.S. marching band with banners that *nearly* say, "US(C) Conquers China."

I will explore the context of an ancient welcoming ceremony at the entrance gate of the city wall in Beijing. A ceremony replicated for international dignitaries in which Chinese diplomats greeted the USC marching band. A ceremony replete with the pageantry and spectacle of artistic Chinese cultural performance—brightly colored uniforms, costumes, flags, streamers, dancers, and music. A ceremony also equipped with the regulatory and military mechanisms that barred everyday Chinese citizens from close access to and participation in the performance of culture that they (themselves) are more meaningfully connected to. I will do a critical analysis of captured images of these everyday citizens trapped behind gated enclosures, protected by armed guards. As well as images of the performers when the frame of cultural performance slipped and their painted-on smiles melted with conceit in the hot noonday sun and the intensity of the tourist gaze.

In future presentations of this work (and other ventures in tourism) I will include photographs; the ultimate tourist evidence of being there. The photos will be strategically projected on the wall behind me as I speak or they will be strategically placed between paragraphs on a page contextualized in my analysis of place, space, culture, and experience. In those pictured moments, the actuality of presence and the forethought of image-taking will further implicate me in the processes of my own objectification and my own cultural analysis. In the pictures the audience and reader will see, as you most undoubtedly have imagined, the staged moments of taking pictures. Bodies, cultural artifacts, and moments pressed together in the viewfinder of someone's desire, whether it is the Chinese person acting on curiosity and documenting experience or me directing my partner to take a picture of the act of taking a picture—not for pleasure but for scholarly critique. Those literal snapshots taken by a Canon or a Kodak, or those mental pictures, taken through foreign irises, regulate bodies while they expand and contract the visual range of knowing, collecting, and consuming difference.

Maybe in this project I am reckoning with the psychic dimensions of cultural placement and racialized displacement.[62] As researcher-ethnographer-tourist, I am complicit in my own positioning and positionality. I am complicit like all those who cross the borders of familiarity to venture into the unknown. All tourists are complicitous in the vicissitudes of experience. For—separate from the planned ventures and packaged tours that guarantee location, views, and bodily exposures—it is the unexpected changes and the unexpected experiences shaping the perception of self and other that become both the trappings and treasures of tourism. And in particular transnational travel, where the materiality of bodies (sex, color, size, faciality, hair, and demeanor) as extended to and sedimented in race, ethnicity, culture, and gender performance—demand a reorientation to the self as other.

The challenge is to decipher the meaning between what you have come to know differently and what you have come to know as always and already the same. In other words, what is the evidence-of-difference and can that difference really be known outside-of-being-felt in the tourist excursion? The tourist excursion is a fanciful foray into a world of otherness and a momentary contact with exotic difference. In this sense, the visuality of tourism allows for a surveillance of structures without really knowing composition; an exposure to place without really knowing space, and an encounter with difference that only offers surface sightings and not the invisible essence of culture.[63]

Maybe this is the key—those moments in tourism, which are in actuality the very core impulse of tourism, where the brokers of cultural travel experiences press bodies together for a seeing of and acting among difference. And if cultural performance and experience in tourism is about situated behavior, then performance theory or praxis becomes a lens through which to view and come to understand the meaningfulness of cultural experience and cultural difference. Della Pollock puts it this way: "Insofar as performance is thus aligned with historicity against history, it is especially capable of disseminating cultural knowledge—of dispersing meaning in time and across difference. In this capacity, performance is increasingly understood as an important site of—even a paradigmatic trope for—cultural resistance" (1998, 26).

By invoking the notion of cultural resistance I am interested in the manner in which tourism, in particular transnational tourism, promotes both an appreciation of and a resistance to cultural difference, which in turn might signify an elemental concern of performative contestation. In this case, performative contestation like the purchase of the round-trip ticket in tourism becomes a strategic mechanism signaling both the direction of effectivity and the mode of effectivity, both the lingering effects of the encounter and the mechanisms that shape the nature of the experience.[64]

Tourism as performance sets and operates on a stage of viewing other cultural ways of being. It depends on the economic ability and necessity of those traveling, as well as the economic need of the people and spaces traveled to. Tourism offers limited performative scripts and stratagems for intercultural encounters (in the form of tour packages, tour guides, tips for traveling, and commercially engaging other cultures). Tourism avoids the deeper structures of intercultural communication that grapple with issues of cultural identity; cultural frames and forms; the structuring norms of intercultural contact; and the tenuous process of learning, negotiating, and appreciating difference.[65] The tourist industry only seeks to ensure a good visit and a safe return to terrains of the normal while possibilizing future border crossings and touristic activity, which primarily signal commerce and not meaningful cultural exchange.

The tourist excursion resists deep cultural immersion and thereby ensures a surface and speculative viewing of other people's ways of being. A viewing that is always engaged through a perspective that is less about participant-observation and more about observation and comparison, as well as entertainment and leisure. Tourism as both act and location is contestatory social engagement, one that negotiates between expectations and reality, between the known and the unknown, between the ease and disease of social travel and human encounter. Maybe in tourism the struggle to find authenticity is also the struggle to avoid one's own sense of familiarity, and authenticity's pleasure is really its absence.[66] Because authenticity cannot be found in places foreign to everyday cultural practices, nor can the notions of authenticity (of the other) ever meet the phantasms of our imaginations.

So, in reference to my trip to China, when friends and family asked, "Did you enjoy it?" I said, "Yes." When they asked: "Did you like it?" I said, "Some parts of it." And when they asked, "Would you ever go back again?" I hesitated in my response and said, "I'm still thinking about it, but probably yes."

Placement and Displacement of Black Identity

The Case of Migration across Borders from Campus to Community

assisted by Javon L. Johnson

One of the arguments of this book is that research or research methodologies are never "objective" but always located, informed by particular social positions and historical moments and their agendas.

—Paula Saukko, *Doing Research in Cultural Studies*

The nation is imagined as limited. . . . It is imagined as sovereign. . . . Finally, it is imagined as a community, because, regardless of the actual inequality and exploitation that may prevail in each, the nation is always conceived as a deep, horizontal comradeship.

—Benedict Anderson, *Imagined Communities*

The idea of "the public sphere" in Habermas' sense . . . designates a theater in modern societies in which political participation is enacted through the medium of talk. It is the space in which citizens deliberate about their common affairs, hence, an institutionalized arena of discursive interaction.

—Nancy Fraser, *Rethinking the Public Sphere*

[Paulo] Freire talks about consciousness as intentionality toward *the world, for both reflection and self-reflection are the basis of*

knowing—of coming to know ourselves and our reality objectively.
Such reflection must, however, be always considered in relation to
our actions *for it is to constitute authentic knowledge. In other*
words, according to Freire authentic knowledge is a praxis. To know
implies to act in conjunction with reflection.

—Michael Peters and Colin Lankshear,
Education and Hermeneutics: A Freirean Interpretation

There is always a story that frames the nature of research. Maybe a personal happening that resonates in memory and motivates further exploration of issues that effect lived experience on a localized, national, or global level or on a cultural, racial, and gendered level. In framing this chapter as such, I am using a variation of Paula Saukko's important epigraph about the undergirding and motivational issues in cultural studies. Issues that tease at and even contest the notion of "objectivity" in research; knowing that in everyday life, like in scholarly endeavors about culture, we are more objectified than we are objective. The positionality of who we are and how we perform is always brought to our attention in the shifting contexts of our cultural engagements. Hence our challenge in the academic life and everyday life is often to make sense of how we have been situated and the shifts we make to find a sense of comfort in place and space.

This chapter takes the transnational issues of cultural contestation as depicted in chapter 1 and locates them in the domestic migration of Black faculty, staff, and students across borders between the university campus and "the Black cultural community." Knowing that each location in Benedict Anderson's term is an imagined community, one that only exists in desire and the practiced/performed norms of social membership. In which case, contextualizing Nancy Fraser's replay of Habermas in the framing epigraph—cultural performance is political participation in specified public spheres. Cultural performance is practical behaviors, signifiers of social membership, and the markers of familiarity that are negotiated as bonds of affiliation and recognition in particular social, cultural, and racial communities.

Through an explication of ethnographic interviews with Black faculty, staff, and students, this chapter is structured around three emergent themes as these research participants and conversational partners reflect on their experiences of moving back and forth between campus and community.[1] The emergent themes—which focus on the constitution of racially defined communities, negotiating the boundaries of identity in place and space, and negotiating what is constructed as double consciousness—are framed with my opening autobiographical narrative. The narrative helps to establish a template for my own bicultural socialization and how I situate myself in the cultural communities that this chapter addresses.

SITUATED DESIRE; OR, BUILDING A DESIROUS SITUATEDNESS

I go back in time for the genesis of this experience, knowing that the effects are always and already at play in the dailyness of my hyphenated existence as a Black-male-professor. The story is about "going home" and about "homecomings." Those times when I have traveled the distance between campus and community, between being home and being at home in those spaces that support particular aspects in my identity and those places that sanction normative performances of my identity. Here is the story:

As a college student and later as a professor, I would regularly make the trip from campus to community to home. I would enter my parents' house and often I would find my father in conversational play with one of his buddies. My father would often take great pride in introducing me through the shifting stages of my academic development. He would say, "This is my son, the college student"; or, "This is my son, the graduate student"; or, "This is my son, Dr. Alexander. You know the one who lives in California?" A Louisiana man with a fourth-grade education, my father would often encourage me to "say something" to his buddies—a request for a performative display of my academic persona as artifact of his parental pride.

But later in the day after his friends had left, I might say something that noticeably had the stench of the academy. Something said that would stimulate or engage what David Howes in his book *Sensual Relations* calls "olfactory vocabulary."[2] For me these are not just words to describe smell but words that have a smell; aromas of articulated thoughts simmered and

conjured in cauldrons of culture located elsewhere. You know what I
mean—a turn of a phrase, a display of vocabulary, a cultural critique, a
commentary, or worse yet a correction. In J. L. Austin's construction of
the performative, words in their embodied presentations of identity do
things.[3] They project and engage what literary critic Terry Eagleton might
also refer to as radical cultural politics and a desperate placement or displacement of them.[4] In other words, after such utterances on my part the
orienting tone of my father would then shift, and he would say something
like, "Don't be talking like no professor to me!"

My father's dictate quickly reminds me that identities are performative
and relational; they do not have a "unitary meaning but a range of competing" contestatory orientations that are sometimes regulated by place,
space, and timing (Mercer 1992, 424). Language is implicated in the con-
juring of particularity to necessitate suitability; meaning language is specific to intent and location. In Judith Butler's construction of performativity these are stylized repetitions of communicative acts, linguistic and
corporeal, that are socially validated and discursively established in the
moment and location of the performance.[5] Can you smell it now, what
my father would call the stench of the academy intervening even in the
telling of its own story?

The difference between my father encouraging me to talk and later regulating how I talk reminds me that I have crossed a border territory in
time and space; one that signifies the shifting relational identities between
a proud parent and a student, and between a father and a son. Informed
by the complicated construals of cultural performance[6] that regulate
behavior in everyday reality, as well as the necessary breach in our own
identity constructions that we all barricade and bridge daily as we move
from campus to community to home. It is a shift that both places and
displaces aspects of identity for the efficacy of our social, professional, and
political relations.

This is a routine performative act. One that is initiated as we all move
through space to the particularity of the roles that we play in the performances, presentations, and practices in everyday life and our location, nay
positionality in culture.[7] It is in my commitment to issues of race and culture that I place the specificity of this routine performative act in the experiences of Black folk, as we move from the specificity of our *habitus* to the
places of our *habits*. Those necessarily politicized places where we live and

the practices that cultivate space (home, neighborhood, and community) to the places where we work, learn, and act out the performative identities of professionalism and intellectualism; all with the hope of igniting social and cultural transformations that bleed the borders between campus and community. Moving toward becoming what critical educators have referred to as transformative intellectuals, engaged public intellectuals, or cultural workers—dedicated to exploring "the relationship among culture, power, and identity" as it is negotiated across multiple borders of social habitation (Giroux 1996, 97).[8]

The university is often constructed as the ivory tower. Not just a space set apart from the surrounding community hovering above as a site of the intellectual elite, but also as an institution presumed to be sheltered from the practicalities of ordinary life. This is especially the case when issues of race and class are introduced into the equation of education, access, and community. In particular, the university becomes a contested terrain where Black folk (and other traditionally marginalized "others") must negotiate competing constructions of identity. Such negotiation takes place between the traditional Euro-American categories of intellectual endeavor[9] that contribute to the notion of the ivory tower and some endemic notion[10] of Black cultural life in *knowable communities*.[11]

Knowing of course that in performative terms the engagement of these behaviors occurs in what Stanley Fish (1980) would call "interpretive communities." These are social sites where aggregates of individuals within larger communities share common values while establishing norms and conventions of everyday life that constitute a performative cultural membership.

These standards of behavior may work in alignment, but are in tension with larger more collectivized constructs of race, culture, or the situatedness of being. Consequently, *community* becomes a contested term in which cultural performances are always determined, regulated, and assessed through the interpretive processes of those who vie for membership.[12] I frame this routine performative act of shifting identities[13] from community to campus to foreground the particularity of racial experience and embodiment; meaning bodies as living histories marked at the intersection of place, space, and time. This is an approach to race as a diffused status characteristic[14] that filters experiences and ways of knowing, how

one is known and how one comes to know him- or herself in the specificity of social commerce.

My emphasis on racialized identities[15] is not meant to halt or deny the
progress in civil acknowledgments as some so carelessly critique when
Black people talk about blackness. The approach is designed to foreground
the meaningfulness of articulated experience, experience that always
guides individual and cultural development, and offer ways of knowing
the self and knowing the world. It is what Huggins, Kilson, and Fox
describe as the way "New World Africans, from their first awareness of
themselves as Americans, have wanted to assert the uniqueness and
importance of their experience," of their travel and situation (1971, vii).
Realizing of course that the reality of remembering is complicated by the
circumstance of conditions—layered sedimentations of experience coupled with the convergence of multiple realities that inhibit the unearthing
of a collectively acknowledged truth.[16] Hence, as a Black cultural critic I
am "seeking both to develop fair but forceful examination of black life,
and to establish a community of interlocutors" who find strength in the
articulation and interplay of experience, and those to whom this knowledge becomes additive and expansive with their understanding of Black
cultural performance (Dyson 2004, 341).

So we engage in storytelling—narratives that explain, persuade, and
stand as exemplars of experience and as a rhetoric of possibility.[17] This is
true both for the specified bodies that this study foregrounds, and for
those whom these bodies are always measured against in the realms of
communal and academic performative relations. In this chapter I want to
foreground the voices of my conversational partners and racial familiars
as we engage in both describing and building community in the places
that we live and work, and finding ways to bleed the borders between campus and community.

This is the story that frames the nature of this chapter with the particularity on migration narratives of Black folk working in the university environment and the notable shifts in our movement from campus to community to home and back again. In this chapter I want to offer excerpts
from the three emergent themes in the ethnographic conversations that I
have conducted with Black faculty, staff/administrators, and students. The
joint themes of community/constitution/camaraderie, negotiating boundaries of identity, and reconciling consciousness all emerge through a par-

ticular definition of migration. While the notion of human migration might be used to describe a one-way directional movement, I am interested in migration (maybe as described in the animal kingdom) as both a transporting and transitory process. Migration as a movement that is necessitated by desire with the promise of return—leaving and returning as a commitment to culture, and migration linked to mobility as a contributing force in the dynamism of cultural processes.[18] I am interested in migration as a movement from place to locality: the fact or condition of being in space and time with purpose and intent.

In her project "Who Set You Flowin'?: The African-American Migration Narrative," Farah Jasmine Griffin (1995) outlines four pivotal moments that structure traditional migration narratives. I modify them here to reveal the ways in which, while her project primarily charts the great Black migration from the South to the North, these are also topoi to understanding the internal bidirectional migration of Black folk between community and campus. First, in the migration narrative there is an event, desire, or realization that propels the movement. Second, the traveler offers a detailed representation of experience in the new locale. Third, an illustration is offered of the social, cultural, and performative negotiation of self in location—the then and there in relation to the here and now—and sometimes an articulated performance of resistance against difference. Fourth, a vision of the promises and possibilities of being in the new locale is offered that justifies or demonizes the choice to leave the point of origin (see also Hintzen and Rahier 2003). In varying forms these characteristics of the traditional migration narrative are represented in this research signifying on a physical movement as well as a psychological shift in the performance of identity.[19]

COMMUNITY, CONSTITUTION, AND CAMARADERIE

In writing about the nation, Benedict Anderson offers key insights to social constructions and constraints of collective identity that often place desire for sameness as unifying force over detected differences that test the fabric of culture. The three terms that articulate this first emergent theme concretize, as they also signal, the ephemeral nature of collective desire. A desire that both yearns for and resists the collective, because within each of these God-terms (community, constitution, and camaraderie) is a socializing agent that establishes norms of identity while displacing individual agency for the perceived comfort of social relations. This tensiveness of being an individual in the company of others, establishes the invisible forces that shape and maintain affiliative bonds within social and political enclaves.

In the interview protocol of my process there were a series of questions that focused on defining the notion and parameters of community, moving from denotative and connotative descriptions to building a more concretized construct of "the Black community." These questions were designed to establish a point of comparison leading to the construct of "the university community" and negotiations of identity here and there. The responses offered a range of complimentary and conflicting responses.

What is your construction, experience, and understanding of "community"?

Most initial constructions of "community" circulated around notions of codependence and neighborly necessity. In particular Zora, a faculty conversational partner, invoked the meaningful construct of the African village in describing community.

> Zora: My notion of the concept of community has to do with the African proverb, "It takes a village to raise one child." So community essentially means a whole body that has different outgrowths that all work together for the same common goal and the same common purpose. And that communities can exist in all types of arenas, for all different types of reasons, but that communities are essentially imagined, they come out of the mind of the people who are working in the community, for the community, of the community.

By invoking Benedict Anderson's notion of the "imagined community," Zora is particularly suggesting that community is held in stasis through a collective will and relational bonds that are situated in a particular locale. In a similar manner another faculty conversational partner, Alice, also grounds her orientation to community based in proximal orientation and relational support. It is an orientation that expands the construct of community from a particularly domestic sight, like the village, to more expansive spaces of social relations.

Alice: Community is the people who you surround yourself with and who you learn from, live with, who you can turn to for support or just count on being there. So community is people, but community also is a space—a physical and social space where you live or where you work. So there can be your work community, and your neighborhood community.

Alice invokes de Certeau's (1984) popular construction that place, specifically in terms of community becomes space, or practice place. For Alice this means that space becomes a place of social activity that establishes the relational associations that is the core of community.

Here I also want to foreground an exchange with staff/administrator conversational partner Abrahm that I believe reveals the complexity in which these issues overlap and sometimes bridge the gaps between campus and community. In particular Abrahm begins to identify how race serves as a bonding agent in the realm of social relations. But also how he has come to negotiate his understanding of community as an expansive construct of human relations that exceeds the limits of race or familial connections. I also include a specific section of our dialogue to foreground the dialectic in this ethnographic interview, but also to signal that the active process of sense-making that becomes a part of establishing a collective community identity—both as people who work in the university environment and more specifically Black men negotiating the politics of community in relation to each other.

Abrahm: Generally when I think about community . . . it's geared toward . . . family and then, kind of the environment in which you live in . . . I think that there are different forms of community but I think for me, personally, community has some type of family concepts attached to it.

Interviewer: Okay, . . . I'm going to play devil's advocate here. Can you have community in a situation where you don't necessarily have family, as in biological family? Or . . . where there is some mixture of race and culture within that sense of commonality?

Abrahm: I think you can have community . . . without having a sense of the family structure . . . I guess when it comes to . . . race and culture, yeah, I, I guess I would probably link community to those . . . I mean, I think to a certain degree . . . [for example] we as men, can be like a community . . . I look at . . . the Million Man March as kind of an example of, you know, a mass community that came together for a specific goal.

Interviewer: Do you define your experience working in a university environment as working within community?

Abrahm: I'd probably say so . . . I have never really taken to that point, but now that I'm starting to define and talk about it here, I would probably say yeah. Because I usually try to bring a family/team . . . philosophy into my work, . . . that's the kind of the environment that I feel that I work best within. So yes, on a small level, you know my department is a community, and even on a larger level, we [at the university] you know, faculty, staff, students would also be a community as well.

What I appreciate about Abrahm's comments is the manner in which he sutures together notions of codependence and neighborly necessity with constructs of proximal orientation and relational support—within the construct of family. His construction of community then becomes inclusive of possible racial, cultural, and biological links—but also shared desire that bridges borders of difference in location to simulate family to necessitate productivity. This was also true in the comments of student conversational partners Maya and Angela. I buttressed these comments against each other only to suggest an ongoing dialogue on these issues even though there was no direct exchange between them.

In our conversation Maya reinforced community as defined by social relations, and Angela concretized the notion of shared desire in the specific offered examples of religion and family as cultural communities.

Maya: Community . . . it doesn't necessarily have to be like a neighborhood, but it could be like an atmosphere where some way, . . . everybody who is in the atmosphere relate . . . because they're in the same neighborhood. As far as school is concerned it could be a community because everybody's got an interest in learning.

Angela: [Community] could be looked at on several different levels. My first community is my church community. That from which I gain my spiritual strength, my integrity, my morals, my values, everything comes from my church foundation. That is my strongest community. Then there is the family community, of course. Your upbringing which all stems from your religious upbringing [laughing] depending on how strong you are in your religion . . . Communities to me are just different cultures . . . that you feel that you belong to . . . My school community . . . [The student mentioned roles and organizations that she claims membership in on campus.]

Within this contribution Angela's perception of communities as cultures deepens her orientation to communities as systems of social interaction governed by particular rules of engagement. Rules of engagement that both establish patterns of social affiliation but also build a homeplace of comfort. In this way, she includes her school community as a place of both work and comfort.

In his use of the Million Man March as an example of community building, Abrahm too reinforced his construction of both family and community across borders of difference, but he also drew on empowering and enabling elements of racial and gendered commonality that could be used as energizing force. In many ways the Million Man March was about a group of racialized and gendered individuals, Black men coming together to build community. To do what Carrie Mae Weems described as an attempt to "make good on their pledge to improve the quality of life in their communities," and in particular to the Black family (1996, 9). They engaged this through a "translation of religious passion into political language and the voicing of religious dissent to political policies and cultural practices in protest rallies" (Dyson 2003, 44).

In a sense this is like Angela's reference to religion as dominating force of community and family as a crucible of beliefs and practices. In my own Black cultural community experience, religion was a cornerstone of everyday life and the family was the bridge between community and school and the relative success of Black students. For it was within the family that standards of social and cultural acceptability were established; views and perspectives on social order that shaped learning and the orientations to processes of teaching, schooling, and education. If the axiom that the classroom is a microcosm of society is true, then the family is the nucleus of learning and the corpus of social identity that schooling seeks to effect.[20]

I engaged this significant validation of the Black family link to education because I believe that in Angela's response, she was actually anticipating the nature of our conversational discourse. She grounded the significance of her identity as a student and more particularly as a Black-woman-student, in the foundational logics of religion and family. This is evident to me in how she ordered her communal affiliations with the religious community as the "strongest community," followed by her family community and then her school community. Knowing of course that the pri-

mary communities of church and family have already informed her participation and membership in what she defines as her school community.

What is your construction, experience, and/or understanding of "the Black community"?

Issues of race have already been implicated in constructions of community (via references to the African proverb, family, and the Million Man
March, etc.). Yet when my conversational partners were asked to define
the nature and influence of "the Black community" as a particular construct, there was more difference and dissonance in the specified coupling
of community and race. On one hand, the notion of "the Black community" seemed to further politicize an aggregate of individuals around issues
of history, oppression, struggle, and upliftment. On the other hand, there
was also some resistance to a tendency within the construct (or how people orient to the construct), that would over-suggest sameness in racial
commonality, thereby becoming reductive or essentializing and denying
ethnic, cultural, and class diversity in the always collectivizing construct
of race. For example, I press these four responses against each other beginning with staff conversational partner Malcolm to foreground the category
of responses to this question about "the Black community."

> Malcolm: "Wow! The first thing that comes to mind is history . . . Thinking
> about shared histories and experiences that people of African descent have
> endured, you know, maybe not personally but just . . . through the genera-
> tions.
>
> Abrahm: The Black community. To me, I think it definitely has an ethnic con-
> notation to it, I think it's a cultural connotation to it . . . you know, there
> is a bunch of, a group of black folks, African Americans, . . . who are just
> together, I think. You know . . . on different levels . . . I think as a whole I
> think it really encompasses everyone out there . . . I think there's a, you
> know, a kind of pro-Black notion that is associated with the Black commu-
> nity, in terms of you know, the Black community . . . should be out to
> advanced itself, and to a certain degree [through] Black business, [and] so
> forth and so on.
>
> Maya: The Black community. Um, Black only. Excluding everyone else.
> [Things] like what we have in common, the struggle, all kinds of things like,
> . . . music. Everything that most outsiders see . . . immediately when they
> hear "the Black community" is what comes to my mind . . . music, [media

representations of] violence, [well] people see, like you know, just the surface things, and that's what comes to my mind immediately. . . . Right, from
my own individual aspect it would be more like the hip-hop lifestyle. How
music influences everything, like almost everything as far as like adolescents
are concerned . . . um . . . like cars, clothing, like speech, like as far as . . .
Ebonics . . .

Angela: Black people . . . people of African American descent.

These responses worked in some very interesting ways to construct "the
Black community" by extending the social and affiliation variables of
community to the specificity of Black experience. In particular, the
responses marked the historical struggle of people of African descent
brought to America with a political sensibility that acknowledges struggle
and survival, "linking Black communities through a common historical
moment or a shared cultural trope" (Wright 2004, 2). While meant to
be an empowering strategy, it is also grounded in an assumed history of
oppression as a means of promoting social advancement through coalition-
building and commerce. Maya (a student conversational partner) then
extends the logic to include the politics of Black cultural performance.

Her response is both simple and complex in ways that signal those visible displays of Black culture like music, fashion, style, and the complexity
of language. Paul Gilroy signals the meaningfulness of her contribution in
his essay ". . . To Be Real: The Dissident Forms of Black Expressive Culture." He writes that black cultural performance traditions were drawn
from critical and creative processes of sustenance and survival.

In embattled circumstances of expressive art acquired a threefold character.
They reconciled their producers to their sublime plight and offered them a
measure of compensation for it, while also providing partial refuge from its
malevolent effects. Their art combined the laments of unfreedom with its
oppressed confirmation. This distinctive aporetic blend founded a tradition
of culture-making that resists the verdict of redundancy to which its own
bleak history points. That observation is as near as the study of modern
black expressive culture gets to producing a metahistory of its own functioning. (1995, 13)[21]

While Maya's comments seemingly reduce notions of the Black community to its visible evidence, what is seen, it is in fact these externalized,

performative, presentational, and enacted representations undergirded by logics of a historically situated sense of self that begin to define the parameters and the varying ways in which Black people have negotiated our current predicament.

In such a case, the meaningful simplicity of Angela's response, "Black people," in defining "the Black community" concretizes and specifies the bodies in question; the bodies that relate to each other through the specificity of time and the location of a living history. For Angela, "Black people" are the make-up of the "Black community"—and thus her construction becomes expansive and not reductive in that she is not relegating community to locality, but maybe back to a construct of nation, a construct that is both inclusive and illusive at the same time.

The very nature of the African Diaspora creates the literal conditions of an imagined community in that members will never know their fellow-members, meet them, hear of them, or come to understand the true constitution of their racialized identities—ties that bind and cosmologies that separate. Yet in the minds of each lives the image of their communion, community, and camaraderie both as an attractive force and resistant dynamic.[22] In reality the consequences and conditions of separation, time, and location have created what Stuart Hall (1998) calls "diasporic identities," which are never really the same or not the same, whether across continental divides or cornerstones that signify neighborhood.

On the other hand the responses of Zora and Alice seek to expand the borders of what it means to be Black, by in fact resisting the very construct of "Black" in the collectivized notion of "the Black community." Theirs is a resistance to some nostalgic notion of "a Black community" waiting to be reunited in the diaspora of people of African descent. Their response begins to address the tensiveness in acknowledging the dispersal of people of African descent and then recollate particular commonalities that tie them together (Wright 2004, 2). Hence, Zora and Alice argue for a sense of community among Black people in which difference has become a socializing agent of communal identity, not race.

So while I want to construct these as opposing voices (Malcolm, Angela, Maya, and Abrahm versus the following voices of Zora and Alice), I also want the reader to help me in seeing that these contributions offer more clarity in claiming and characterizing the confluence of identities within community, and less dissent over the construct of community as a collectivizing unit. In fact, I believe that the logics that are offered here actually build an argument for a diversity of ideas and identities that contribute to the productive association within communities.

> Zora: Well Black for me is really an interesting kind of word, in that I think that Black is created as a Western concept, as the antithesis to White. Which even though it has been taken as [let's say] Black power, and black beauty; and reclaimed by this community, who was labeled that way. It still essentially carries with it a lot of very very negative connotations because of the way in which it was constructed.
>
> So that when I say, "Black community," what I usually think of is a community that has come from *Blackness*. And the Blackness of the Black community would have to be slavery. That the Black community represents a community that is existing, that is surviving, that is built on and comes from the experience of slavery and that many of the attitudes, ways of living, modes of speaking, style of dress, comes from that oppression of slavery, with remnants and remembrances from a past life in Africa.
>
> Alice: I don't like the construct of "the Black community." Because I think that it essentializes what it means to be Black and it reminds me in particular of when . . . Mayor Hawn didn't want Bernard Parks to stay as police chief [in Los Angeles] and there was this kind of statement that "the Black community" is upset by this . . . when it really meant the middle-class Black establishment/community, not the progressive young aspect of the Black community. So when I think of "the Black community" the first thing I think is there is no such thing as "the" Black community.

In both cases I pressed my conversational partners to clarify the nature of their positions on the issue of "the Black community" in relation to their previous constructions of "community." I believe that Zora and Alice were making an argument similar to Michelle Wright's critique of Henry Louis Gates: "Gates' reliance on the term 'black' to signify a homogenous set of practices and/or experiences elides philosophical, cultural and historical differences, and, in insisting on either absolute difference or none, denies us a framework in which to understand 'Blackness' as a unity of diversity" (2004, 5–6). In particular, I believe that Zora and Alice are arguing both against a conflation of identity (as in the problematic construction that "all Black people are the same") as well as for some referential lexicon of "Blackness" that can signal the particularity of racial designations without collectivizing cultural character. So here it might be necessary to look less at being Black as the dominating signifier of unity, and more on *Blackness as performative agency* in organizing Black people in community.

In particular, I asked Zora and Alice to reconcile in some way what seemed to flow as celebratory constructions of community that foregrounded the variables of codependence and neighborly necessity with proximal orientation and relational support. This is in relation to their strained hesitancy in dealing with the constitution of race as a defining variable of community.

Furthermore, I asked them, if possible, to offer me an alternative and more personally suitable construct that would *racialize community* without the element of essentializing or invoking problematic relational politics. In the process I asked them to identify those communities that they claim membership in or the places that they call home; knowing of course that home is also a contested space.[23] Their responses are worth noting at length.

> **Zora:** Home (community) for me. I belong to three different communities. I belong to the community of motherhood. I belong to the community of academia. And I belong to the community . . . of woman, but not only am I a woman. I am a New World Yoruba woman. I am a New World indigenous woman, that is what and who I am. My place here [at the university] was influenced a couple of years ago, or maybe it was just a year ago. When I had a conversation with an esteemed friend and colleague of mine, as I sat and said, [playfully lamenting] "I am the only Black girl . . . I am the only Black girl . . . what to do?" And my colleague said, "Perhaps you are supposed to be the only Black girl as you welcome the other Black girls and Black boys and people of color across the line into the ivory tower. Maybe you are the welcome committee." So that is the reason why I am here in the ivory tower. Me coming from my indigenous, grassroots, New World, Miamian studying background. My purposes is to help the other Black and brown girls, other Black and brown boys, other Asian—Latino/a, European, Celtic, Druid, people find what I have found, which is humanity inside of culture and inside of this [academic] community.
>
> **Alice:** I definitely think that there are common experiences and interests. There are *some* common experiences and *some* common interests—among Black people. But I think that it is largely shaped by class . . . but I think that

the most common experience that almost all of us can share across class is experiences with racism—feeling excluded in certain settings, like maybe in our work-place, having people treat us unfairly, or certainly in public spaces like restaurants or government buildings . . .

The neighborhood that I live in I consider . . . I kind of think of that as the "Black community." . . . It is diverse . . . at this point in Los Angeles there are not a lot of places that are Afrocentric anymore, there is not a lot of places where there is a high concentration of African Americans and in addition . . . there are the people who live there and then there is also a cultural aspect—in terms of restaurants that are Black owned, and stores that sell African clothing and hip-hop oriented events and spoken word by predominately Black people. So the history that is there [longevity]. It has been there a long time . . .

Honestly I did choose to move there because it was a Black community. Having lived in West L.A. for most of my time in L.A., I really felt so unvalidated in that previous place that I wanted to be in a place where I felt recognized. And it really has been that way. People are proud of me . . . People care about me . . . People let me know—like if it's street-cleaning day and I need to move my car—someone knocks on my door. I never had that experience in West L.A. People would even hardly even say hi or even make eye contact.

In both of these responses the women tease out and tease at the intricacy of what they mean by community and their positionality in community; their political location within space and in relation to people in place. In particular, like Angela (the student) outlining the communities in which she claimed membership (religion, family, school), Zora delineated aspects of her communal identities as mother/motherhood, New World Yoruba woman, and professor–welcome committee–emissary. Zora did this not necessarily to order her identity or the communities in which she claims membership, but to in fact show how they inform each in the specified context of the university.

In her response Alice offers a particularly direct manner in which to envision "a" community of Blacks without essentializing a monolithic notion of "the Black community." I appreciate the manner in which her rearticulation moves through four stages of logic: First, she claims points of connection in the lived experience of Black folk, but then implicates class as a variable or a point of disconnect that distinguishes the conditions of experience—if not the perspective of racial experience. Second, she offers the overarching construction of racism as shared experience, a somatically felt inequity and oppression based on the materiality and historicity of bodies that might be a common link, though a differently encountered variable that connects Black people. Third, she offers a specific example of her lived community, which she conceives as "a" Black community—based on the people who reside in the area, as well as the practical proliferation and performance of Black cultural life via places, activities, and cultural arts. Fourth, she offers insight to affirmation in "a" Black community by describing her experience as a "felt recognition."

Felt recognition becomes both sensate experience and relational site. A location where the visual recognition of blackness is validated and her personal sense of worth is appreciated and celebrated in ways that the materiality of her body, the content of her intellect, and her academic accomplishment are unified as meaningful contributions to race, culture, and community. Ostensibly she says that in her particular Black community— the "[Black] People are proud of me . . . [Black] people care about me . . . [and Black] people let me know it."

This type of racialized and gendered acknowledgment of a Black woman in community cannot be reduced to an ingratiating and insipid Sally Fields acceptance speech. You remember. "You like me, you really really like me." This is an acknowledgment grounded in histories of oppression of Blacks in general and the specific invalidation of Black woman labor and accomplishments. Such appreciation comes from others with similar histories of struggle (aligned by race or gender); those who seek to acknowledge and to uplift community. This might also be an actualization of what Neckerman, Carter, and Lee (1999) identify in their essay "Segmented Assimilation and Minority Cultures of Mobility" as a kind of support system in the Black community that validates the accomplishments and self-worth of middle-class Blacks who negotiate the workaday world in White institutional environs while still suffering the pangs of racial distrust and indifference.[24]

NEGOTIATING BOUNDARIES OF IDENTITY

The notion of public and private spheres might serve as apt comparison between campus and community; one designated as a space of work (academic endeavors, formality, and protocol) and the other constructed as the domestic site (home, community, and family).[25] Of course these are not really distinct and separate categories of experience; both are fraught with the politics of identity that establish particular patterns of behavior, performances of sociality, and pressures of expectation. In varying ways these are the prevailing themes of talk that emerged with faculty, staff/administrators, and students when asked to speak of their shifting sense of self as they traverse the boundaries of campus and community; all of which I concretize as the performative act of negotiating boundaries of identity.

While the notion of the public sphere might be constructed as a communal force against the state, for my purposes I am interested in the ways in which the directionality and politicalness of our conversational talk is not directed against the state (or the university in this case) but designates a theater of cultural performance, located in the borderlands of our existence. Borderlands in Gloria Anzaldúa's construction of a "vague and undetermined place created by the emotional residue of an unnatural boundary . . . [and] those who cross over, pass over, or go through the confines of the 'normal'" are neither there nor here because of desire and necessity (1987, 3). In this sense, we are those who cross borders, those imaginary yet sedimented lines that define places and characterize spaces as boundaries of acceptability and territories of terror.[26] Our conversation is about locating ourselves in those in-between spaces, set off against the often-reifying identity politics of location—between campus and community. In conversational play of these ethnographic interviews, we explore the truncated reality of our similarly shared experiences as we negotiate our existence in the borderlands.

Does campus or community life place particular demands or constraints on your performance of race, culture, identity, or sociality?

The cluster of questions that organized this line of discussion was geared toward having my conversational partners offer narrative descriptions of experience in campus life. Many of them prefaced their comments by acknowledging the logical fact that we all shift aspects of our complex identities to foreground a particular suitability to the social and relational contexts in which we enter. They then moved into specific examples. I want to frame this section with offerings by faculty conversational partner

Alice and staff conversational partner Malcolm—because they foreground a performative resistance to the social pressures and expectations of/in community.

> Alice: In my neighborhood I don't really want to play up . . . my educational training and my research interest or the kinds of things that I write about. I find other aspects of commonality that I have with the people in my community and a lot of them are teachers, in my direct building, so I can connect with them on that . . . and a lot of them are single women, single Black women in the current situation that we live in, so I can connect with them on that . . . Whereas in this setting at Cal State I am—my reason for being here and what I do here is—all about my training. I [have to] emphasize my educational experience, I emphasize my research interests and my kind of ambition and ambitiousness—whereas I don't emphasize my ambitiousness in the community. Because it is seen more as . . . being egotistical, where as here it's seen as "that's how people know what you are doing." [It is] how people know whether you should be appointed to different committees or whether you should be advanced in promotion.
>
> Malcolm: In the community I think at times . . . when you're black, and you are considered part of . . . the university world . . . it kind of places some responsibilities or burdens on you . . . , Like oh he's going to be the smart one, he's going to be the one who solves all the problems, or he knows it all . . . And there are times when I don't want to carry that, and so I might tend to, not necessarily dumb myself down, but maybe not speak up so much, like in community meetings, or . . . when I volunteer for something . . . because I don't want to always be perceived as the problem solver.

Alice and Malcolm offer particular narrative constructions that chart their positionality in the intersections of campus and community. In both responses there is a tensive negotiation in their academic persona in community. While Alice signals issues of appropriateness as related to relational communion, her resistance to speaking of her academic life in community is captured in the performative construct of *ambitiousness*. This construct signals a trait of personal motivation that is often celebrated (ambition), as well as suggests a degree of being overzealous that turns into egoism.

In her experience—and in my own experience in "the Black community"—ambition linked to motivation and uplifting self and community (if not sometimes constructed as *uplifting the race*) is seen as a positive trait. But ambition linked with revelry in the self-accomplished is seen as elevating the self above community (above race, above other Black people), and that is demonized as a trait not congruent with building and sustaining community. In other words, showing ambition is a performative act of desire about transforming and bettering the self and is always linked with the sustained logic of struggle in Black cultural life. Ambitiousness on the other hand, suggests a state of being (arrogance), an elemental aspect of character that is read as end product rather than as process. In her response, Alice goes on to suggest that these performances and presentations of self are interpreted, validated, and invalidated differently between campus and community—one being appropriate and encouraged while the other is seen as less than humble, less than a part of the people.

In a similar way, Malcolm speaks about toning down references or performances of his academic accomplishment or professional affiliation. This is both to deflect negative critique, which can become isolating and work against the notion of "the real"—in terms of a delimited Black masculine performativity. It also deflects the pressure of performance; having to pay the high competency tax that is sometimes demanded because of education and the exhausting ways in which community sometimes demands service. Even with his high commitment to culture and community, Malcolm modulates his performance and presentation of self in order to regulate the relational orientations of others to him as he crosses from campus to community.

Yet I find that the commentary offered by both Alice and Malcolm falls short of critiquing the Black community. I believe that the very nature of their descriptions acknowledges that community (the Black community in particular) and the cultural performances through which it sustains itself are a sociopolitical complex; a system of harmonic and aharmonic discords, unspoken rules, and social relations that govern membership. Whether in the specified location of a neighborhood or within the larger realm of visuality where seeing-is-believing, and marked bodies are subject to a particular critique and cultural performative expectation. This becomes evident in both Alice's and Malcolm's commitment to community coupled with the daily performances of compromise and resistance that goes into maintaining any cultural membership.[27]

From a different perspective a student conversational partner and a

staff conversational partner foreground two important issues that I want
to describe under the construct of pivoting propriety. Propriety describes
"the manner in which one is perceived and the means constraining one to
remain submitted to it" (de Certeau, Giard, and Mayol 1998, 17). Like the
experience of migration, while propriety shifts, one is always grounded
in the memory of other rules of engagement. Cultural rules that, unlike
governmental policies that dictate human sociality, can be displaced in the
mind but not from the body.

> **Maya** (student): When I come to campus I know I have to build up, talk about
> school work; my mind is on school, period . . . though my mind might be
> set on . . . social aspects, but the social is still about school . . . But then
> when I go home, I'm not going to lie, my mind is kind of, it's just back to
> my neighborhood and where I'm from. But I still have to keep school
> engraved in my mind so I can still go back to school, ... you know . . .
> **Lorraine** (staff): A lot of that would be in relation to policy issues . . . what is
> proper and what is not. . . . not just policy issues as in defining things, but
> just to be able to interact with others in a professional setting, as for as what
> in general becomes appropriate or issues—or . . . for instance, if there is an
> issue of concern—you are able to go here, but you are not allowed to go
> there . . . whereas outside you would go directly to [the source].

In the student's response I like the notion of "building up"—having to
literally construct the persona of the student when she enters campus. This
is a performative act accomplished through talking about schoolwork and
focusing her attention on things that relate to the school experience. Yet
while she initially constructs the campus as a place for work, which would
relegate the community as a site for social activities, she rescues that idea
by saying that "the social is still about school." In this way she reconfigures the social (as play) in terms of maybe meeting friends, partying, and
cocurricular activities to social (as work) as a necessary component in the
educational experience. Also, her response foregrounds shifting cultural
scripts between campus and community as well as the investments in performative mandates that secure membership.

Lorraine's response focuses primarily on the ways in which the campus
environment mandates a proceduralism that is both practical agency and
political protocol. She clearly acknowledges this in terms of appropriate
procedures and behaviors within a professional environment, but proce-

dures and protocols that she might not practice and follow outside of the context of work and campus. What is particularly important about this response is that it reminds us that protocols of human sociality are often dictated by political mechanisms; chains of command that regulate not only procedures but also levels of directness in human contact. This is true for formalized organizational and bureaucratic systems like the university, as well as cultural communities that exhibit the same elements of systematic and rule-governed social affiliation.

Does the knowledge of the people in the community where you live about what you do at the university have a perceived impact on your relationship with them?

The answer to this question was alluded to in a number of the above responses, in particular Alice and Malcolm's reference to the perception of ambitiousness and the demand for community service. Yet the particularity of Zora's extended narrative that follows offers a unified connection between campus and community. The narrative response reveals ways in which the duality of campus and community identities are not bifurcated or isolated, but unified as racialized character and possibility.

> Zora: The other day I was coming home from Trader Joe's; I had just done some shopping. I have a neighbor, and of course I love all my neighbors. (They're good to me.) And we have a community, like in our neighborhood we do. So I am coming home and my neighbor's husband's son—he's grown, he's my age. He actually comes to this school, here at Cal State, Los Angeles—and their daughter comes here at Cal State, Los Angeles. And so I am getting out of the car, I am taking my bags up, and he is talking to my upstairs neighbor. And he is like, "Hey Professor [Zora]." And I am like, "What's up with you padnah?" And so then my upstairs neighbor is like, "Uh huh . . . She is just [Zora] to me. I ain't calling her no professor [Zora]." Right? And so I looked at her and I looked at him, and I said, "You don't have call me Professor [Zora], nevertheless, you know that is who I am. O.K.?" And so they both just looked at me and fell out laughing. And it was like, "You crazy. If your students saw you when you be coming outside in your pajamas they would not be happy." [laughing]
>
> The most beautiful part of the interaction was [the young man saying] "Don't do nothing professor. Let me take those bags into the house for you." And I was like, "aaah you make me feel so good. I feel like a queen." And he was like, "As you are, as you are." So that I watched this big strong

strappin' man, OK, student, Cal State L.A. student, no less, carrying all of
my bags out of my car into my living room in one swoop . . . That made
my morning and my day magnificent.

There are many things that I appreciate about this narrative. I appreciate how the playfulness, respect, and care of this interaction are informed
by the social, cultural, and political components that designate and regulate the bodies in play. These are qualities that are about community life,
campus identities, and the knowledge of how each plays with and against
the other. Maybe this is the counternarrative to how Alice and Malcolm
spoke about community and maybe, in fact, it is the very essence of these
types of interactions that they embrace in their own experiences in "a
Black community." These are also part and parcel of my own experiences.

In the narrative I appreciate the dueling aspects and the relational play
between neighbors. I appreciate the young man carrying Zora's bags and
the historical reference—from a Black-male-student-neighbor to a Black-
female-professor-neighbor—of Black women being queens in another
land, another life, and in that configured relationship. This is not stated
in nostalgic defiance but chastened, the statement stands as they stand in
reciprocal relation to the particularity of each other: a teacher and a student, a Black man and Black woman offering respect and comfort in the
company of each other, in community (Posnock 1998, 21).[28] This is a
moment of sincere cultural performance and respect. Moments like this
reconfigure the borderlands between campus and community in which
the inhabitants are not brutish slaves subverting the normal, but empow-
ered individuals performing the altogether real in the company of each
other.

I appreciate the manner in which these characters perform this cultural
theatric; the players—the strappin' young man, the sassy upstairs neighbor, and the teacher-neighbor-friend—play with the ordering of identity,
which is and/or should be foregrounded in the particularity of the community. The difference between "Professor Zora" and "She is just Zora to
me." Mediated by the knowledge of "That is who I am." The playfulness
of this cultural exchange, like Zora's construction that she has a "community in her neighborhood," delineates and connects these associations.
Neighborhood as a geographical "space of a relationship to the other as
social being" (de Certeau, Giard, and Mayol 1998, 12), with community

being a particular relational dynamic of congeniality that goes beyond the constraints of propriety to include an element of care and celebration in human social relations.

Like Michael Eric Dyson's reading of John Singleton's *Boyz N the Hood*, "neighborhood is community precisely because it turns on the particularity of racial [and gender] identity," while acknowledging position and positionality as possibility and promise that uplifts race and social conditions (2004, 341). The upstairs neighbor's reference to Zora's students (seeing her in her pajamas) and their subsequent laughing, speaks to how the real and imagined borders of place and space can be penetrated with the knowledge of the other. Thus resulting in humbling acts that humanize identity as it crosses borders that divide and connect. The reference (to students seeing her in her pajamas) is in fact a performative that does what it suggests, and the laughter is not solely about what could be, but what is always and already in the realm of their knowledge of each other and how they negotiate their social, cultural, and political relations.

RECONCILING CONSCIOUSNESS

The construction of this thematic label, "reconciling consciousness," is intentional on my part. While the phrase might suggest references to W. E. B. Dubois's classic discussions of Black "double consciousness,"[29] I am not particularly interested, at least not here, in the fullness of that discussion about the Black inability to reconcile Blackness and an American identity. Though of course I realize how the elements of that discussion are pertinent to a bifurcated sense of self between campus and community with the identity politics of both sites holding its inhabitants hostage. What I am most interested in here is the manner in which my conversational partners articulated their awareness of a performative and representational shift in their identity as they move from campus to community and the ways in which they work to reconcile that shift.

Hence "reconciling consciousness" becomes a more empowering construct about agency and not solely about a debilitating sense of a bifurcated self. In each of these situations, my conversational partners signaled their conscious awareness of self in space; and while the notion of "conscious awareness" might seem redundant, I am referencing how they negotiated their positionality (or rather the politics of their position in place) with a responsiveness toward adapting or asserting the particularity of their character in space. Such awareness is prompted in the following question and responses.

Do you perceive yourself making shifts in your identity as your move from campus to community, and back?

> Alice: Yes I do . . . I have worked on trying to be more whole in all the settings that I am in. . . . So I actually probably do it less than I used to . . . for example. Sometimes I will use slang in the classroom as a way of being who I am and also trying to connect with the students.

> Malcolm: Okay. I try to be myself, and I try to be real . . . on campus, you know, even with a set of responsibilities I have to the university and to students, you know. I'm still [Malcolm] who loves pop culture, [Malcolm] who watches television, and things like that, and I share those pieces of myself, . . . with my coworkers, [and] students, and things like that.

These two responses are both framed within a desire for wholeness, an acknowledgment and resistance to a bifurcated identity that marks them as different in the shifting locations of campus and community. In many ways they ground the nature of this shift in performance, the strategic enactment of choice and behavior. For Alice that is noted initially in her comment about using slang in the classroom, both as an expression of her "true" self and as a strategy to connect with students—students who might use similar language while also recognizing her effort to connect classroom content, cultural expression, and aspects of the personal.

For Malcolm it is reflected in his efforts to be himself and, maybe more importantly, "to be real." In Black vernacular "to be real" is not only to be true to yourself; it also suggests a culturally and communally constructed notion of authenticity. To speak the language and politics of the Black community as in the theorizing of Henry Louis Gates Jr. (1988), to represent and signify Black culture as embodied performative practice within and across borders of difference. Yet in a later extension of this thought Malcolm admits to the limits of being real in the university environment.

> Malcolm: I think to some extent, you know . . . black university administrators or faculty [or staff] can be real, but only to a certain extent, . . . university politics, university policies, . . . will demand that you be another person. . . . I think, that . . . within [the] university, you can only . . . be yourself to a

certain extent . . . um, without bumping up against a glass or brick ceiling, you know . . . And so I think that . . . being real might be true to yourself, ethnicity wise, [maybe] in terms of class or gender, [yet] you know again, there are those . . . powers that say—you can be yourself but only to a certain extent, if you want to achieve this or do that or something [else].

In many ways Malcolm references the broader construct of mediated realities, which is a core argument within this entire chapter. *Mediated realities* reference the ways in which the actuality of being is often dictated by the specificity of location. Not simply where someone is positioned but also how one is positioned. In referencing university administrators, Malcolm states that "university politics," and the particularity of university procedures dictate identity performances that separate the specificity of racial or cultural impulses from that of university protocol. His use of the phrase, "bumping up against a glass or brick ceiling" is the metaphoric reference to both reduced possibilities and limited advancement as well as the type of performative cultural mandates that often discipline individuality and difference.

In his response he attempts to suture racialized and ethnic identities with the professional pressures on identity, yet acknowledges that those possibilities are sometimes limited. He then signals the nature of the compromise that many Black administrators might make between advancement and "being real." Of course these are very contentious issues that are intervened and complicated with the "politics of being real," which most often are constructed by the collective and competing powers of culture and community. Hence the Black administrator stands betwixt and between competing mandates on cultural performance—administrative protocols and racialized mandates of the real.

When I posed the same question about shifting identities to student conversational partner Angela, she offered me a response that revealed a different strength of will and character, accompanied by a logical strategy of locating self in space. To the thought of shifting, she immediately said,

Angela: No, cause I am [Angela]. I am gonna be [Angela] regardless. I know how to be behave, I am well educated and a part of being [Angela] is being able to adapt in certain situations. A lot of people always tell me, they say, "[Angela] you are always wearing so many different hats. One minute you're like this, the next minute you're like that." That's because [Angela] knows when to act and when not to act.

Within her response of "knowing when to act and when not to act" of course she is talking about appropriateness of behavior and the agency to perform. I asked her to elaborate on the notion of adapting in this context, and she responded with a trope, an associational and behavioral comparison. She stated:

> **Angela:** I will use the analogy of a chameleon—how when you put them in certain environments they are suppose to be able to change, and adapt to that environment. It is a way of conforming but at the same time you are not losing who you are.

I like this response, but more than just liking it I respect the level of sophistication that I read in her utterance; the chameleon is a sly and clever creature. A creature that nature (if not history or nurture) has endowed with the ability to change color not simply to adapt, but to adopt performative traits and the forethought of materiality (color) with a purpose: to learn, to hunt, to feed, to go undetected, to appear to be a natural part of its environment; to camouflage.

The chameleon analogy subtly challenges fixed and essentialized notions of Black character, identity, and possibility. Angela's comments work in the realm of what Clarence Lusane describes in the foreword to *Beyond Identity Politics: Emerging Social Justice Movements in Communities of Color*: "identity politics [in any community] evolves as part of an arsenal of weapons," that is, skills and stratagems required to sustain self in community and across borders of social travel. This chameleon-like skill that Angela talks about is really a series of performance choices that are more so engaged "as a matter of necessity [than . . .] a matter of choice" (1996, 2). As Angela says, while this could be seen "as a way of conforming," what she considers to be her core identity (remembering that she constructed her identity in the communities of religion, church, and the Black community) is consciously consistent. This even if she chooses to vary external performances and presentations of self.

In many ways the response given by Zora, one of my faculty conversational partners echoes Angela's (student) response, but places it within the specificity of what she describes as being "a Black girl," which for Zora is both a description of bodily materiality and a political positionality. I offer an extended excerpt from her contribution to focus on multiple issues. These issues range from the construction of a historical identity in relation to a local construction of the self, to the notion that while identity is often considered a social construction there is an agency in self-definition that serves as an act of self-empowerment. This becomes particularly important as Black people move between campus and community, spaces where there might be a seemingly fixed sense of racial and gender identity performance.

Zora: Well actually for me . . . I use to feel myself doing that quite a lot [shifting], but now it's starting to all meld together. [Why?] Because I have been at the club and felt students tap me on my back, and be like, "Did you grade my paper?" [laugh] That has happened to me because people know who I am. Because I know who I am and so that now, my performance in my community and my performance at the university become the same thing, an opportunity to teach, to lead by example, to say "you know?" This is who I am. I am a real Black girl. Right! . . . You might roll up on me playing some Jon B early on Saturday morning with some two buck chuck from Trader Joe's. . . . I am a real Black girl. When I say real Black girl . . . you know what I am saying? I know my cultural connections. But I also know that America is a very big part of me. Even though I have to know the other part of me as well. So that is why I say I am a *real* Black girl. I am an indigenous Black girl. I was just born here and speak English.

I use this as an opportunity to show people what Black really is . . . .really beautiful. That it is the silk of the Nile. That Black is not the Western construction of evil and devil and scary and threatening. That it is hard working. That it is Harriet Tubman with her boots on praying, willing people back and forth, thirty years old knowing that she had a period and didn't have no *Always*.[30] Strapped with a gun on her waist talking about, "Look nigga . . ." because that's what she used say, when people/men would tell her "I can't go no further." She would say, "Look nigga make a choice. You gonna be free or you gonna die. Which is poppin? Now if you gonna be free let's get steppin' cause I smell the hounds. They comin', let's go."

And so I have to be that. I can't be any less than these women. I can't spit on Harriet Tubman; I can't spit on Sojourner Truth. And I can't spit on Queen Latifah either; I can't spit on none of them. So I have to walk and talk and be a certain way at home, in my community, and at home in my

community/professional/academic worlds, at home and at play at the same
time. I have to be representin' at all times. And so that everything is coming
together for me as the same performance, an opportunity to teach by
example.

Zora's response offers a series of important examples of how the borders and boundaries of her identity are separated only by porous mem-
branes that allow a fluidity of self within the multiple locations of her habitation. In particular, her example of encountering students "at the club"
suggests that she must, as they expect, negotiate her relationship with
them both as teacher/student and as people in the community enjoying
themselves. While identities might be mediated and invoked in particular
situations, the reality of that moment (in the club) strips bare the human-
ness of both parties. Her laughter in offering this narrative suggests just
how ticklish such situations can be. Hence, for her, there needs to be a
consistency in her character and self-presentation in both campus and
community that creates the possibility of her being in the dailyness of her
life—regardless of where she might encounter students.

In Zora's self-description of being "a real Black girl," she invokes the
construct of "realness" to suggest both the actuality of her performative
engagements and a point of origin that positions her racialized and politicized identity. Her comment uses aspects of Black vernacular to signal
what are, for her, performances of blackness that are easily recognizable
in the Black community where she lives, as well as the Black communities
in which she circulates. Yet in her self-description as "an indigenous Black
girl . . . [who] was just born here and speak[s] English, " she is establishing
positionality. Remember that it was Zora who earlier identified herself as
a "new Yoruba woman." Hence her reference links notions of being "real"
and being "indigenous" to bridging more expansive borders that might be
defined in terms of nation and geography.

For Zora, her embodied presence and performative engagement of self
is about her understanding and performing allegiances to African culture,
the terror of the middle passage, and the current predicament of her location in the Western world. While in earlier conversations she resisted the
notion of "Black people," she embraces it here as a construction rich with
the sediments of an African origin, "the silk of the Nile" as she puts it.
Hence, as she moves on in her narrative she signals and calls forth refer-

ences that navigate a historical terrain crossing the Nile, the confrontation with difference in the Western world, work as both labor and tenacity, and the willful struggle for survival. In such, she presents her embodied sense of self as a remedy to the perceived problem of Black femaleness—bridging gaps and suturing wounds that have long been infected with social discontent.

Zora's expansive response to the question about double consciousness does not reveal a tension or confusion that is most often associated with the construct. Her comment reconciles the multiplicity of those historical and contemporary representations of Black struggle and survival in a cogent performance of her own self-presentation. In offering the tripartite reference to Harriet Tubman, Sojourner Truth, and Queen Latifah—"Black" women with mythically historicalized and problematized legacies—she positions herself in the company of the diversity within the subject category of Black woman, who have negotiated the borders and boundaries in the materiality of their presence, the social construction of their identities, and the necessary borders (literal and figurative) that they needed to cross in order to realize their possibility—while also establishing a radical template of sociality and performative agency for others.

BLEEDING BORDERS

There is always a story that frames the nature of research. Maybe a personal happening that resonates in memory and motivates further exploration of issues that effect lived existence. As my conversational partners told their stories of migration they often said, "You know what I'm talking about." These were not questions or conversational prompts but confirmations of shared experiences—either literal or the ways in which our narratives engage tropological allusions that we can each relate to; bleeding the borders between campus and community, between researcher and subjects. These stories are about "going home" and about "homecomings." Those times when we have traveled the distance between campus and community, between being home and being at home in those spaces that support particular aspects in our identity and those places that sanction normative performances of our identity.[31]

I want to leave you with two excerpts from a migration narrative offered by a student conversational partner whom I will call Martin. In the narrative I want you to read yourself into the text as protagonist or antagonist, as audience member or participant, as teacher or student, as Black or the otherwise "raced" reader of these narratives. I invite you to travel with him as he crosses the border from campus to community. Here is Martin's story:

> **Martin:** I recall one of my philosophy classes in which I was the only African American, and as we addressed issues of Blacks and Blackness, everyone turned to me as if I was the ambassador for all things that are Black, to all things that weren't. I felt isolated, alienated, and otherized. I felt things that words can't even describe. I felt alone. On one particular occasion we were discussing free speech, its limitations (hate speech), and questioning whether or not there should be any . . . [limitations on free speech]. During this discussion we arrived at rap [rap music], . . . questioning whether or not it's harmful, and if so, could it be banned under the *clear and present danger* clause in the First Amendment. A young white woman, backed by a heavy portion of class and a very opinionated Asian young man, asked me [directly], "Why do Black people even listen to rap, why do they act like they do (specifically referring to the images of rap and rap videos), and why are so many of them gangsters?" I replied in a manner that made those questions seem as foolish as they were. I told them statistically Whites spend about three times as much [money] as Blacks [do] on rap music, [and the] images that you see of how Blacks act . . . are mediated images of an institutionalized oppressive system which serves to create Blacks as second-class citizens . . . And besides, Black people are not this one big homogenous culture. And as I critiqued the class I realized that I had been reduced to nothing but race. I was that African American again, that Negro again, that Black man again, that colored again, that blacky again, that coon again, I was that nigger again. . . . [always and already]. . . .
>
> In college and in academic life, I feel alone, but in the home place, the African American community, I feel appreciated and celebrated for my accomplishments, but I also feel alone. I feel appreciated and celebrated when I'm labeled "the smart one," when I come home with a report card full of A's, or when I'm in [the public eye for other achievements] . . . But I feel alone as I am constantly critiqued by my family as not being "a real nigga," because the way I dress, my pattern of speech, or my mannerisms are not consistent with theirs, or the rest of the world's preconceived scripts and notions of how Black masculinity and identity should be performed. Or as my mother, and all of her five sisters would say, "You can take the

nigga out of the hood, but you can't take the hood out of the nigga." I realize now that critique is an act of love, and that even though I feel alone during these critiques, because they're grounded in pointing out my differences, they are my family's way of telling me that I must stay grounded and always recognize where I come from.

The problematic construct of "being a real nigga" that Martin's family engages is a very familiar charge in "the Black community."[32] It serves as a disparagingly positive regulatory device that establishes both the trap and the paradox of authenticity.[33] The trap is that the complicated cultural construction of "nigga" both acknowledges the problematic historical origins of the reference, while engaging in a radical reappropriation of that term—suggesting family, familiarity, and affiliation. [34] The dubious reference when directed by Blacks to Blacks both signals a desired and affective performative identity, while also establishing a particular evaluative criteria on which such embodied and enacted performances are measured. The descriptive speculation of "being a real nigger" of course both empowers and marginalizes at the same time. The difference is whether the phrase is used as affirmation or disconfirmation of identity and racial membership.

On the other hand, Martin (a Black male college student) is trapped in the paradox of authenticity. He is located some place between being a Black male in a still-racist society and being a student, who is expected both to represent the critically sanitized performances of academic inquiry and to serve as a racial resource—a representative and a visual aid to/of Blackness. In such a case, "The paradox, the dilemma of authenticity, is that to be experienced as authentic it [a person or performance] must be marked as authentic, but when it is marked as authentic it is mediated, a sign of itself, and hence lacks the authenticity of what is truly unspoiled, untouched by mediating cultural codes" (Culler 1988, 159). Hence Martin is trapped betwixt and between a social construction of himself and the actuality of his being; negotiating the balance of what it means to be real in the shifting territories of his social engagement. Territories inhabited by cultural communities with differing performative expectations to sustain membership.

Martin's narrative about the classroom experience acknowledges the tensions that still exist in the social construction of Black identity and the ways in which Blacks in the ivory tower are sometimes called on to both defend and define our racial and cultural identity. In his own response, Martin identifies how those moments of social encounter establish a place of entrapment. A place of entrapment that may clarify the racist constructions of Black cultural life while risking to reify those perceptions in the magnitude of a defensive response; which may confirm stereotypes of "Black male rage." This may or may not be an accurate assessment given the conditions of the encounter. (I play out this dilemma in different ways in chapter 3 under the construct of "good man/bad man.")

Within the closing of Martin's overall contribution he uses a variation of bell hooks's often-cited construct that *critique is a form of love.*[35] Of course, when Martin uses this construct he is, as I believe hooks is, referencing critique in a context of love. Critique in the context of relational security. Critique in the context of home or pedagogical encounters where relational conditions (adult to child, teacher to student, or colleague to colleague) signify intention mediated by care. Critique in the context of an interpersonal relationship in which both parties understand (as much as that is possible) the intentions of the offered commentary—to inform, to strengthen, to support, and to empower. This is in opposition to *critique as a practice of power*—to denigrate, to diminish, or to regulate behavior. Martin uses the phrase "critique as a form of love" in reference to his family and not to the students in the classroom situation. Hence, his defensive response to their descriptive accusations and assumptions about Black culture (through the frame of rap music and hip-hop) acknowledges that their critique is not about love.

In the two narrative examples that I offer from my conversation with Martin, he strategically marks a conceptual and relational challenge between campus and community. A challenge that must often be negotiated as the perceptual difference in a social orientation to people, race, and culture as regulated and signified in space. Hence Martin is cast as both the insider and outsider, as he occupies a tenuous location in both campus and community (Puwar 2004, 8). Yet I suspect that Martin, like many scholars, acknowledges that authenticity is a social construction.[36] As social creatures we are all implicated in performing for community and performing culture in community—the benefits from which we accrue and establish our own positionality in the dynamic of human social relations. The nature of this chapter reinforces this notion by contextualizing the performative logic of shifting identities between the contested borders of the ivory tower and the Black community.

Throughout the migration narratives in this chapter, my conversational partners articulate the ways in which they encounter the differing performative expectations between campus and community and, in some ways, how they manage and maneuver in order to negotiate their own identities in place and space. In particular, the narratives position the tellers in relation to their desire—the academic arena with its promise of professionalism and promotion, and the domestic sites that they call home—circulating constructions and investments in the notion of "the Black community." In the narratives they depicted moments of cultural encounter and confrontation that occur as they enter the academic arena. This was followed with personal and cultural challenges that necessitated performative recalibration between the sensate awarenesses of Black cultural life, the acknowledged protocols of academic life, and the necessary adjustments when crossing the border from campus back to community.

My conversational partners spoke in some very provocative ways about how they negotiate the challenges of place and space with the particularity of why they engage these performances in shifting locations. The justification is confirmed less in the difference between place and space, and more in what is acknowledged as their own bicultural identity and the desire to draw from the strength of both communities in order to ensure their own possibility. In this sense, such a border crossing should be constructed as both contestatory and compensatory in the construction and maintenance of fluid social identities across disparate territories of desire.

3

Passing, Cultural Performance, and Individual Agency

Performative Reflections on Black Masculine Identity

The concept of the masculine subject is useful, then for two reasons. First, it highlights the multiple discursivity that posits individuality on the subject, while also acknowledging the performative character of this constitution. . . . The second benefit associated with the concept of the masculine subject is that it critically connects "man" as a political category with masculine identity work. In so doing, this connection exposes the political implications of masculine-oriented performativity. To be sure, the self is fragmented, multiple and contingent, our identities being processual within subject positions rather than being singular and accomplishable in any final and closed sense.

—Stephen M. Whitehead, *Men and Masculinities*

The aim of my analysis is to present enabling forms of consciousness that may contribute to the constitution of the social, economic, and political relations that continually consign the lives of black men to psychic malaise, social destruction, and physical death. It does not encourage or dismiss the sexism of black men, nor does it condone the patriarchal behavior that sometimes manifests itself in minority communities in the form of misdirected machismo.

—Michael Eric Dyson, "The Plight of Black Men"

Why hadn't she spoken that day? . . . Why had she allowed him to make his assertions and express his misconceptions undisputed? . . . Why . . . had she failed to take up the defense of the race to which she belonged? . . . Irene asked these questions, felt them. They were, however, merely rhetorical, as she herself was well aware. She knew their answers, every one, and it was the same for them all. The sardony of it![1] She couldn't betray Clare, couldn't even run the risk of appearing to defend a people that were being maligned for fear that the defense might in some infinitesimal degree lead the way to final discovery of her secret. She had to Clare Kendry a duty. She was bound to her by those very ties of race, which, for all her repudiation of them, Clare had been unable to completely sever.

—Nella Larsen, *Passing*

These three epigraphs establish an impulse that runs throughout this chapter. The first two quotes, from Whitehead and Dyson, progressively offer insights to the social and political category of "man," the performative nature of masculinity, and the ways in which these operate within the specified social conditions and constraints of racial identity. The third epigraph is for me a small yet pivotal moment in Nella Larsen's influential novel, *Passing.* The moment, which occurs near the beginning of "Part Two: Re-Encounter," establishes the conditions of a critical choice about performance, agency, passing, and the fictions of identity.[2] The character's contemplative query is a response to the complex contestation of racial confrontation and the positioning of self and other, and self as the other.[3]

The novel as a whole is a stirring case study in passing that focuses on Blacks unmarked by racial signifiers, who are thus able to assume a performative identity of Whiteness. Yet these performances are about "making not faking," to invoke Victor Turner's popular aphorism. Jane Blocker clarifies my particular application when she writes: "Performative identities are not false; they are not the function of the kind of artifice or masking that implies a hidden 'real' self; rather they challenge the coherence of that presumed real" (1999, 25). In actuality, the performative accomplishment of passing is a dialogically negotiated act between the one passing and those who would accept or deny, support or sanction, that passage. Each must buy into a prescription of racialized materiality giving way to a set of social and performative executions of identity that maintain a farce in human social relations. So, as the characters in Nella Larsen's novel might attest, while passing is an adaptive tactic it is also one that is filled with an anxiety of engagement and discovery.[4] The primary characters in the novel, like those who pass in everyday life, must negotiate the possibilities and consequences of performing the presumed actuality of the self, in relation to those assumed qualities that come with racial identification.[5]

In this chapter I use the notion of "passing" as a transitive trope. I apply it not to cross-racial movement but as an acknowledgment of the performative nature of assuming particular and expected racial-cultural-gender traits, and to the process of having performances deemed appropriate or inappropriate, to both a skewed sense of authenticity and the manner in which racial performances and performances about racial identity unveil the facile evidence of knowing self and the other—causing (as in chapter 1) a confrontation with our own complicity in the social construction of racial politics. Furthermore the chapter concretizes the traveling/bidirectionality (in chapter 2) in the construct of passing. In both chapters, there is an assumption of particular norms with differing benefits—though all circulate around a constellation of acceptance, acknowledgment, and the acrimony of contested intentionalities.

This chapter is structured around three divisions: a brief discussion on cultural performance that outlines some of the theoretical perceptions on maintaining cultural membership that guide my thinking, an autobiographically based performative script in which I use the construction of "Good Man–Bad Man" to note the delimiting binary that governs the perception of Black men and the sociocultural politics of performative Black masculinity, and a meditation on the process of defining the self as a unitary whole in spite of the fragmentary nature of human identity.

Within this chapter I use a critical and performative method that I am referring to as an integrative and reflexive ethnography of performance. This experimental approach is grounded in Norman Denzin's construction of reflexive critique. A "text [that] is reflexive, not only in its use of language but also in how it positions the writer in the text, and uses the writer's experiences as both the topic of inquiry and a resource for uncovering problematic [intercultural] experience" (1997, 216). In particular, I articulate an actual experience translated into a performance and then I reflexively comment on the ways in which people responded to the performance as an element of the performative replay of the actual text. The method further extends conversations on reporting performance knowledge[6] and performative reflexivity.[7]

I ground the nature of my work both in performance studies and in cultural studies, hence the approach of an integrative and reflexive ethnography of performance also allows me the opportunity to address questions about and responses to culture and performance. It allows me to further theorize the mechanisms that undergird both performances in everyday life and how I (and others), reconstruct and critique those occurrences in the academic arena. Hence I feel that the fullness of the engagement between the performer, performance, and audience (whether on the stage or on the page) demands a close reading of and through experience. Knowing of course, that the text and context of performance is always and already implicated in the production of culture, but that I am interested in "different forms of sense making, within various settings, in societies incessantly marked by change and conflict" (Green 1996, 126).

PASSING AS CULTURAL PERFORMANCE

The notion of cultural performance is as contested as the subject matter to which it refers. The definitions range from units of observation and forms of social critique and maintenance to a means of dramatizing our collective myths and history.[8] Yet a particularly telling interpretation of cultural performance that is pertinent to my arguments in this chapter is that cultural performance privileges one social marker above others.[9] In particular, this interpretation of cultural performance is a reference to the engaged performance of expected norms of behavior for the purpose of social agency[10] within a particular cultural context. It also acknowledges the unidirectionality of cultural performative agency, whether as a fulfillment of cultural traditions that build community or reappropriating racial stereotypes to advance beyond social roadblocks. The notion of passing can be extricated from this definition as both a means of maintaining cultural membership, by assuming the necessary and performative strategies that signal membership, as well as the conscious and unconscious choice to engage other performances that situate racial identity. In this way intercultural dynamics are maintained primarily through recognizable performative practices. Social relations are sometimes contingent on the validation of those cultural performances. The accusation of passing is thus an assessment of cultural performance whether as subversion or the presentation of the real.

Cultural performances are framed events; they are also important dramatizations of the codes and ethics of living in specific cultural communities. They enable cultural members to understand, critique, and transform the worlds in which they live, while also providing outsiders cues to understanding cultures that are not their own.[11] And while most of the work of those writing on cultural performance focuses primarily on communal ritualistic practices that transmit social culture, self-awareness of cultural performances in everyday life offers the same level of possibility of seeing the self and other in the negotiation of cultural membership.

These cultural performances are indeed designs for living.[12] In the case of passing, the design for living is the performative move that assumes the identity and the specified benefits of being the other within a particular context. For example—gay men who "pass" as straight attempt to avoid the social and cultural strictures against homosexuality; or light-skinned Blacks "passing" for White assume the social and cultural privileges of being White, and avoid the stigma that is sometimes socially associated with being Black. In either case, passing is a performance of suppression that is associated with the origin of the denial. It is a performance whose success depends on not overacting.[13] In which case overacting would call attention to the fact that performance is in actuality being used as artifice to racial identity, as opposed to performance as the actualization of the real and the embodiment of the known.

Passing is a product (an assessed state); passing is a process (a constructed and active engagement); passing is performativity (depended on a ritualized repetition of communicative acts known and interpreted within specified social systems); and passing is a reflection of one's positionality (politicized location, which is always relational to people and that which is being passed)—knowing that the existential accomplishment of passing always resides in liminality.[14] This is not the process of becoming but the state of being betwixt and between two performance communities, the point of origin and the territory of desire; with the performative expectations of both communities serving as mediators in a tensive feud (or maybe a fraud) of identity—acceptance and denial. For while performance can make manifest the subject of its focus. It does not modify the materiality of embodied presence and the social investment in race.

"GOOD MAN–BAD MAN": PERFORMATIVE AGENCY
AND CHOICE

I'm a man.
I'm a Black man.

The Black male body is polemical. It is a site of public and private contestation; competing investments in Black masculinity that are historical and localized affecting notions of intellect and character, as well as virility and fertility. The diversity that exists within the character of the Black man is not acknowledged, hence he is relegated to a stereotypically pathologized position, in which any variation might be constructed as inauthentic or not being real, passing for something that he is not. I offer you some of those frames with an eye on felt experience.[15]

In the classroom as a student I am a "Good Man," a sometimes-cultural representative and resident exotic other. I stand as a Good Black Man in contrast to the problematized and media-produced images of my brethren. Instructors, from time to time, have even sought my opinion on issues of a delicate racial nature. I am "a kind of native informant, lurching about the island and showing Prospero its sweet and secret places, serving to provide data with which Prospero can then rule" (Karamcheti 1995, 142). Typically, as a teacher, I hear at some point from a good-non-traditional-White-woman-student-bigot, "You're a very nice Black man, a credit to your race."[16]

Crossing over and crossing under that invisible divider, the wall—the border that separates the white ivory tower from the larger often depressed surrounding cultural community, I sometimes enter perceived as "Bad Man." I enter as "John Houseman in racial drag" (Karamcheti 1995, 143). I am perceived as a Black man trying to transcend his "natural" state, elemental and unsophisticated. I am perceived as a Black man who is trying to pass for White, not based on appearance but in the metaphoric drag of linguistic performance and wearing the garments of academic accomplishment.[17] I am deemed Bad Black Man because I seemingly do not perform the expected role of indigenous Black man, authentic Black man, real

Black man—someone who is perceived to be organically connected to the Black community in ways that are deemed appropriate.[18]

In this context the qualities that make me a Good Man—being relatively articulate, relatively intelligent, relatively polite, a "gentleman"—transform me into "Bad Man." Here I am critiqued on a different standard.

(A "stereotypical" Black brother) "Listen to the way he talks." Faggot.
"You don't have a girlfriend?" Faggot.
"What do you mean no basketball?" Faggot.
"You're a teacher?" Faggot.

My performance of "Good Man" is read as Bad Black Man or at least different. Read as odd. Read as strange. Read as queer. In this case the expectations and possibilities of being a Black man are conflated into a limited series of performative displays—you are or you are not—as if performative displays somehow transcend physical beings.[19]

Black men who participate in this form of masculinity view this double negation as a positive and ultimately as a form of power. Because of the security, power, and attention that come from embodying phallocentric Black masculinity there is strong resistance by those who have adapted this form to alternative models. The logic might suggest that Black masculinity itself was forged out of resistance against White institutional practices; anything less would be performing "less manly."

There is a resistance to rethinking masculinity that is embedded not only within the psyche and lived experience of Black men alone but within women as well. Bell hooks writes: "Heterosexual women have not unlearned a heterosexist-based 'eroticism' that constructs desire in such a way that many of us can only respond erotically to male behavior that has already been coded as masculine within the sexist framework" (1994a, 111). So even a heterosexual man who engages in a sensitive awareness of feminist issues, and in humanistic caring alternative performances of Black masculinity, is demonized for not being a strong, take-charge kind of guy. This dilemma is more problematic for Black gay men, who in addition to rejecting particular forms of masculine performativity are also rejected for issues related to desire.[20] Indeed, Black male identity is often constrained by these borders that are neither fluid nor flexible.[21]

The notion of "Good Man–Bad Man" is often embedded in a culturally linguistic transconfiguring move in which bad becomes good and good becomes bad. The performative elements of masculinity are then situated locally and mediated by context. Masculinity as a performance is set to a musical score; a dirge orchestrated by culture and social design. It is an audience-based construction of movement, choreography of talking the talk and walking the walk. It is a performance of self for others.

The accusation of passing and the assessment of "Good" or "Bad" is a reduction of identity and delimits the possibility of expression to specified sanctioned performances. To pass is ultimately to acknowledge that identity is not static. To pass is to test and challenge the fractured and multifaceted aspects of identity identified with race, designed by culture, and subverted in desire.

The hyphen between Good Man–Bad Man is really a continuum of varying shades of light and dark; a rehearsal process; a descent into madness, into anger. It is a construction, a deconstruction that begins with something like:

> (Very polite and soft-spoken) "Excuse me, may I have some service?"
> (Ignored by White-girl worker)

It initiates itself as a sincere yet unacknowledged effort to connect, to communicate.

> (More irritated, a little more strident) "Excuse me, but I've been waiting for
>   some time now . . ." (Sentence cut off short as the White-girl worker turns
>   to another White customer)

Acknowledging the tensions that may exist within the lifescripts of those involved, it becomes a little less tolerant, more insistent.

> (Escalating in tone) "Excuse me, I need some help here!"

And finally it realizes that niceness (Good Man) won't work; or, as my brother would say, "You want to see me act like a nigger? I can act like a nigger!"

(Explode in anger, direct challenge) "Can I have some God damn service now!"

(White-girl worker is frightened and maybe embarrassed) "Oh I'm sorry sir. I didn't see you. How can I help you?"

Contact at last!

The question from those in polite society is "Why do you have to be that way?" or, "What do you get from that?" The answers are simple, yet complex. Simple because I get:

"Service."

"Attending to."

"Visibility?"

Even if I have to cross under, even if I have to be a subversive, even if I have to tap into negative stereotypes that fulfill fearful expectations from others, to be "other" to myself. I do this to pass; not to pass for White, for my dark-brown skin and the dreadlocks growing out of my head prevent that racialized possibility; but to become other in order to pass through particular racial-cultural roadblocks; and this is the core of my argument.

I assume the performative role of "Bad Man" when really I am "Good Man." Somehow the simple act of social acknowledgment has to be reduced, or escalated—to this kind of racial-cultural attention. It is the very lack of reflexivity of those who ask the question, "Why do you have to be that way?" that evidences how they are implicated in and call forth such a performance.[22] Whether it is specific to the situation outlined in the performance or in moments such as this, when I am expected to defend myself and explain my behavior for their comfort and ease, which is an expected performance of "Good Man."

Without the presumed-to-be-natural presentation of my Black masculine identity, I am not seen—though I am standing in clear view. Ralph Ellison captures this social dematerialization of the Black male body when he says, "That invisibility to which I refer occurs because of a peculiar disposition of the eyes of those with whom I come in contact. A matter of the construction of their inner eye, those eyes with which they look through their physical eyes, upon" (1995, 4). So it is the social construction of my identity that works in opposition to the reality of my being.

"Oh I'm sorry sir. I didn't see you. How can I help you?"

Referencing the darkened imaged of O.J. Simpson on the cover of *Time* magazine June 1994, Phillip Brian Harper in "The Limits of Race and Social Regulation" describes a strategic mechanism for maintaining the social construction and image of the bad Black man:

> *Time*'s cover image serves as twofold corrective, disciplinarily reaffirming Simpson's "actual" blackness while underscoring the criminality inherent therein. For this positing of Simpson as constitutionally "wrong" to operate simultaneously as a crucial setting "right" of the social order suggests that even more rests on the congruency of skin color and racial identification. (1996, 131)

In particular, Harper's argument rests on the logics that Simpson's image was darkened to suggest some presumed pathology and the suspicion of black maleness; hence the darkened image performatively suggests a darkened character that is particular both to Simpson and to Black men in general. This works in opposition to the more acceptable image of O.J. "The Juice" Simpson as the beloved luggage-leaping former football star in the Hertz rental car commercials, who worked his way into the archives of Americana and even earned the privilege of honorary White-man in his marriage to the White wife he was assumed to have killed. This is not a defense of O.J. Simpson as much as a signal to how his visual representation shifted to foreground the presumed Bad Black Man in him.

And so within this public establishment, I symbolically darken my face and escalate my volume, as is expected—and engage in a loud blackface performance for the complex social desire of the other. The answer to the question—"Why do you have to be that way?"—is complex because it is an odd mixture of expected fear and the signification of otherness that maintains a certain order, distance, and maybe even comfort between self and other. And whether I literally perform "Bad Black Man" or not, I am always and already perceived as engaging that performative mode by those who have made it a relational standard. So the perception of me as "Bad Black Man" has become a practiced and performative inculcation of beliefs by others.[23]

In traditional blackface minstrelsy performed by Whites, "The Black mask offered a way to play with collective fears of a degraded and threatening—and male—Other, while at the same time maintaining some symbolic control over him" (Lott 1996, 13). So in this moment of necessity (or desperation), I reciprocate and at the same time subvert this performance tradition, as I figuratively darken my already dark face and become other to myself, in order to ensure the same benefits as the other, who historically performed me.[24] In other words, the success of my performance of "Bad Man" is predicated if not anticipated on the stereotypical forms that anticipate and fix the conditions of black male possibility.[25] This is my acknowledgment of racial stereotypes and my use of those stereotypes as a means to an end. This is also the reflection on bodies and racism that I referenced in chapter 1 as an impulsive response to interracial social engagement.

Allow me to play these issues through a scene in the novel *Passing*, a scene between the primary character Irene (a light-skinned Black woman) and her husband Brian (a prominent, darker-skinned Black doctor). In response to her husband's projective conversation with their sons about the social practice of lynching "coloured people," Irene expresses her distaste for what she constructs as "the race problem," and her hope that he would not have the conversation. While Irene's motivation is framed as an attempt to protect the innocence of her sons, it is undergirded by her own growing paranoia about issues of passing. Brian's response is key to a particular argument that I am developing here about the historicity of bodies in social relations and the consequences of particular encounters. The character says,

> You're absolutely wrong! If, as you're so determined they've got to live in this damned country, they'd better find out what sort of thing they're up against as soon as possible. The earlier they learn it, the better prepared they'll be . . . At the expense of proper preparation for life and their future happiness, yes. And I'd feel I hadn't done my duty by them if I didn't give them some inkling of what's before them.[26]

While I am using the utterance of a "fictional" character to concretize an actual instance, I am also keenly aware of the manner in which Nella Larsen crafted these characters to reflect an all-too-real social relation. I

find that Brian's character is not promoting racism as much as he is promoting an understanding of the social conditions that regulate race relations; a dynamic in which we are all implicated. The story that Brian
wishes to tell his sons is referenced as the narratives that anticipate and fix
the condition not only of Black possibility but of Black-White relations. I
perceive the performance of "Good Man–Bad Man" to operate in the
same manner. And while the novel does not realize the conversation
between father and sons, I imagine a discussion that speaks through the
complications of racial difference and focuses on the reality of choices
made through racial logics. Such a conversation and such a performance
might serve as a template for meaningful sense-making of problematic
racial encounters.

So the question, "Why do you have to be that way?" that the White
critics of my performance asked speaks to issues of agency as if to ask, "If
you find the performance so problematic, why do you engage it? Why do
you use it as a means to an end and then critique those who presumably
initiated the performance? When it is in fact your choice to engage it?"
"It" being the stereotypical performance of Black male rage. In responding
to these actual questions and critiques, I am interested in how Stephen M.
Whitehead speaks to and through Michel Foucault's construction of the
discursive subject; a subject that is created through discourse, sometimes
in relation or in contradistinction to the materiality of the body, and how
this is linked with alternating practices of power. "Thus the symbiotic
relationship between power and the subject is revealed both in the individual's subjection to those 'laws of truth' that constitute various discursive
regimes and in the simultaneous marking and identifying of the subject
as an individual—an enabling, positive moment of (self)-creation" (2002,
101).[27] So, they who ask the questions engage in a critical, albeit short-
sighted, reflexivity without the benefit of questioning why the performance was successful, or even questioning the conditions that gave rise to
the performance; they demonize me for demonizing them, which is in
actuality a stratagem that maintains the social order through a practice of
their own power over me.

While they demonize my critical observation along with the described
performance they fail to understand, they fail to understand that while I
problematize my own performative choice, these (the performance and
the critique of the performance) are both practices of power that help to
transform me from the objectified invisible other into the identified (visi-

ble) subject that gets attended to. But not just attended to like a petulant child who craves attention. The performance becomes a political act that always undergirds Black masculine–oriented performativity[28] and illuminates the racial politics that are already in play—both in the actual scene depicted in performance and in the critique of the scene in performance.[29] Unlike Peggy Phelan's (1993) arguments about the illusive *Unmarked*, we (the me and the not me)[30] are both clearly identifiable social agents, and the power of my embodied presence, which is clearly marked, is merely extenuated through and by performance.

The performance of "Bad Black Man" and the critique of the conditions that gave rise to the performance that lead to a moment of self-creation[31] that provides agency. I will acknowledge though that outside of this critical engagement of writing about the performance of "Bad Man," that practiced form of agency (in everyday life), can be a place of entrapment for many Black men. It can be a performance that perpetuates the expectations while it services their (and my) desire. And therein lies our sad compromise, playing into "the spectral and the spectacular in racialist representations of black men" (Wallace 2002, 30).

The performance of "Bad Man" is less cannibal and more crafted, canned, and contrived. It is conniving, coping, and controlling. It is contending with the conditions in the circumstance.

So I wear my Mean Black Man face from time to time as a defense mechanism; as a performance, and even as a stratagem to get or cross over.

I wear the expected Mean Black Man face like a sign of membership or a signifier of identification, to those who buy into that socially constructed performative expectation.

I wear the expected Mean Black Man face as I would carry a fake passport, a documentation of citizenship in some (not so) imagined world in which my identity is dictated by others.

I wear it knowing of course that my body is always and already marked and that sometimes it is not only what I look like but also how I act (read through the performative lens of desire and disdain).

So, from time to time I make a spectacle of myself to fulfill the necessary qualifications/conditions for the immediacy of service. Knowing that spectacle is the "principle symbolic context in which . . . societies enact and communicate their guiding beliefs, values, concerns and self-understandings" (Manning 1992, 291). It is a magnified performance for display and serves as a rhetorical act promoting a particular social positioning.

I also know that it is not really a compromise. The moment of my decision to engage the performance of "Bad Man" (and I can only assume this to be true of other Black men in similar circumstances) is one that has been historically rehearsed. It is a stock performance in the repertoire of most Black men that is called forth in a moment of desperation. It has "a distinct developmental history, along with a definable set of expert 'end state' performances. [Most Black men] do not exhibit their intelligences 'in the raw'; they do so by occupying certain relevant niches in their society, for which they must prepare by passing through an often lengthy developmental process" (Gardner 1999, 38). In that moment I hesitate, contemplate, and even practice a certain restraint; as I filter the scene through my own sensibilities and then decide how I want to proceed.

Here I am arguing against the perception that the performance of "Bad Black Man" is exclusively reactionary, for the slightest reaction of one individual to another is pregnant with the whole history of these persons—in their specificity and in their historical social relations within these shared social spaces.[32] In this sense, I have also faced accusation and critique by others, who suggest that the performance of "Bad Black Man" is premeditated in ways that exceed the constructed nature of all human behavior as performative. For them, it is a form of ambushing or bushwacking White folk. And if it is, then I am hiding in plain view, and my place of concealment is really the socially constructed space of my *habitus*, in relation to their own *habitude*. They demonize me for negatively characterizing the White-girl in the scene, without regard to how I am demeaned and must further demean myself for service.

In the act of calling the other to attend, I know that I am not consciously giving up my agency by giving in to performance that demeans me in the act of calling the other to attend. I experience the performance of "Bad Man" as a double-voiced act, in the way that Gary Saul Morson elaborates on Mikhail Bakhtin's concept of the double-voice.[33] It is a performance that works on multiple levels for a particular effort. He writes the following:

> The audience of a double-voice word is therefore meant to hear both a version of the original utterance as the embodiment of its speaker's point of view (or "semantic position") and the second speaker's evaluation of that utterance from a different point of view. I find that it is helpful to picture a

double-voice word as a special sort of palimpsest in which the uppermost inscription is a commentary on the one beneath it, which the reader (or audience) can know only by reading through the commentary that obscures in the very process of evaluating. (1981, 108)

So in the moment of the performance of "Bad Man" I want the White-girl worker to audience the performance and respond with my desired effect. I also want her to understand how the performance of "Bad Man" is layered on top of the performance of "Good Man" that she ignored. In fact, passing in this context is a way of avoiding the enclosures and significations of race, class, or sexuality that limit the possibilities of iden-tity.[34] Yet I do understand that my double-voiced performance may fall on deaf ears, if in fact the audience for this performance reads only a rude behavior and not the sophistication of my intent.

The performance, that constructed premeditated behavioral enact-ment, is designed to display my performative flexibility in light of her rigid and limited engagement of me. In this sense my conscious performance of "Bad Man" becomes a display of an often unnoticed, socially invali-dated, and collectively demonized form of intelligence in many Black men—that is, the ability to read a situation and respond. As with the very nature of a palimpsest, the historical construction of the Black male body becomes the site where there was an attempt to erase an original cultural inscription and to replace it with another. Yet the earlier inscription was never fully erased so over time the result of Black male identity is a com-posite—a palimpsest representing the sum of all the erasures and over-writings.[35] And the body remembers.

In the performance of "Bad Man" it is the me and the not me, in the moment of the enactment and in the face of history, calling forth a histori-cal construction of the self that facilitates a particular desire in the moment of the social engagement. Referencing the work of performance artist Ana Mendieta, Jane Blocker writes,

In the performance of identity, and in identity as performance, Mendieta is and is not "herself." She negotiates among identity possibilities that them-selves emerge with the act of performance. No one true identity exists prior to the act of performing. No one identity remains stable in and through performance. Understanding identity as having these "performative" quali-ties enables a discussion of gender, color, nation, and ethnicity that bypasses essentialist categories. (1999, 25)

I negotiate among the identity possibilities that emerge with/in the act of performance. I know that no one true identity exists prior to the act of performing. I know that no one identity remains stable in and through performance. Understanding identity as having these performative qualities enables me to engage a discussion of sex, gender, race, and power that bypasses essentialist categories, even those essentialist categories that I have defined for me and others.

The establishment of such categories is a way of making sense of the world and our place in it, regardless of how right or wrong they might be. I know that the "performance of Bad Man" has different purposes and effects for different audiences. I know that the performance of masculinity is often connected with aggression and violence as an act of performative sustainability within the culture and community of men. Hence the performance of "Bad Man" might be seen as good, not "normal," especially when this performance is in defense of masculinity and in opposition to the feminine, as is most often the case in performative masculinity.

> Not to mention the desirous construct of the "bad boy,"
> that some women (to invoke a heterosexual construct of desire),
> Black and White (to acknowledge racial distinctions and similarities),
> find appealing as a social subversion of acceptable performances
> of being polite,
> of being docile,
> of being safe,
> and of being sensitive.

I know that many men including myself struggle with the performative character of masculinity and what we gain and lose when we adhere to those expectations.[36]

I know that aggression by men is often used to maintain dominance over women (and gay men) in ways that diminish worth and value. Maybe that is the effect but not the intent with the White-girl worker in this narrative. In this case, I also know that the historical specter of Black male aggression and its relation to presumed White-woman-vulnerability is invoked. Though of course White women have also historically exerted their own form of power and privilege that has often gone uncritiqued.[37]

In this way, we are both stuck in the sediments of history and neither one of us can be easily rescued.

I know assertiveness is sometimes viewed as a valued social construct linked with motivation, success, and self-reliance.[38] I know that in a strategic calling-forth, the performative and historical construction of the Bad Man, that I am also signaling the contested and racialized constructions of being a Black man. In particular, the images that were used as marketing tools and rhetoric by White men in promoting African (Black) bodies; African bodies as prime stock or chattel, or disembodied notions of virility and ferocity that translated into the African slave's being a good stud, a good worker, or a good fighter—but not a human. Like the marketing of the African female as being a baby-making machine and built for speed, both in the field and in the bedroom. These are the same images and rhetoric that were used as persuasive evidence to justify slavery and a specious sense of intellectual and humanistic superiority; a performance of divine sanction that abolitionist Frederick Douglass rightly signaled in his self-described transition from "a slave . . . [to] made man" (1845/1982, 107).

I know that the performance of Bad Black Man has the potential to instill fear in ways that might perpetuate the stereotype of Black male aggression. Like the many stereotypes of Black men either grounded in some actual instance or a culturally agreed on assessment that is strategically differentiated from aggression (e.g., assertiveness) when performed by White men.

I know that (this) performance is a constructed thing. In this moment, the moment of the performance and the moment of talking about the performance of "Bad Man"—it is an intellectualized choice spurred on by an internalized reorientation to myself for an external validation. This is not a validation of who I am, or even who I want to be, but what I want to effect in the moment of its engagement.

I know.

Yet I still question to what degree in this moment of deconstructing performance am I engaged in framing the space of my own marginality for the close scrutiny of (the) other(s). To what degree do I confirm the tensiveness between the idea of marginality, in relation to a fixed center, while at the same time arguing that my disposition as a subject or a self-as-object with agency is anything but fixed? [39]

Maybe this is a core element of the very contested nature of such performances. Performances that seek to subvert fixtures of social relations, while (seemingly) simultaneously reifying them. Yet within this particular context of performing badly, I acknowledge that I practice a racially subversive power that is also socially constructed and allocated. It draws its strength and potency out of the relational wreckage that constructs self and other; whereas the proprietors of civility are held captive to their own construction of the uncivil (the Bad Black Man, to put a face on the specified construct of my focus) and their fear. So the performances of "Bad Man," those performed for the shifting audiences of men and women are not equally performative—for the roles are socially scripted, and the outcomes are seemingly expected.

I suspect that most Black men know that this is not a legitimate power, grounded in our position or status; but a referent or coercive power that is only and always relational, based on the materiality of bodies involved in the specific social negotiations.[40] The forces of singularity that exist within the event horizon of our experience do differ.[41] Hence the borders of marginality shift and sometimes others are also on the outside of the comfort zones of their own socially constructed reality. My project becomes a concern to illuminate the positionality and complicity of bodies in those specific yet shifting locales.

In responding to their questions, I know that I am engaging in more than a text-based academic call and response.[42] I seek out opportunities to engage myself and others in a critically reflexive process of seeing ourselves and the ways in which race, gender, and power are always and already in play—in the act of performing, audiencing performance, and responding to performance.

What is truly at stake for me is not the sole necessity of scholarly production. It is the real-world consequences of how these issues play out on the stages of everyday life, and how my body is sometimes an unwilling participant in acts of social violence; destructive forces pressed against the will of my desire. Knowing that in this academic and far from safe mode of social exchange it is the irony of my hard-fought privilege as a Black male scholar[43] that affords me access to extend my personal and political agenda into this venue. I know that the backlash of audience-critique is always forthcoming, and even that can sometimes further a certain critical reflection on performative practice while helping to expand the parameters of discussion for performance pundits.

Critics of performance, in an often-unsuccessful staged act of delicacy, try to isolate the specificity of their critique (the tenor from the vehicle, the text from the person who generated it). I find that in my response to questions and elaboration on intent, both theirs and mine, that I cannot separate what is often constructed as an intellectual engagement over an emotional response. Not knowing if there is really a difference and not knowing what I would get from that endeavor, especially when the parties involved know the issues that are at/in play. And because many of the questions and concern-filled critiques about this performance came from Whites, "white power [attempts] to secure its dominance by seeming not to be anything in particular," just an intellectual speculation not informed by the materiality and subjectivities of those asking the questions (S. Jackson 1998, 5). Though the particularity of bodies offering critique (whether in staged performance or the performance of everyday life) in relation to the bodies that are critiqued always implicate the thoughts and attitudes expressed.

Signaling the performance work of Amanda Denise Kemp (1998), the black body in question is my own . . . a body that is "settled into a web of social relationships" (127–128). Considering that theories of the flesh[44] define the very domain of performance and that the lifescript, the sedimented experiences of people that both guides and dictates action, filters their experience of performance—we are all complicit in performances that critique and illuminate racial and cultural politics. We are trapped in what Primo Levi calls "the gray zone" (1988, 54). And how Debarati Sanyal extends his construction to describe that "moral topography of [social exchange], a zone of violence and ambiguity in which victim, perpetrator, accomplice, and witness [are] 'bound together by the foul link of imposed complicity'" (2002, 1).[45]

I also understand that I am engaged in critically reflecting on my role (my own culpability) in the (re)staging of this historical scene. I understand that like the very nature of performance studies as alluded to by Dwight Conquergood, I am "struggl[ing] to open the space between analysis and action, and to pull the pin on the binary opposition between theory and practice . . . [to] embrace . . . different ways of knowing [myself. That] is radical because it cuts to the root of how knowledge is organized in the academy" and historically, what I have been expected to know (and not know) about myself (2002, 145–146).

Maybe this is why I embrace the project of performance studies not only as a preoccupation, but as a vocation. Through a process of critical self-reflection, a process of interrogating the locations of my multiple subjectivities and the allegiances that inform how I live my life. Performance becomes a radical methodology that I use to engage an act of decolonizing my own mind.[46] So maybe in this essay, I am feeling my melanin[47] and articulating a racialized identity that is both a part of who I am, and the way I have been socially constructed to be. Knowing of course that my agency signals what I am willing and not willing to claim.

But most of the time, my face is just my face.

My face is Black and notably not mean—though that is my own assignment. It shows my joy and my pain. It reveals my disposition—of angst, of frustration, of fear, of overwhelming insecurity, and, more often than not, my joy, passion, and compassion. "Regardless of how I perform identity, my body is marked with signs that signify identities that exist outside of my desires, signs that exact (mis)recognitions. It is these (mis)recognitions that actuate the border patrol, that necessitate border inspections" (Esposito 2003, 240). The visage of my sometimes stern Black male expression (in staged performances or in daily wear—which are almost indistinguishable) always seems to be jarring for some. Even to those who claim to know me and see me narrowly as "Good Man," a distinction that is its own place of entrapment. In this case I am relegated to a limited space within a margin of their comfort with me and with Black men in general.

Their narrow view of me is a performative dualism that they deny acknowledgment of in themselves. It is an extreme myopia that prevents them from seeing their own "Bad" performances, which are often projected as power, interpreted as strength, and used to mark difference and assert control.

Or, maybe it is a cultural performative dexterity
that they do not have to engage,
a performance that they don't need to engage,
in order to cross over or cross under,
to pass through.

Perhaps it is a regularized performance that they give, that is never read as "Bad White Man" or "Bad White Woman"—for maybe they (those who engage such performances of privilege and propriety) set the sliding standard, the shifting territories of identity on which all else is measured.

I think about what it means to be a "Good Man" and I look to the contemporary men's movements, the Promise Keepers and mythopoetics. To look at them I see that possibly to be a "Good Man" might be to tap into the "Bad Man" in me, the controlling man, dominating man, patriarchal man, *Iron John* (Bly 1990).

Maybe it is to chant,
to scream,
to drum,
to beat . . . (pounding on the chest) . . .
to rape, . . . to pillage? **NO!**
What passes as a real man?

Well, maybe *that* kind of performance is only privileged by the middle, not to be mistaken for the margin. The middle, as in middle of the road, as in middle class, as in middle-aged-White-heterosexual-men, who claim spirituality and religious doctrine as their justification to be:

(The sign of the cross is made as a form of benediction)
"Good Man."

As a Black man, I am always in the margins of those social constructions. Those same performative practices:

to scream,
to chant,
to drum,
to beat (drums) . . . for me, are always deemed as bad (native and bestial) and in this case bad ain't good.

ATTEMPTING TO DEFINE A MEDIATED SELF
In this performative vernacular of Black masculine identity I offer a working definition of self through a process of negation. Contemporary Black

men must systematically and instantaneously survey and deny the prevailing stereotypes that demonize our bodies and pathologize our characters. This is followed by the painstaking process of reconstructing in the minds of others an identity and image that is reflective and representative of who we are and wish to be. This program of self-identification is an "on-going performative process" that works against a historical backdrop and the prevailing sociological and classist intentions that mark and minimize us (Butler 1990b, 271).

Yes, Judith Butler rightly argues that the body is a "materialization of possibilities" (272). In this notion the fluidity of identity is acknowledged, and the body becomes an emergent landscape. The landscape of my body, like that of my mind, is not dictated by my race or my sexual identity delineating one territory from the other, in which a border crossing is negatively constructed as passing. Nor does a social script that may delimit my expressive possibilities (as a Black man) also dictate the specific topography of my body. It is a site in which the borders of my identity are only limited by the reach of my desire. When I cross over those borders I pass—not passing as in denial, but passing as in extending. I pass—not passing as in faking, but passing as in making myself known:

> To pass as in "gaining passage despite obstacles."
> To pass as in "to move past in time."
> To pass as in "to be transferred from one to another."
> To pass as in "to undergo transition."

In this way, according to Martha J. Cutter, "only when 'passing' becomes a subversive strategy for avoiding the enclosures of a racist, classist, and sexist society does it become truly liberating" (1996, 75). So I pass.

The contemporary Black male agenda is not to unweave the cultural tapestry that tells the story of our history. It is to reconfigure and offer alternate perceptions to those who view the display, and those who blind themselves in the veil of oppression. The idea is to show the texture of our lives, to reveal the dimensions of our characters, and the beauty in our souls. Within this vigorous program of self-identification and determination, the materialization of possibilities is revealed in a nonessentialized fabric of many hues. The scale of perceptions of Black men, good and bad, will be expanded beyond the binary to include the multiple and varying shades of identity, and the performative dexterity that it takes to be unique within a cultural system.

In the process we see the hyphen between Good Man–Bad Man as a bridge. Following the example of Cherrie Moraga and Gloria Anzaldúa (1981) in *This Bridge Called My Back*, I offer an uncompromised definition of my Black masculine identity—which may resonate with you (the reader) in some ways. This definition of self is both articulate and sociably polite (Good Man?) and blunt, in your face, and downright rude (Bad Man?). I find that I exist somewhere at the intersection of the two.

My Black masculinity is not a "dick-thing masculinity," in which I fuck my way through the world as some form of social orientation (hooks 1994a, 111).

NO!

My Black masculinity is not some pugilistic combative representation of the Black male in which my mere presence threatens to kick your ass if you look at me in the wrong way.

NO!

My Black masculinity is not a performatively stoic identity that denies felt experience, waiting to explode as some uncontrollable Black rage.

NO!

My Black masculinity is not floating in some liminal transitional space teetering on the hyphen between Good Man–Bad Man, waiting for some ritualistic or biological determinant to push me over the edge.

NO!

My Black masculinity is a human positionality firmly situated in individual choice. It is a choice to move, to cross, and to pass over the socially constructed and restrictive borders for my identity. Yet within that movement, my Black masculinity carries with it the resonant traces of a rich cultural heritage. If that sounds like pride, it is. Adrienne Rich suggests,

"Pride is often born in the place where we refuse to be victims, where we experience our own humanity under pressure, where we understand that we are not the hateful projections of others but intrinsically ourselves"(1994, 787).

My Black masculinity is mediated by an academic enlightenment. I am engaging the close scrutiny of the self and "other" that is necessary in any process of social and cultural renewal. The process demands a confluence of understanding from the intellectualism of the academy and the articulation and liberation of our enfleshed knowledge. That mediation, like the hyphen between Good Man–Bad Man serves as a bridge to our multifaceted selves. We do it for ourselves, refusing to have others continue to intervene in the construction of our identities. We are attempting to resolve the difference within our selves, the Black community, and our individual lives while commenting on others.[48]

My identity is influenced through social discourse. I acknowledge that varying aspects of identity are socially constructed and that through dialogue these can also be socially reconstructed in ways that are liberating. It is the nature of my work and that of other Black scholars interested in the social construction of identity and the relationship between race, sex, and gender that we act in dialogue with each other to influence change and awareness.[49]

My identity is enacted as an alternative performative masculinity. This alternative performance ameliorates and challenges the static interpretations of how I should be, interpretations that inevitably oppress me in both academic circles and my own racial-cultural communities. The homophobia and anti-intellectualism of the Black community, coupled with the racism of the academy, demands that those who would wish to concurrently claim membership in these disparate communities find ways to reconcile the tension that exists in passing back and forth. This reconciliation might engage performative practices that sustain personal worth, while challenging the contested notions of what constitutes cultural membership in both.[50]

PASSING AS BORDER CROSSINGS

In the novel *Passing*, the characters of Irene and Clare, two light-skinned Black women—one passing and the other haunted by that passing, signify a tension both about the evidence of cultural performance and about the social promises and pitfalls of racial identity. In his essay "Succeeding with passing" Thadious M. Davis writes: "The internal worlds of the two characters are inextricably interconnected with their external worlds, and their physical appearances are reflections of their attitudes towards individuality, race, and women of color, as well as projections of their bifurcated inner selves" (1994, 308). Within the novel the two women negotiate the knowledge of their racial identity, which is held in a tender terror about the possibility and probability of passing and being discovered, of taking chances and servicing each other's anxiety, as well as chancing the consequences of an unforgivable border crossing.[51]

The White-girl that I depict in this chapter and I—in our encounter— are of course not like Irene and Clare. Yet the materiality of our bodies (Black male and White female), clearly depicts the landscape of socially defined territories that give historical consequence to our specific encounter. Our inner worlds are inextricably interconnected with our external worlds, which might establish the conditions for the reading and misreading of each other's intentions. I know that I am operating from the location of my own resentment at being ignored, without taking into consideration her intention (which the orderly procedurals of customer service already mandate). But this is neither apology nor explanation. I believe that we all operate from the specificity of our own orientation to any given situation as informed by lifescripts that document already played scenes and that offer stage directions for future encounters. While those scripts can be subverted, we must play the roles in which we are cast—trying to find moments of empowerment that are not necessarily oppressive to others.

I also realize that by referring to her as "the White-girl," that I reduce an aspect of her identity to the literality of her body, which of course is part and parcel of my critique of her orientation to me—once again confirming our joint complicity in replaying a problematic historical scene that circulates within the confines of White privilege and Black rage. Yet I must note that, while my reference to her as "the White-girl" signals race, I am also signifying a particular performance of Whiteness that she engaged. One that Peter McLaren refers to as "a form of discursive brokerage, a pattern of negotiation that takes place in conditions generated by specific discursive formations and social relations" (1999, 40). This embodied in the discursive production of the Good White Girl is a performance of identity that generates its potency in the actuality of social and racial contact.[52]

This scene also evidences that the two, meaning White privilege and Black rage, are not inextricably disconnected. In other words, my performance of "Black rage" itself is a discursive strategy engaged as a specific response to a performance of White privilege; one that the White-girl worker afforded to other White customers who entered the store long after I did, but who were attended to on their request. Mine is a performance *to* Whiteness that is not particularly entertaining or satisfying for either of us. But like most performances in everyday life, it is functional and strategic, void of aesthetic pleasure but replete with a/effect that lubricates the machinery of social exchange.

After the original publication of (a version of) this chapter, I received from "well-meaning" friends the critiques that frame this conclusion; critiques about my representation of "the White-girl," along with a concern that her voice was not represented in the performance or the essay. For them this is an ethical issue that undermines the validity of what they presume to be some democratic dialectic that should undergird auto/ethnographic writing, which is not purely evident in their own work. This critique came either as a dubious presumption that all scholarship offers equal representation of voices, or simply to establish particular grounds of accountability for me. Which signals the (not so) residual traces of how power, race, class, and positionality circulate in the realm of scholarly production seeking to regulate particular voices or more specifically, seeking to regulate the telling of particular stories.

I am conscious of the manner in which I have reinserted their comments into this overall chapter. It is less to antagonize those well-meaning friends and colleagues than to reveal the necessarily vulnerable process of engaging reflexive ethnography that must acknowledge the mechanism of its own production.[53] Just as those who read ethnography must also analyze the structures of knowing the other, the power of constructing the other, and how their own desire is implicated in their interpretation of meaning and experience in ethnographic reports.

Yet in entertaining their critiques I come to realize that in many ways "her" voice is represented in the larger construction of this integrative and reflexive ethnography of performance; if only given credence through her defenders, who demonize my orientation to her and my depiction of the scene. Though her defenders are responding to a narrative depiction of the actual happening, their critique is meant to discipline me—both in the specificity of my performative scholarship and in the actuality of my orientation to them—through the particular encounter of the White-girl in the narrative, who now serves as proxy to Whiteness. And in this sense, like Michelle Fine in "Witnessing Whiteness," "I find myself trying to understand how whiteness accrues privilege and status; gets itself surrounded by protective pillows of resources and/or benefits of the doubt; how whiteness repels gossip and voyeurism and instead demands dignity" (1997, 57). All of which, is in opposition to the ways that I am oriented—both within the narrated scene and in the wake of the narration.

The notion of passing suggests a movement, from one cultural community or social disposition like race or sexuality to another like Black to White or gay to straight. Either is accomplished and maintained through performative practices—the use of language, racial-cultural stylistics, associations, activities and relations. [54]

> To pass is an assessment of performance.
> It is to say that the appropriate performance has been engaged.
> It is to say that people have deemed the performance as authentic if not plausible.
> It is to suggest a denial (or cloaking) of that which has been passed.
> It is to challenge the notion that identity is coalesced into a pure essence that is governed by race and culture.
> To pass is ultimately to cross borders.
> To trespass across borders where your presence is not warranted by privilege or authority.[55]

These borders are constructed and sedimented within the lived experiences of cultural communities. And those associative and disassociative practices of human engagement that mark difference between categories of identity. In actuality "passing . . . draws attention to the problem in the politics of identity, for passing accentuates what the masquerade must hide: the pre-existing social relations that facilitate disguise in the first place" (Hitchcock 1994, 3). Hence the performance is a covert action, operating below the radar and yet within the spectrum of the social investments in performative racial identity separated from the materiality of bodies.

The hyphen between Good Man–Bad Man acknowledges that we all "cross over into realms of meaning—maps of knowledge, social relations, and values that are increasingly being negotiated and rewritten as the codes and regulations that organize them become destabilized and reshaped" (Aronowitz and Giroux 1991, 119). The hyphen both joins and separates; it decenters as it remaps. The terrain of our lives becomes inextricably mapped to the shifting parameters of place, identity, history, and power. In essence, we all have border identities.

> The border is that imaginary, yet felt, location where the public and the private meet.
> It is that practiced place of history where we remember trauma and possibilize relief.
> It is that positionality where the political and the personal do symbolic battle.
> It is that space where our fractured selves are examined.
> It is that place where we are expected to pass customs—even when passing is constructed as both an act of assuming and consuming the other, as well surmounting the other.[56]
> And so I agree.

I agree with Herb Green when he says, "In my opinion, identities are far too complex to be reduced to pure essence" (1996, 253).

Good Man–Bad Man. Both? Neither!

The hyphen between Good Man–Bad Man becomes symbolic of a border crossing in which the fluidity of identity allows passage into specified territories and situations. But the hyphen is always a site of tension—a difficulty in negotiating separateness and connection.

In her essay "Hyphen-Nations," Jennifer DeVere Brody states: "By performing the mid-point between often conflicting categories, hyphens occupy 'impossible' positions. . . . They mark a de-centered position that perpetually presents [those who occupy that space] with a neither/nor proposition" (1995, 149). Passing, regardless of its political and racial implications, is a performative act in which cultural members cross borders of identity, both real and imagined. It is an act of performing the me and the not me in relation to others and in particular situations; performances that tempt and contempt, as well as test and contest the relational and perceptual borders of actual and perceived identity.

Like the character of Irene in *Passing*, we are all "bound . . . by those very ties of race, which, for all [our] repudiation of them, [we] have been unable to completely sever." These are racialist discourses, bodily orientations, and cultural performances that help in regulating social interactions and our sense of self in the company of others. So whether or not I was successful in my performance of "Bad Man" is only measured by the acquisition of my intention. I got service. Such performances are both contestatory as well as compensatory[57] in that they emerge in the confluence of racial strife and serve as evidence of competing intentions. Yet they never really make amends, as they take us to the limits of our possibility and marking our bodies with the bruises of social contact. These are encounters that regulate bodies and borders. These performances of passing through race and culture that are as much about agency as they are about necessity.

4

(Re)Visioning the Ethnographic Site

Interpretive Ethnography, Performing Drag, and Feminist Pedagogy

Theory, writing, and ethnography are inseparable material practices. Together they create the conditions that locate the social inside the text. Hence, those who write culture also write theory. Paraphrasing Clough (1994), there is a need for a reflexive form of writing that turns ethnographic and theoretical texts back "onto each other" (p. 62).

—Norman Denzin, *Interpretive Ethnography*

At best, it seems, drag is a site of a certain ambivalence, one, which reflects the more general situation of being implicated in the regimes of power by which one is constituted, and, hence, of being implicated in the very regimes of power that one opposes.

—Judith Butler, *Bodies That Matter*

As feminist studies enters the classrooms . . . , the challenge of developing and implementing a pedagogy consonant with our goals and objectives becomes critical. If some of our goals are to promote interracial understanding, to highlight the ways racism, classism, and sexism/heterosexism continue to divide, alienate, and oppress people, and to evaluate alternative models for social change, then we must, as many feminists are now realizing, upset the "normative" balance of power in the classroom.

—W. S. Hesford, "Storytelling and the Dynamics of Feminist Teaching"

I often begin my performative scholarship with a personal moment—a narrative or a confession. This reiterative moment in my work is a signal to myself and to the audience (the reader), that I am personalizing the text. It signals that I am engaged in a reflexive project of seeing myself see myself, in both the moment of the academic utterance and the awareness of owning what I say. So, I begin this chapter with a confession, because I think that interpretive ethnography is partially about self-disclosure; it is "autoethnographic, vulnerable, performative, and critical" (Denzin 1999, 510). It is about articulating one's views and perceptions. It is about detailing experience and offering storied histories of lived experiences. So I confess, for some time I have been interested in drag performance and how that relates to identity and more specifically, how it relates to the authentic character and identity of teachers in the classroom. My interest in drag is not exclusively relegated to the reductionary and reifying discussions of sex, sexuality, and gender or the polemics linked with subterfuge and deception, or even the contested performative accomplishment of allusion versus impersonation. Though these issues inform my thinking of drag performance as they have informed my interests in passing (chapter 3). My interest in drag performance focuses on the sensuousness of experience, the challenge of display and representation, and the risky and risqué nature of performing and critiquing drag in the classroom; drag as an exaggerated performance of redirecting the gaze—both that act of subverting what is seen and presumed to natural, and that strategic manner that presupposes a knowledge of the real, displaced by the surreal.

Within this chapter, I am interested in the contested notion of discussing issues of sex and sexuality in relation to the sometimes sanitized discussions of pedagogy and classroom practices. This chapter picks up and extends logics from the preceding chapters. In particular I take the notion of passing (from chapter 3) and place it in the context of gender, and place the issues of negotiating boundaries of identity (from chapter 2) in the subversive identity politics that occur between teachers and students.

In constructing the notion of pedagogy as a performance of drag, I would like to offer three theoretical constructs that help ground my joint interest in pedagogy and drag, and how I am relating this to and through interpretive ethnography. First, in *Passing and Pedagogy* Pamela L. Caughie states that "pedagogy often defined as the 'art' of teaching, functions more like interpretation; it provides students with the means to accomplish something" (1999, 64).[1] In that sense pedagogy is like teaching good manners, "which signals the practical synthesis of the question 'What should be taught and why?' with considerations as to how that teaching should take place" (Simon 1992, 55–57). Like good manners, pedagogy is always something that is relational. The beauty of the performative accomplishment is only truly appreciated by those with an articulate understanding of intention and effect, and those with investment in particular affects.

Second, in *Drag: A History of Female Impersonation in the Performing Arts* Roger Baker offers a conceptualization of drag performance that speaks not to the practice of donning the clothes of the other but to the effect of the engagement. He writes, "Drag is about many things. It is about clothes and sex. It subverts the dress codes that tell us what men and women should look like in our organised society. It creates tension and releases tension, confronts and appeases. It is about role-playing and questioning the meaning of both gender and sexual identity. It is about anarchy and defiance" (1994, 18). Baker suggests that drag is about disrupting notions of the normal or the expected. It is about both performances of resistance and resistant performances of gender. Drag is based in the assumptions about the normal and its opposite.

Third, in this sense I want to use Judith Butler's clarification of performativity by switching metaphors—from gender as drag to gender as an assignment. She writes: "To the extent that gender is an assignment, it is an assignment which is never quite carried out according to expectation, whose address never quite inhabits the ideal s/he is compelled to approximate" (1993, 231). The combination of these utterances could suggest that the teaching persona is rife with expectations and those teachers who assume the expected assignments of character in a denial of their ideal selves are performing in drag. Linked with Butler's construction, Del LaGrace Volcano and Judith Halberstam's interviews with drag king performers suggest the difference between male and female impersonation. "The male impersonator [a woman performing a man] has to take things off . . . while the female impersonator [a man performing a woman] has to add things on" (1999, 35).

In constructing the metaphor of pedagogy as drag, I want to suggest that, like drag, pedagogy is about what we as teachers reveal and what we conceal in the classroom and why. It is about the construction of our personal identities and how we filter knowledge through experience. I suggest that teachers engaged in interpretive ethnography are filtering knowledge through experience, revealing aspects of themselves often left hidden. So while the context of this chapter is focused on the links between drag (performance) and pedagogy, I must also reveal my own experiences with and positionality in these performances. To that extent, throughout this chapter, I will offer a series of descriptive excursions that take me away from the formal construct of the classroom, but always bring me back to the constructed nature of pedagogy as drag performance, blurring the boundaries between place and space, and the intentionality of particular performances. In this way I seek to complicate what Suzanne de Castell and Mary Bryson call "the often contradictory implications of theoretical debates concerning identity politics/essentialism juxtaposed with the embodied actualities of producing, negotiating, performing, and troubling difference/s in educational contexts" (1997, 1).

Excursion #1: The Queen as King (or, the Making of a Man?)

I have attended gay clubs and seen women doing drag.
They are often dressed in men's suits, with false mustaches
and an Elvis-like charisma,
or Billy Idol–like lust.
But this particular performance is different.
S/he walks onto the stage and the 5 to 1 ratio of male to female audience is
    quieted.
There is music in the background, but no one notices it.
All that I notice is he/r^2—
a sculpted body, a hard body.
S/he is not masked in elaborate make-up.
This is a performance of revealment not concealment.

S/he's not swaying with undulating hips, but walking with purpose,
"straight" with a control of focus,
taking up space,
booted feet landing firmly in he/r tracks.
S/he surveys the room and makes he/r mark.
S/he commands our attention.

The 1 percent of lesbians in the bar begin to hmmmmm with delight—
the first of such sounds in the evening.

Unlike their critiquing whispers of the drag queens that preceded he/r,
they engage the performer in a methodical seduction that
is slightly lost on me, but not really.
Well maybe.
For you see, for me this is Victor Victoria—it is a woman, "pretending" to be
    man—
or is she? The tension that exists in my desire and my aesthetic appreciation
    suspends me in that query.

S/he has short spiked hair that s/he passes her fingers through.
S/he's wearing a tight T-shirt "with her breast firmly under control."[3]
He/r shoulders are broad, he/r chin square.
S/he's wearing tight jeans.
One hand is strategically placed on he/r crotch—
but seemingly not as suggestion of what is not there—as in parody,
but a gesture to what is there—a signal to her sex;
pointing direction to desire.
With he/r other hand passing through he/r hair s/he looks like
either James Dean
or the Venus DeMilo
(if she had arms, or when she had arms.)

He/r's is a performance of absence—
Signaling what is not there magnifies the potency of what is,
an organic masculinity.[4]
S/he has a slight mustache, just enough to seem "real."
S/he has sideburns that frame an intense expression.
He/r body is unfettered.
S/he sits on a stool and spreads he/r legs
in that manly pose that suggests masculinity,
but really just signals comfort, confidence, and control.

S/he mouths the words to some male love ballad,
and I believe he/r.
It's not in the words, but in the delivery.
I see he/r care for detail and he/r focused attention to the women
in the audience.
He/r's is not a "performance" of masculinity,
like putting something on—
she has taken something off to reveal
an essence of directness and desire.

The performance is a moment in which a woman
strategically "transforms" herself to look like a "man."
Yet s/he knows that the women looking at
he/r as a "man" knows that s/he is a woman—
the sexual object of their affection, mimicking the presumed image of
the feminine heterosexual gaze.
S/he also knows (she has to know) that in the "gay bar"—
gay men are looking at he/r
as the object of their male desire.
Yet, s/he is a trickster—directing and redirecting gaze (gays).
I suspect that in the exclusively lesbian bar that the project is more direct,
the audience specific.

The song continues, but it doesn't really matter,
it's not what s/he says,
it's what s/he does.
Well maybe not: Little girls are supposed to be seen not heard. Right?
He/r admirers approach the drag king and pay the monetary homage
that has become custom when in the company of royalty.
The men offer their appreciation of the aesthetic.
They are allowed to lean in and kiss he/r on a turned cheek.
Women who offer their appreciation are engulfed in a "manly" hug
with an appropriate display of affection.
The kiss and the touch are like secret fraternity/sorority signals
of membership and desire.

INTERPRETIVE ETHNOGRAPHY AS REFLEXIVE PEDAGOGY

Using Norman Denzin's (1997) construction of interpretive ethnography
as guide, this chapter also seeks to further the discussion of the classroom
as a situated cultural site. It is a site that places the teacher as both participant and observer in an intense social negotiation of attitudes, beliefs, values and practices. The nature of this kind of research "shifts the focus or
research from the perspective of the ethnographer as an outsider to a discovery of the insider's point of view. Ethnography is not merely an objective description of people and their behavior from the observer's viewpoint. It is a systematic attempt to discover the knowledge a group of
people have learned and are using to organize their behavior" (Spradley
and McCurdy 1972, 9). Hence, teachers can be seen as ethnographers sur-

veying the terrain of their classroom culture. This research furthers the significance of storytelling by teachers, by grounding it in the thick description and critical reflection of experience that is ethnography.[5] This chapter argues that since teachers are always and already positioned as participants and observers in the process of education, we are uniquely situated to engage in writing interpretive ethnographies as a means of both documenting our experience and providing insights to others.

The typologies and provisional unities that I use in this chapter demonstrate a meaningful discontinuity between what I am advocating as a critical interpretive ethnography at the service of pedagogy and what some might read as merely a venture into creative writing.[6] And yet, creative writing has benefit in the social world. While grounded in aesthetics, creative writing like interpretive ethnography is committed to the critical social processes of meaning-making and illuminating experience through descriptive language. Interpretive ethnography is considered a theory of writing. It is also linked to a theory of intent.[7] Within this sense, I must admit a fixation on the reflexive that is both a germinal element of interpretative ethnography and helps to theorize the politics of my own production, which is always a requirement of scholarship. Reflexivity is also the cornerstone of critical teaching. Critical teachers engage reflexivity as an active mediation of their in-class practices, and as a meditation on the effectiveness of their practices, which serves as the very nature of praxis.

I fully practice what Denzin outlines as six levels of reflexive engagement: First, a subjectivist reflexivity in which I engage in my own self-critique. Second, a methodological reflexivity in which I try to sustain and argue for a methodological purity. Third, an intertextual reflexivity in which I add my voice in relation to a larger conversation of these issues. Fourth, a standpoint reflexivity in which I claim a subjective involvement with the subjects of my reflection while also maintaining an objectified sense of purpose and process. Fifth, a queer reflexivity in which I identify myself as a gendered subject with agency and self-identity. Sixth, a feminist-materialist reflexivity in which I question the very nature of writing about others in light of my own fragmented identity.[8] While these are characteristics of the poetic or narrative text, I find that they also establish meaningful orientations of teachers to students, curriculum, schools, the classroom experience, the process of publicly articulating experience, and our own dense particularities. Interpretive ethnography demands a reorientation to self in relation to time and space.

Ethnographers cannot be expected to know everything about a particular culture. So in writing interpretative ethnographies, teachers might focus on specific moments of experience in order to extrapolate meaning. Teachers might focus on those rare moments when teaching really works, or those particular moments of conflict and struggle in the classroom.[9] "The history of such oppositional moments needs to be written, but it only becomes legible against the more hegemonic set of discourses and practices in which vision took shape" (Crary 1999, 7).

Hence the classroom is a cultural site. It is a space that is socially negotiated and socially constructed. To make this acknowledgment is in fact to acknowledge that the classroom is what we make it, either a space of oppression or a place of possibility based in the competing intentionalities of society.[10] Yet, unlike traditional ethnographies, where the ethnographer travels to the wilds of exotic sites crossing disparate geographical borders in search of the other—or crossing over to the metaphorical "wrong side of the tracks" in search of experiences other than their own—the classroom is ever present in the experience of teachers and students.

The classroom is a site in which diverse lived experiences and disparate ways of being and knowing come together to negotiate the sometime collectivizing cultural practices of traditional education. The teacher thus becomes the ethnographer of her own experience and that of the classroom environment. The classroom becomes a space for tracking these movements. The classroom as a practiced place offers rich opportunity for interpretive ethnographic reflections and analysis by teachers. And while the work of Peter McLaren has called our attention to the classroom as a cultural space, interpretive ethnography offers a journey into the personal experiences and reflections of teachers within that space to not only describe but also to illuminate.

Here I focus on an in-class student performance that forced me to re-vision the nature of teaching and how my dense particularity as a Black gay male teacher demands a certain accountability on the part of students, who negotiate the content of classroom experience, in relation to their own lives, and my material presence in the classroom. Making this realization places me both on the inside of the outside, and the outside of the inside of my own classroom experience.

A STUDENT PERFORMING DRAG IN THE CLASSROOM

I received the analysis paper for his prose performance in my beginning Oral Interpretation of Literature class and I was amused by his selection, an excerpt from Meryl Cohn's (1995) *Do What I Say: Ms. Behavior's Guide to Gay and Lesbian Etiquette.*[11] This is a trade book in the camp etiquette genre. He constructed his performance around his vision of Ms. Behavior, an overly exaggerated hyperbolic drag queen dishing out advice to the would-be drag queen and the ill-advised "natural" woman.[12]

I am amused when he prances into the performance space like a high-stepping carnival performer on six-inch stiletto heels, his stylized version of femininity. Other than his shoes and his affected manner, his drag was suggestive, as all drag is suggestive. He wore black corduroys and a red shirt—of the "polo" variety. He resisted shaving his facial hair—a vandike (his male drag). If the dualism of his appearance forestalled the believability of his drag, he circulated pictures of himself done up—his face beat with make-up, full dark lips, wearing a larger-than-life black wig and a form-fitting black dress that emphasized his ample bosom. The size of his faux breasts and the thinness of the dress revealed a white brassiere—a documented fashion faux pas that competed against his pedagogical credibility on drag etiquette.

In this performance I am amused at how he reconstructs the audience from students in the classroom to audience members at a drag show, blurring the lines, knowing that the classroom is always a site of performance and that drag is always relative. And I begin to think about the shifting roles of teacher-student, performer-audience, spectacle and spectators in the classroom. I begin to think that pedagogical positions are like drag performances, the dawning of particular personas for the pleasure of others or some internal fulfillment of desire.[13]

I am intrigued by this pedagogical performance. He continues to instruct the class on the proper decorum for being a drag queen. His method calls attention to the spectacle of instruction while it speaks to the spectacle of gender performance. But I am less interested in his campy delivery—this bigger-than-life queen who has found he/r way on the runway of my classroom—with unsuspecting and captive viewers. I am more interested and amused by the other students in the class. They are a motley crew. During previous discussions related to issues of sex-sexuality-gender they have silently asserted their heterosexuality by performing *het-texts*.

Stories of male-female desire, masculine zeal and fatal femininity, as if to extend the expected heteronormative standard of gender performance into my classroom as an insurgent act of performative resistance, against what they know is my queer identity.

I am musing on their response to Ms. Behavior. They giggle and guffaw as she walks in her stiletto heels allowing the point and balance of that performative act to dictate her body gesture. They issue embarrassed smiles when s/he talks about the dilemmas and challenges of finding size 15 pumps. They direct resentful stares when she speaks of the negotiation of dressing rooms—praying for a sign that says, "unisex" so that s/he does not have to make the choice. But he, the performer, has made some clear choices.

I see one of my het-boys sitting in the back of the room. In class he previously did a performance of Hercules—his idealized masculine idol in a text by James Baldwin called, "The Choices of Hercules" from *The Book of Virtues* edited by William J. Bennett (1993). In his performance (of gender) he preened and flexed his sculpted physique and beamed over an idealized feminine construct in the text. He is eye candy for the girls in the class (and for some of the boys). But now Hercules is cowering in the corner, his body angled to the wall as he takes sneak peeks at the spectacle of femininity that is Ms. Behavior. Ironically, in his own performance text, his character makes a choice between two women: the first called Labor, the second called Pleasure. Whereas Pleasure was "beautiful as a summer day," Labor "was not as beautiful as the other, [but] had a countenance pure and gentle." He chooses Labor over Pleasure.

Ms. Behavior speaks about the labor that is gender performance. Yet Hercules (the character and the student) is performing resistance. In both his performance and the one he is viewing woman is a concept-metaphor, a comparative and relational performance used to signal sexual and gendered relations.[14] In his performance he used the descriptive of woman to set off his own masculinity as linked to heterosexual desire. Yet Ms. Behavior (the character and the student), reveals the copresence of sex and gendered performance in a manner that envelops the concept-metaphors of man and woman in a simultaneous performance of possibility that shakes regimes of the normal. Hercules looks back and forth between the picture in his hand, the drag queen—every bit the femme fatale, and the male in performance—they are the same and not the same. He smiles then passes the pictures on quickly, as if embarrassed—this time refusing to make the choice of Labor over Pleasure, which is now made manifest in Ms. Behavior.

And I am musing at the women in the class who perform a tensive audiencing of their drag queen big sister. S/he both challenges their comfort in femininity and confirms the constructedness of femininity and their own enculturation into a cult of beauty. When Ms. Behavior instructs them on the danger of blue eye-shadow, the negotiation of their first pair of heels, and the process of finding the right dress—they nod and giggle like sorority girls acknowledging secret fashion tips.

At the end of the performance all students rush to ask questions. The men want to know about the negotiation of wearing heels (and how long it took him to learn). The women confirm the performance of gender— not this man-teacher in drag, but how his instruction parallels their own performance of gender. They begin to spinstory, sharing their own personal successes and failures. Yet, to find their comfort in the complex issues of gender performance and sexuality—as presented by Ms. Behavior, they must reject the pedagogical trigger of their body memory—as same and not the same. They invalidate the meaningfulness of the message by relegating the performance as spectacle—as they say, "That was funny. You're so funny."

For them, spectacle is something that amuses, shocks, and dumbfounds—but does not inform. Spectacle is only something that draws attention and marks the difference between the normal and the not normal, performance and performativity, the thing and the thing done— establishing distance between the drama of the actor and the aesthetic distance of the spectator. For this audience Ms. Behavior troubles the boundaries between biological category (sex) and performative behavior (gender), in ways that they may not have questioned before but that they are surely invested in. Ms. Behavior causes them to question the categories of sex and gender and how performance is implicated. Their dismissal of the performer in relation to Ms. Behavior is their own performance of resistance to the performative nature of gender.

And it is in that moment that I must intervene. I intervene knowing that I am going to make a spectacle of myself, hoping that they don't see me exclusively as a gay-identified man coming to the rescue of a drag queen in distress. But that they see me as their teacher (who is gay)

engaged in a moment of instruction, which can also be a moment of rescue and recovery. I feel the need to address his performance as it meets
the assignment, the performance as a construction and deconstruction of
femininity, and how this relates to the nature of their comments. I feel the
need, as I often feel the need, to deconstruct my position as teacher in
moments in which the sociopolitical aspects of curriculum or course content come in tension with the personal aspects of how I carry myself in
the world and the things that I value. I need to remind them that for our
purposes performance has to be *dulce et utile*, sweet and useful—the aesthetic crafted with intention. Like my teaching, that must be carefully
crafted to inform about content matter, while signaling larger issues of
decorum and the social politics that dictate our lives.

How does the performance of Ms. Behavior inform us? Of course we
knew the presenter was gay; he'd mentioned it often. I have created a space
where that is commonplace. For surely, if I am going to be comfortable in
my own gay identity, I must find ways to fuse that aspect of myself with
everything else that I am including in my role as teacher—and thus give
space for others to walk in relative ease in the classroom. It is not my
desire to flaunt the implicit and or explicit nature of my difference, but to
present myself as authentically as I can to be fully present in the classroom
and to use the fullness of my identity as the tools with which I teach.

His performance of gender helps to denaturalize the everydayness of
gender performance. He magnifies the constructedness of gender by placing his body on those illusory borders that separate and signify what it
performatively means to be a "woman" and what it performatively means
to be a "man." As teachers we also place our bodies in the instructional
gaps negotiating the tensions that often exist between our teaching persona and the fullness of our being. Our sexualized and racialized bodies
always signal a history, an enfleshed knowledge that may or may not (to
our students) inform our pedagogy and our orientation to the subject
matter.[15] Yet, in this pedagogical performance we come to see not only
how Ms. Behavior narrates gender performance, but how we are implicated in that process as actors and spectators engaging our own performance and reviewing the performances of others.

His performance opens up a space where we can come to question the
very notion of "misbehaviors" as they relate to the expected performances
of sex, sexuality, and gender reduced to issues of heteronormativity.

Knowing of course that within a technocratic construction of education[16] and the teaching body, the body of the teacher is constructed as straight—if not neutered—conferring intellectual knowledge without "libidinal complications" (Roy 1995, 119). The pedagogical performance of Ms. Behavior forces us to realize that as teachers/performers in the classroom, we are trapped in the spectatorial gaze of our students. We are positioned somewhere in the binary between parody and reality, between the real and not real, and the choices between our personal Pleasure and the Labor of pedagogy.

Excursion #2: Drag Droppings (or the Making of a Woman)

The performative arena of a male drag show is like no other.
The female "impersonator"/performer receives
many accolades for his illusion,
For his construction and deconstruction of masculinity and femininity,
in the site of the gay bar where that is the ongoing embodied activity.

What does it mean to be a man watching a man in drag?
What does it mean to be a man pretending to be a woman while men watch?
It is a fabricated farce.
It is a moment of suspended disbelief.
But this is not Victor Victoria.
The viewer knows that it is a man pretending to be a woman,
not a woman pretending to be a man pretending to be a woman.
It is the embrasure of a gay aesthetic,
a grassroots theorizing on potential male performativity
and the subversion of a delimiting possibility of masculinity.

The performance is a moment in which a man strategically transforms himself
to look like a woman.
Yet he knows that the men looking at him as a woman
know that he is a man—the sexual object of their affection,
mimicking the presumed image of the masculine heterosexual gaze.

In the dressing room the drag queen adds padding in strategic places in order
to simulate feminine features.

> Creating hips where straight lines existed.
> Creating an ass where a flat bottom has lingered.
> Creating breasts where a hairy chest might have been.

With make-up applied, he slenderizes his manly nose
into that of a petite fem.
He gives the illusion of high cheek bones, full lips, and eyes that pop out
maybe with vibrantly colored lenses.

His body is shaved, plucked, cropped, and topped with a wig or
an elaborate head dress.
He dons an after-five gown—for of course that is what "real" woman wear
in this UnReal performative arena.
He steps into the pumps as he steps into his identity—transforming himself
from Burt or Victor to Priscilla, Victoria, or Eartha Quake
or some other transgendered earth-shaking transformed persona.

With his penis "firmly under control,"
he stands on his spot waiting for the music to signal his entrance.
The music begins.
The curtain opens.
He assumes the appropriate feminine persona—
based on the outfit and the music of course—
because a lady is always properly aligned.
To the beat of the music he either shakes and shimmies,
or sachets and saunters into the arena.

With whoops, hollering, and applause the men in the audience,
some who look like men and others who are drag wannabees,
validate the transformation, the illusion, the performance of hyperfemininity and
     suppressed masculinity.
Those who are so moved, approach the drag queen and pay the monetary homage
     that
has become custom when in the company of royalty.

In the course of he/r performance,
a vigorous gyrating of hips and tits to a rock 'n' roll beat
or a statuesque crooning of a love ballad,
(undoubtedly by Celine Dion or Madonna),
the drag queen may drop a dollar bill or an earring,
a tassel from he/r dress or any other part of he/r pastiched image.
These are called *drag droppings*.

Though the typical gender performances in this arena are subverted—
chivalry is not dead in a gay bar.
A courtly gentleman from the audience will always offer assistance.
In exchange he may be rewarded with a kiss or the simple touching of finger tips,
accompanied by the diverting of eyes
and the coy smile that signals a shy feminine mystique,
which we are told is the mark of a "true" lady.

A TEACHER PERFORMING DRAG IN THE CLASSROOM

When Jane Gallop talks about pedagogical positions as drag she is talking
about role-playing. She is talking about the sensuousness of getting off on
"playing teacher." And she is talking about the tensions between "oppos[itional] pairs teaching/sex, understanding/conflict, duty/gratification,
experience/representation, gender-blind/hypergendered, reality/pretense,
labor/play" (1992, 217). Drag for her is literally teetering on the line
between the her and not her in the "infantile pedagogy" of her childhood
remembrances and in her dailiness as a "Full professor"(p. 215). She
engages an uncomfortable struggle with the notion of teachers and students as lovers, the inability to delineate pedagogical desire from carnal
lust, or pedagogical incest with students—whether imagined or realized.

Though Ms. Behavior possessed her own appeal, my construction of
teaching as drag has nothing to do with costumed constructions of the
real (or surreal). It has nothing to do with a lustful desire for my students,
or my inability to tease out the differences between the enjoyment of pedagogical engagement and an inappropriate desire for my students. For me
the notion of pedagogical drag is about representation. It is about a carefully crafted teaching persona that is either designed to foreground aspects
of the personal, or to cover them up. It is about those moments of slippage
or detection in the classroom when, either by accident or intention, we
reveal our biases, or our students detect our biases, and articulate their
detection through questions of fairness. In my construction of pedagogical
drag I am interested in those active pedagogical moments of response in
which teachers are engaged in the dual process of constructing their personal gender/sexual identity as it relates to in-class performances. Like
Gallop's construction of oppositional pairs, I am now interested in how
student questions seek a clarification between bias/desire, affinity/rejection, and pedagogy/propriety.

In a written evaluation and reflection on the performance given by Ms. Behavior, Hercules questions whether or not I was easy on the performer (in my critique) and harsh on the class because he is gay (and because, he suggestively writes—"and you are gay.") He questioned whether or not the performance met the criteria of the assignment and whether or not the choice of material could be considered "literature." While he vigorously defended himself against accusations of homophobia, he also questioned whether or not the character presented in the performance was believable, and whether the selection and the manner of presentation was celebrating, if not advocating, a subversive and delinquent homosexual agenda. His concerns question the risks in pedagogy and the notion of promoting politics in the classroom, as if the classroom is not always and already a site of cultural and political proliferation. But his concerns are questioning my personal politics as related to the issue of my sexuality.

As I ponder his questions I see myself standing up in front of the classroom with my pressed white shirt, appropriately matched tie, nicely creased pants, intellectually sleek glasses and appropriately didactic manner (my professional drag). I am talking through the issues of this performance as filtered through the assignment and audience response. As I am standing in front of the class engaged in the pedagogical performance of commentary and critique, I am thinking about the imaginary picture of myself in drag that is circulating around the room, the me and the not me. Somewhere between my praise of the performance and the admonishment of the audience the students see my biases and my allegiances. They see the imaginary slip of my drag subjectivity showing, if not literally dragging beneath the presumed objectivity of the teacher.[17] And I wonder if for them somehow my queer identity competes against my pedagogical credibility? While credibility is an audience-based perception, I know that my academic knowledge and my understanding of pedagogy offer me a foundation on which to build, if not solicit, credibility.

Somewhere between my comments on the selection and my clarification of the issues, the gay man in me has challenged the impression of the straight teacher and the sanitized nature of classroom discourse around issues of sex, sexuality, and gender that had so often signaled my classroom experience as a student. This knowledge was considered dangerous because it destabilized established commonsense worldviews that encouraged sameness and shunning difference under codes of morality; dangerous because it pulled the veil away from oppression, discrimination, and suffering, making for uncomfortable confrontations with the realities of living;[18] and dangerous because the classroom is now seen not as a safe haven that we have assumed it to be, but in fact the dangerous place that it has always been. A place where ideas, beliefs, and values are challenged in ways that shake the very foundations of socialized practices and cultural ways of knowing. The classroom as a place where minority voices have always been silenced and dominant ideologies have been upheld with a vengeance.

And now in the classroom, I am positioned in the tensive negotiation of viewing and responding to performances of sexuality and sexualized performances, and how my own desire and disdain becomes a politicized variable. Yet I know that this is not so much a trap as it is the quest of good pedagogy—to question not only what to teach and how to teach it but also why. The condition of tensiveness does not so much signal strife and resistance as it reveals the contrasts and conflicts in which teachers infuse their teaching; an academic intellectual knowing tempered with a personal sense of being in the world.

So I must respond to the questions and accusations, both those of the student and my own.

RESPONDING TO QUESTIONS IN DRAG

Dear Student,

In this class I speak from the position of the teacher and a person in the world. In this class I speak with the express intent in clarifying issues, challenging thoughts, and encouraging critical introspection. In this class I speak as a teacher who has accomplished some degree of academic accomplishment, but not at the expense of the person that I am or would like to be.

In this class I speak as a teacher, but as a teacher who is Black, and a teacher who is gay. My academic knowledge is filtered through the person that I am. Sometimes that knowledge influences other aspects of my life, but most often the history of my being, the history of being Black in this country, the history of being gay in this country, tempers and directs my understanding of academic issues and directs my teaching. It happens to help recoup the past and redirect the future. So my comments related to Ms. Behavior are not designed to promote a "homosexual agenda," but a critical examination of the performance as it met the assignment and the accompanying social critique it offered on the construction of gender.

While I appreciate your questions, I would ask that you reflect on why you asked the questions. Does the performance of "misbehavior" challenge you in some way that questions your notions of the normal? Would you prefer to silence such dissent? To question whether Ms. Behavior and I are trying to promote a homosexual agenda is also to have us question whether you are promoting an agenda of heteronormativity that would deny our voice, and therefore you become some legislator of what is moral and normal. Are you setting yourself up as the arbiter of good taste? And since I am Black and Ms. Behavior is Latino and we are gay, and you are a straight White man asking the questions, should these be factored in our discussion as well?

How does this performance work in tension with your own? Here I am speaking directly to your performance of prose, not the constructedness of your gender performance? Do you see the relationship between this text and your own choice, "The Choices of Hercules"? Can you engage in that critical endeavor?

PERFORMING PEDAGOGY/INTERPRETING EXPERIENCE

I am deftly aware of the importance of compassionate and yet critical commentary to my students. The intentions are grounded not only in a quest for humanity but also in the idea that our students can become better without becoming bitter. Similarly, an interpretive ethnography must be grounded in an ethic of care. It is not engaged in a narcissistic process of sense-making as the fulfillment of inward desires or as a practice of power. It must engage the critically reflexive process for the benefit of self and other in a morally imaginative process.[19]

Within interpretive ethnography there is a tensively held moral obligation toward the subjects of reflection and the intention of the reflection and commentary. And in this sense interpretive ethnography works in alignment with compassionate care that always guides and undergirds good teaching. An ethic of care that is designed to inform and engage without harming, to promote and deter without silencing, to offer information and knowledge—knowing that it is an offering and not a mandate.[20] The intimate engagement of reflection and description that is interpretive ethnography demands a felt involvement that cannot help but motivate and transform the author and those who read it. So in order to make interpretive ethnography meaningful beyond the scope of the individual experience, the insights gathered must be translated into action; it must be used to transform our educational praxis and the experience of students.

Excursion #3: Gender Markings

On March 1, 2000, I performed a program entitled "Gender Markings" at the University of California, Santa Barbara (UCSB). The performance was scheduled as the last event of Black History Month and the first event moving into Women's History Month. The event was sponsored by four organizations: the UCSB Multi-Cultural Center, the Center for Black Studies, the Queer Resource Center and the Queer Student Union. The positioning of my body and the performance at these intersections created varying expectations for those in attendance and pulled me in multiple directions. For some it was an entertainment event, for others it was about representation, for still others it was a pedagogical moment—all of these expectations converge in the traditional classroom. The audience was mixed, with me reading a lot of same-sex couples and a series of singles— older and younger. There was a mixture of faculty and students with pens and pads taking notes.

In the performative presentation I included the two pieces on drag performance mentioned before: "The Queen as King (or the Making of a Man?)" and "Drag Droppings (or the Making of a Woman?)." After the performance, a highly "masculinized-pretty-dyke-girl"—with short cropped hair, spiked in the front, with a chiseled jaw line, wearing a black leather coat draped over a white t-shirt, sitting up front with her legs crossed in square fashion asked me a question. She said something like: "I am very interested in your depiction of drag king performance. Could you talk about that some more?" I answered her by saying that in interviews with drag king performers, Volcano and Halberstam note that the performers suggested that the difference between male and female impersonation is that the male impersonators (women performing men) have "to take things off . . . while the female impersonator has to add things" (1999, 35).

When asked, "What is a Drag King?" Volcano replies that a drag king is "anyone (regardless of gender) who consciously makes a performance out of masculinity" (1999, 16). Volcano continues,

> I had been doing (female) drag for years. It was only by making a "perform-ance" out of femininity that I was able to inhabit a female persona, a femme suit that was seldom a comfie fit. But when I donned a Drag King persona it didn't feel like much of an act. I was astounded by how natural it felt to be a guy and be free of the anxieties I had lived for years around not passing as a "real" woman (16–21).

So, the question of feminine and masculine identity-construction in drag performance circles is seemingly reduced to the layering of the effect or the paring-down of the effect. "The drag king takes what is so-called natural about masculinity and reveals its mechanisms—the tricks and poses, the speech patterns and attitudes that have been seamlessly assimi-lated into a performance of realness" (Volcano and Halberstam 1999, 62). The drag king's performance is a performance of absence—signaling what is not there magnifies the potency of what is; an organic masculinity. The performative challenge of masculinity thus becomes to simulate a kind of raw simplicity and natural macho charisma. "A Drag King is a performer who makes masculinity into his or her act (yes there can be male Drag Kings)," those men who parody the very notion of what has been socially constructed as masculinity for the amusement or approval of others (36). Within the radical performative arena of drag there is a resistance to the notion of gender as fluid, "as a recreational pursuit or as no more than a choice between different wardrobes" (39). These women, most of whom are lesbians, are not merely exploring but embodying meaningful compo-nents of their own gendered selves. Many of them seek to "blur [not only] the lines between on and off stage, but that porous boundary [that] shifts and warps" their reality (41).

Later in our discussion the "masculinized-pretty-dyke-girl" in the audience cites Judith Halberstam and Del LaGrace Volcano, as do I. She has done the homework on her own identity construction. She seems to appreciate my commentary. In our discussion she does a *reading* of my performance of *viewing* drag king performance. In her observation, she forces me to acknowledge what is my seemingly contradicting desire—but not really. She forces me to see that the "gay boy" in me appreciates the aesthetic of drag queen performance and the layering of identities; the subversion and the sometimes salacious deliciousness of the feminine mystique recreated and embodied in drag on the male body. It is also the "gay man" in me whose desire for the masculine attracts me to drag king performance. But unlike in drag queen performance, my appreciation for the drag king turns into desire—even though I acknowledge the layered limitations of that aesthetic.

I find in talking to this "masculinized-pretty-dyke-girl" that while both depictions are respectful and celebratory, the documentation of my spectatorship is different, because I am positioned differently at each performance event. At drag queen performances I am implicated as a gay man in the company of gay men engaging in queer performance that simulates the heterosexual gaze (men looking at women)—how queer is that—but not really. In her essay, "Desire Cloaked in a Trenchcoat," Jill Dolan offers some thoughts on the difficulty of the female spectator of pornography geared for the male gaze, in which the female image (body) is the object of lust. She says, "According to the psychoanalytical model, since male desire drives representation, a female spectator is given two options. She can identify with the active male and symbolically participate in the female performer's objectification, or she can identify with the narrative's objectified female and position herself as object" (1993, 124–125). I want to rework this quote playing on the male drag performer's objectification of women, or maybe more specifically, the objectification of femininity and how the gay male "straight acting" spectator positions himself as spectator.

While the notion of a "straight acting" gay may seem like a oxymoron, it nonetheless serves as a reoccurring description of the gay man who does not identify as feminine in his daily carriage, and is hence masculine—as those terms are narrowly placed as a dichotomy. The phrase, "straight acting" is also coded language that begs the question of performative sexuality, social conformity, and the notion of gay men "passing" as straight by assuming the socially sanctioned *heterotropes* of masculine performance, engaging what Judith Butler has referred to as compulsory heterosexuality, which is not only an enacted engagement of sexual practice but a performative display of those performances of masculinity and femininity that are narrowly distinguished between the sexes.[21]

Performative heterotropes of masculinity might easily be defined in opposition to what I like to call the stereotypical and often parodied *homotropes* of queer identity. I use the term *homotropes* to refer to the recurring expressive displays used by queers to identify themselves or those stereotypical ways in which we are represented within heterosexual spheres. The performative references might include: lisps; sibilant *s*'s; limp wrists; oversensitivity; the use of double entendre; snapping; throwing shade; swishy walking; chants like "we're here and we're queer"; references to bull-daggers or queens, truck-driving dykes or hair-dressing fags; the reductive positioning of desire, as in the references to someone as a "top or bottom" (pitcher or a catcher); and so forth. Similarly I use the term *homotropes* as Moe Meyer describes *camp*: "the total body of performative practices and strategies used to enact a queer identity," and consequently, I would add, to identify someone as queer, whether appropriately and respectfully applied or not (1994, 5). Meyer says, "it is the only process by which the queer is able to enter representation and to produce visibility" (11).

But nonetheless the question in the moment is how does the "straight acting," hence masculine, gay man position himself in the audience of drag queen performance? He is given two options. He can identify with the active male in performative drag. Thus, he symbolically participates in the parodic recreation/commentary on femininity, thereby furthering the objectification and alienation of women in this performance of desire. Or he can identify with the narrative's object, which is to acknowledge the sexualized suggestion of dualism, male and female, simulacra and simulation—which is also to acknowledge that the projected simulation is a reflection of a male image of the female that does not exist (Baudrillard 1994).

The act of gay men dressed in drag performing for other gay men is less about women and more about the situated desire of the performative aesthetic. In Diana Taylor's description, performance as a strategy "allow[s] for agency, which opens the way for resistance and oppositional spectacles" (1994, 14). I use her articulation to comment both on the spectacle of drag performance and on the spectacle of audiencing drag performance. And like Roland Barthes's entangled articulations borrowed from Jacques Lacan,[22] the viewing of drag "does not transmit a meaning, but fastens onto a limit situation: 'the one where the subject is suspended in a specular relation to the other'" (1978, 148). (Link this logic back to my discussion in chapter 1 of the gaze in tourism.)

On the other hand, in drag king performances not only am I implicated in queer company, but the specificity of my desire is evoked in their performance. I am reminded by Jill Dolan that "the gaze in performance, although not as carefully controlled as in film, is also based in a narrative paradigm that presents gender and sexuality as a factor in the exchange of meanings between performers and spectators" (1991, 14). Whether I am the ideal audience for drag king performance is questionable. My attraction to the embodied performance of masculinity is forestalled by the reality of the sexed person in performance. It is in this way, knowing that my own slip might be showing, that I skirt my way around Judith Butler's conversations of drag. For while they signal the nature of my discussion, they do not easily accommodate, contain, or explain the "variety of receptions drag might have for different audiences" (Brown 2000, 34).[23]

So, in responding to the highly "masculinized-pretty-dyke-girl"—the lesbian-woman spectator of my gay-male spectatorial report—as a gay man I must actually admit my desire for women pretending to be men, performing desire for the spectators most appreciative of that aesthetic. I must admit that in my performance, my description of the drag king is imbued with that desire, while my description of the drag queen is an appreciation of the performance, void of a visually stimulated sexualized desire for the feminine. And this is not an oppositional stance, but one grounded in my own respect and desire.

In this pedagogical moment of question and answer, I also come to realize that the specificity of this question is not so different from the types of exchanges that teachers often have with their students. The questions are always geared toward unveiling that which is concealed, and the answers are always a careful negotiation of the personal and the public through the materiality of bodies and the embodiment of particular pedagogical philosophies. So maybe this is a place for another excursion that focuses on the articulated manners of my teaching through the racialized fog that accompanies the entrance of my Black male presence in the classroom.

PERFORMING DRAG AS FEMINIST PEDAGOGY

To some, my engaging in feminist pedagogy is like my performing drag in the classroom.[24] This private and public act is so subversive that I have only recently been willing to assert its name and publicly admit to engaging its salacious, political, and emancipatory pleasures of drag. Through the frame of performing drag the assumption is that, as a feminist teacher, I (as a man) enter the classroom donning the socialized markings of femininity—a dress, make-up, a particular presumed manner, and the performative sensibilities of a sex other than my own. Hence for them, like so many critiques of gay male drag, I am engaged in a misogynistic parody of women in which my presentation is seen as ridicule.[25] Or that as a man claiming to be a feminist I am trying to assert a particular power over women's political voice, women's scholarly production, and appropriating women's social theorizing.

To some, my engaging in feminist pedagogy might also suggest that, as a Black man, I am engaging in some radical re-articulation of myself. Specifically, denouncing my own once (presumed) misogynistic ways by engaging rhetoric and socializing practices that demonize historical male behaviors and advocate a kinder, gentler performance of masculinity.[26] These assumptions are actually far from my own intent in approaching and embodying what is referred to as feminist pedagogy, or what I prefer as just compassionate teaching; teaching to/on the pulse of those who are present and presenting myself authentically in the classroom with both care and caution. Which I think should be the hallmark of all of those who strive to be "good teachers."

These are the things that I understand about feminist pedagogy that both eschew such critiques and open a space for my own authentic engagement:

I understand that feminist pedagogy is a specified approach to teaching that seeks an end to institutionalized systems of male domination and privilege. Those systems that are reflected both in the course content/curriculum and in the manner in which particular voices (those of women, minorities, and opposing views—as inflected by class, race, and gender) have been historically silenced and marginalized in the classroom.

While my sex category of male may seemingly predicate a particular privilege, such presumed privileges of sex have been historically marginalized and demonized under the regimes and politics of race (my Blackness). Also, the perception of my gay identity, under the structures of heteronormativity, has been used to undermine the salience of my voice and my equal access to particular social privileges (relegated to heterosexual marriages and military service—if I were interested in either).[27] In these ways, I am implicated but not fully included in the very regimes of power that I oppose (Butler 1993, 125).

My practice of a feminist pedagogy is really a reconnaissance mission of surveying the educational terrain of my own oppression. It is a personal rescue project. It engages pedagogical performance practice not only as a method but also as a site of opposition (hooks 1995). It works toward transforming personal, political, and social relations by using the classroom as projective microcosm of society. The classroom becomes a site in which diverse ways of knowing are engaged and long-silenced voices are practiced—that of my students (based in issues of race, sex, and gender) and my own voice, which was so strategically silenced in the classroom locations of my educational experiences. In this way my engagement of feminist pedagogy is not about "the feminine," or particular branches of "feminism," but about the nature of my own experiences and a refusal to perpetuate violence in the classroom. In this sense, maybe I am engaged in a radical intervention of identity politics in the classroom through an embodied educational praxis (De Castell and Bryson 1997).

I understand that in feminist pedagogy power is not a commodity with unequal tiers of distribution, but is a social force of democratic influence through the lens of lived and embodied experiences that cross borders of difference. In this way, feminist pedagogy strives toward including a diversity of inputs/ideas in the negotiation of knowledge. And because Black folk have long struggled for these same rights and conditions for living, I engage a feminist pedagogy as the heralding of my own positionality and possibility and that of my students. I strive to create a classroom space where opposing ideas and experiences can be offered in an understanding of their points of confluence and divergence. I strive to create a classroom where my teacher-power is not necessarily dissipated in some (false) presumed notion of equality between teachers and students, for the allocated authority of our position always forestalls that possibility.

I understand that the test of a humanistic orientation to power is not in its location but in its application and distribution. Hence, I attempt to practice power in negotiating the tensions that often arrive when different voices, motivations, and investments in academic and cultural knowledge converge in the classroom. In this way, I also understand that "the feminist classroom—is and should be a place where there is a sense of struggle"

(Schacht 2000, 3), but that this struggle is not over issues of power, control, dominance or domination, but is a collective struggle over the social processes of knowing and coming to know self and other (and sometimes self as other). Within this sense I attempt to create a space in the classroom where students can practice voice. And through critical questioning and the juxtapositioning of ideas and locations, I use my teacher-power to work with students to think critically and reflexively on their own positionality in the realm of human social relations.

I understand that in feminist pedagogy teachers practice a careful balance between critique and commentary; a system of acknowledging both theoretical constructs and the products of students' intellectual labor with a care that teases at the meaningfulness of articulation without demonizing the positionality of someone's convictions. But I also understand that teachers should not practice a false value-free stance,[28] which potentially undermines their own intellectual credibility and sense of being in the world. In practicing a feminist pedagogy I clearly teach through the personal, revealing to students issues and conditions that affect my ways of knowing and where I stand on particular issues and why (Gallop 1995).

I tell them not so as to overpower their own opinions but so that they may know that in a human society we always exist in relation to each other. I tell them so that they understand that our situated roles as teacher and students do not dominate or negate the wholeness of our beings. That the political nature of intellectual knowing does not trump the personal—and the personal as influenced by race, culture, and class does not override social responsibility. When there is tension between their articulations and my own, their sense of being and my own—and when their attitudes, beliefs and values (especially those that appear as racism, sexism, and homophobia) rub against the already bruised aspects of my own identity, I tell them. I tell them so that they know that their thoughts, manifested into action (public policy or racial antagonism), have consequences. I tell them lest they forget that I also live in the world outside of the classroom.

For example, while my students often talk about my privilege as a tenured faculty member in relation to issues of power and the machinery of the university, I often respond with the following basic exemplar that concretizes the limits of such privilege. I tell them that while I enjoy being Dr. Alexander in the light of day, after a late-night class when I am walking to my car alone, I am just a Black man walking in the darkness hoping not to attract the disdain of some random passer-by. And en route to my home through Los Angeles, I am just another man "driving while Black," thus subject to the same racist scrutiny in which I am suspect by virtue of my embodied presence.

I tell them and create a climate in which they can tell me about the variegated variables that influence and effect the social negotiation of their identity. I try to create a climate that I believe feminist pedagogy encourages—one that is filled with the emotionality of everyday human interaction. Emotionality equated with personal human investment not hysteria, that "incapacity to differentiate between reality and illusion" often problematically associated with the feminine (Schutzman 1999, 9). Also this is a reference to emotionality as the tempered and controlled articulation of feeling with respect to the acknowledged conditions and pressures under which we all labor. It is in this sense that the classroom becomes that often-touted microcosm of society; a politicized location where we begin to establish templates of sociality, standards of social engagement that govern the conditions of living in a democratic and compassionate society.

I understand that feminist pedagogy advocates and engages a consciousness-raising process directed to social transformation and liberation.[29] This is integral to the mechanism of teaching students not only to practice voice in the classroom, but also to practice voice with the thought of applying it in the dailiness of their being in the places that they live and work. It is about making students aware of the forces that oppress and restrict their possibility. It is about teaching and engaging students in the process of critically interrogating their locations, their identities, and the allegiances that inform how they live their lives.[30] It is about helping students to see their potential and possibility. It is about creating classroom space as community space and activating the tenets of a democratic citizenry.

Conversely it is about having students understand the classroom-as-microcosm-of-society metaphor as synecdoche to their lives. Cases, in which voice represents democracy, participation represents social membership, and articulating wrong represents acts of social transformation and activism.[31] And while these undergirding impulses of feminist pedagogy are central to a variety of feminist logics, they are far from being exclusive to women. They signal the possibility of an informed humanism, one that acknowledges the basic elements of living in a democratic society.

As a Black man, I am invested in the promises of that possibility and I work toward its fruition.

In making this case for/of my specified embodied performance of a feminist pedagogy, I also realize that I am not engaging in the problematic project of desexualizing feminist pedagogy. That would be a project in which I would attempt to forsake the trajectory of a compassionate pedagogy from the embodied and political specificity of its origin. In fact, maybe I am furthering an argument for the libidinal complications of linking sex and pedagogy. Maybe I am strengthening and further complicating the investments that all teachers must engage when acknowledging the materiality of their bodies and the historicized legacies that they either bank on or divest themselves of in their teaching.

For me feminist pedagogy, like feminism, is a series of ideological perspectives on social relations and, while it circulates in the body of some women and enlightened men, its actual manifestation is in the realm of social relations (see Cohee et al. 1998; Coffey and Delamont 2000; Maher and Tetreault 1994; Stone 1994; Deats and Lenker 1994). These are issues of performance in interpersonal and political negotiations with self and other, and in the pedagogical situation—between teachers and students. They are related not only to issues of sex and sexuality—but the ways in which the sedimented realities and histories of gender performance, through the embodied presence of the teacher, are made manifest in the classroom. It is an acknowledgment that raced and sexed positionalities inform human sociality; it is an acknowledgment that particular ways of knowing and experiencing the world filter and distribute content and curriculum, compassion and care, as well as desire and disdain in the classroom.

Excursion #4: A Black Man Enters the Classroom

When I walk into the classroom at the beginning of a new quarter there is a moment of pause. It is a simultaneous pause that exists between teacher and students. It is a moment in which students with whom I have had no previous contact see me as a Black man first. When I introduce myself as Professor Alexander they then must negotiate the reality that I am their teacher. I imagine that their negotiation exists in the tensions between the historicized images of Black men and their individual experiences with Black men, and between the historicized image of the White university professor and the embodiment of the Black male teacher that stands before them.

It is a moment when I face the social reality that the body exists and intervenes in the moment of its own engagement. In that I mean, as I enter the classroom as Professor Alexander, the social construction of my Black male body that resides in my students' minds intervenes and maybe precedes my articulation of my identity. And while I believe this to occur with all teachers, I imagine that the experience is different with the White male body that enters the classroom. A White male body is expected and anticipated in the professor-role, a body that while it may not offer comfort (to all students) does present an aspect of the familiar or expected, which is a sense of the known. I imagine that for White men this is an odd space of empowerment and entrapment that they need to negotiate.[32] This logic might also work with the presence of the female teaching body; while resisting issues of sexualization, domestication, and maternalization, the struggle for voice and authority offers its own sense of the known in the classroom. Varying feminisms often seek to critique and unpack the ways sex and gender identities are implicated in the classroom.

This construction, the comparative images of self and other, is part and parcel of my own fears and anxieties when entering the classroom. It has been reinforced with those staid glances and raised eyebrows, nonverbal dissing, and disconfirmations of my physical presence, as if my credibility as a teacher has already been evaluated based on my embodied presence. These are expressions that I sometimes read in the range somewhere between shock and bemusement, and between disappointment and curiosity on the faces of my students as I enter the classroom.

I suspect that it is not only the disposition of my body as much as the location of my body in the classroom that becomes startling for some. Keeping in mind the ways in which society has historically documented and concretized, so as to sanction particular ways of being by making the link between location and the specificity of bodies in action, in their activities, and in their actualities.

The location of a Black male body on the nightly news not in the classroom,
The location of a Black male body in the city jail cell not in the classroom,
The location of a Black male body in the athletic arena not in the classroom,

The location of a Black male body in the church pulpit not in the classroom,
The location of a Black male body on the streets of civil unrest not in the
classroom,
The location of a Black male body in the bedroom not in the classroom.

And yet the classroom becomes all of these for me. The educational
endeavor located in the social negotiation of the knowing and the known,
a space that contains and directs this endeavor, and a tensive dynamic
constructed in the utility of its engagement. While the university classroom is a specified place located in the walls of the ivory tower, signifying
class (the realm of higher learning and those who can and cannot afford
it) and social cost. It is also a space that magnifies intentionality and the
focus on the historicity of particular bodies and particular ways of knowing. So,

As on the nightly news, the range of my behavior as a Black male teacher in
the classroom is always under public scrutiny. I am evaluated and exist in
the interstices where race, gender, and professionalism collide. With some
wondering if I will allow race to foreground the pedagogical endeavor—as
if it does not always and already.

Like the city jail cell, the classroom becomes a place of confinement in
which I sometimes feel that I am doing time. I am doing time while I practice a liberating pedagogy not only for my students, but also for myself. An
endeavor in which I seek to unshackle my perceived image and that of other
"colored bodies" and release our regulated voices from their prisons of
silence.

As in the athletic arena, in the classroom I must practice a particular skill
and finesse that strategically negotiates knowledge and knowledge claims. I
must engage in particular language stylistics, theories, and social relations
that are at once the same and not the same as the imagined images of my
racialized and gender identity that precedes my pedagogy. I must engage
the acrobatics of Black male performativity while redirecting the gaze of my
students from what my body is, to what my body says and does.

As in the church pulpit, in the classroom I must preach the promises and
possibilities of being and becoming while avoiding the pitfall of overprosel-
ytizing, which is often associated with claiming a racial oppression and the

perceived overly animated image of Black male rage. I must engage a strategic body (book) of knowledge that offers my students a particular view of the world and their location working within and transforming it.

As in the streets of civil unrest that many minority feet have trod, in the classroom I too must walk the length of the classroom engaged in a performance of resistance to the uncritical acceptance of certain presumed social truths, for my own salvation and liberation, as well as for my students. In the classroom I must figuratively and sometime literally carry the picket signs that signify the object of resistance while engaging rhythmic chants that echo in the ears of those in the distance of my voice. Chants that articulate a desire that transcends my current position.

And resisting the taboo topic of linking pedagogy and passion—as in the bedroom, in the classroom I know that I cannot be a selfish lover. I must work toward an intimate negotiation of sensuous play (and foreplay) that allows for mutual satisfaction.[33]

I find that in that moment of pause when I enter the classroom, a moment that sometimes extends throughout the quarter—I find myself working within and against a social construction of who I am and who I am perceived to be. And while my personal approach to teaching seemingly comes naturally, nestled within the nature of my character, the processing of my academic training, and the influence of other teachers, I know that my actual performance of a feminist pedagogy is imbued with a desire to transcend the social limitations that are projected on my individual character, the character of "the teacher," and the character of learning. I know that my engagement of a more compassionate teaching, a more sensitive orientation to students, a more personal performance of sociality in the classroom, and a more politicized foregrounding of racial issues is as much a defense mechanism as a sincere performative engagement.

I know that my performance of teacher is a strategic performance designed to challenge the public construction of all Black men, of all marked others who have been minimized based on issues of race, sex, gender, and embodied presence (especially in the classroom). It is to challenge the expected experience of pedagogical discourse; an experience as a student that often left me feeling battered and bruised when someone else's desires were forced on me. Like the pedagogical equivalent to sexual assault, I was forced to say, "I like it. It feels good. Give me more baby. Give me more." Only to nurse the physical and psychological bruises of those encounters later, when time and distance had created borders between the experiencing body and the critically reflexive process of knowing the self again.

My engagement of feminist pedagogy resists the dick thing masculinity of traditional pedagogical processes and the ways in which such a specious power has been attributed to Black men. My engagement of feminist pedagogy moves toward engaging voice and volition of my own Black gay male identity as teacher, and encouraging the same in and for my students.

A BLACK MALE TEACHING BODY AS SOCIAL SUBVERSIVE ENTERTAINMENT

In establishing the metaphorical link between teachers as performers, many theorists have sought to acknowledge levels of craft and aesthetic in teaching separated from facile notions of teachers as entertainers, and hence teachers as spectacle.[34] I know that the relationship between teaching and performance share a unanimity of space and intent, meaning that in the particular place of their production teaching and performance seek both to inform and engage. They use both aesthetic and logical structures that direct attention to specific efforts and the subject matter of their engagement. In this way, I also know that the teaching body is always spectacle, a magnified and performative presence that calls attention to itself as the effect of its labor. Hence I know that spectacle can inform.

Yet in some ways, I want to claim the space of my Black-male-teaching-body for both entertainment and as spectacle. Not entertainment as in my Black male body involved in some forced self-deprecating parody or skewed imitation of myself that parallels the history of minstrelsy in this country (see Bean, Hatch, and McNamara [Lott 1996]). This would make real the historical imitations and stereotypes of my Black identity that I already struggle to combat, and those that I fear as I enter the classroom. Such an approach would reduce the nature of spectacle to "an act of self mockery, a replacing of subjectivity with something so grand, so oversignified, as to suggest hypersubjectivity" thereby truly becoming a fool's discourse (Schutzman 1998, 135). Nor am I talking about entertainment in a particular engagement of enjoyment and play—though of course there needs to be a place for enjoyment and play in the classroom.

I want to engage teaching so that students might entertain the implications and complications of my Black male teaching body and the ways in which my knowledge, experience, and the individuality of my care culminates in an engaged pedagogy.[35] An engaged pedagogy in which I am committed to a process of self-actualization transcending my own imposed and those socially allocated limitations on my possibility. I want them to entertain my on-going project of myself, while empowering them toward their own processes of self-actualization. I want to entertain and I want my students to be engaged in that active process of entertaining possibility (mine and theirs).

> To entertain: to hold the attention—focused on particular subject matters and the specificity of the vessels from, in, and through which such attending is signaled and engaged.

> To entertain: to extend hospitality toward—as in the peaceful socializing engagement of embracing the diversity of ideas, people, and manners in ways that reinforce inclusivity, compassion, and care.

> To entertain: to mull over; contemplate—both the subject matter of social discourse and the embodied presence of those engaged in social discourse. As in engaging new possibilities, or even to hold in mind the comparative relations between what has been known to what one is coming to be known—and how.[36]

In terms of making a spectacle of my Black male teaching body, I want them to read into the activity that provides the insight. I want them to possibilize what makes things work and to imagine other valuations of Black male possibility in daily enactments.[37] In this way I want to use *performing culture in the classroom* not only to foreground culture, but to move toward reforming culture in the broadest sense and in the narrow and yet fertile spaces of the classroom where such seeds must first be planted.

The politics of representation always circulate within the context and confines of the classroom. The danger of such circulations is that they also land on particular bodies, their place of contact leaving social scars that are visible and made concrete through social discourse and human interaction. My Black-male-teaching-body becomes the repository of such destructive points of contact. It also becomes a source model of examining such social projections onto my body. Stigmas and stigmata such as Black man as bestial, Black man as violent, Black man as mean/uncaring/unfeeling, Black man as sexual predator, and so forth, are deflected by a teaching persona and manner that advocates and embodies just the opposite. Through engaging a compassionate pedagogy I am dedicated to equalizing voice and negotiating possibility in the classroom. I am dedicated to engaging a student-centered, communication-centered, empathic, and engaged pedagogy that encourages the practice of voice—for both teachers and students.

At the end of every academic quarter there is a moment of pause. It is a simultaneous pause that exists between teacher and students. It is a moment in which I ask students to reflect on the nature of our experience together. I ask them to reflect on the theoretical and intellectual content of the course—what they have come to know. I ask them to reflect on the intimate and personal aspects of the course—how they have come to know. I ask them to see the act of knowing and coming to know as an intimate exchange one in which we negotiate the delicate tenderness of each other's beings—offering both pleasure and challenge. I ask them to reflect on what they have come to know and how—without teasing them apart.

And somewhere in that process I know that, while my initial apprehensions, or their apprehensions, or my apprehensions of their apprehensions of me—were valid, they have come to understand me through the context of my teaching; in that what they have come to know about themselves through the methods of my approach. I know that we all arrive at new places of understanding the possibilities in learning without bruising; relational epistemologies of shared knowing (Thayer-Bacon 2002).

PLACING VALUE ON EXPERIENCE

Interpretive ethnography places value on seeing and reflecting on experience in particular contexts. This ocular epistemology presumes the primacy of visual perception as the dominant form of knowing. Perception however, is never pure. It is clouded by the structure of language that refuses to be anchored in the present—the site of so-called pure essence.[38] The ethnographer always realizes his or her subjective position in relationship to his or her subjects, co-researchers, the focus of desire and reflection. So within this chapter the specificity of interpretive ethnography applied to the classroom experience, the metaphoric construction of performing drag, and the politicized frame of feminist pedagogy offers perceptive but not concrete answers to the complex negotiations of gender, embodied presence, and the relational politics of pedagogical interaction.

Using Denzin's construction of standpoint reflexivity, the critical narrator is then he who acknowledges his own positionality in the telling and the told. Or she who acknowledges that she "produces a partially situated text that opens up a previously repressed, ignored, or overinterpreted corner of cultural life" (1997, 221). Hence, interpretive ethnography is a personal and critically reflexive process. And "it is a situation-specific, author-specific, fallible method. It asks more questions than it pretends to answer, and its chief product is a perspectival understanding of the truth created by and constituted in a transient rhetoric" (Goodhall 1994, 151). A transient rhetoric that opens space through and of talk, so that teachers begin to give voice to desire and tease through the meaningfulness of experience.

If the classroom is a cultural site and a geographical locale, how do teachers map their experience in the classroom? How do we articulate and describe our travels and what we have learned? Maps articulate place and positionality; they also offer direction to determined destinations.[39] What is the directional model of our classroom practices? What guides the nature and content of our pedagogy? And while it may be easy to repeat the tired aphorism that "the classroom is a microcosm of society," to what degree are teachers cartographers, mapmakers designing their own desire for the classroom? These are questions that we must all face as we plan pedagogy and navigate the terrain of education.

The notion of "performing drag in the classroom" used in this chapter is of course metaphor. It is a metaphor to describe the ways in which teachers and students sometime subvert the scripts of everyday performative pedagogical discourse, revealing not the abnormal, but the all too complicated normalcy of direct human contact, this is *the drag effect*.[40] If to some, my engaging in feminist pedagogy is like my performing drag in the classroom, then they are referencing the historically dichotomized relationship between femininity and masculinity and the historically demonized copresence of one in the other. As a Black man I presume that their sense of drag might also project me in White face—hence becoming a White woman—and in the sense of the historicized sanctions of the Black man/White woman dynamic—this is a rather far stretch that further alienates me from myself.

If I am to assume the role of performing drag in the classroom, it has to be an organic performance, not of putting things on but taking them off to reveal the essence of my desire.[41] The power of the drag effect linked with pedagogy, whether premeditatedly performative or socially assumed, allows the appearance of duality to fulfill its natural place in the realm of human relations while it foregrounds the possibility of a structured and sutured identity that leads to compassionate human engagement in the classroom.

The notion of interpretive ethnographies of the classroom helps teachers to acknowledge their own designs on the classroom; places where they have located the landmarks and landmines of their own desire and how this becomes manifested and inscribed on the bodies of their students. In my own performative scholarship, I find myself trapped betwixt and between, in that liminal space of scholarship and my own highly personal and critical processes. I know that I am involved in the construction of messy texts.[42] Hence for me drag performance and pedagogical performances are messy texts—texts that cannot signal or signify a singular author.

And to what degree are all scholarly documents messy? The nature of what we do as teachers and scholars is always messy—messy with self-disclosing personal insights and disguising them as research; messy with supporting our own felt experiences with a litany of other voices in the reference pages, footnotes, or the back stages of our own scholarly performances. They are messy because when we deal with anything related to human nature we are mandated to get our hands dirty, to get involved and process through experience.

Fading, Twisting, and Weaving

An Interpretive Ethnography of the Black Barbershop/Salon as Cultural Space

My dreads cannot be ignored. My dreads are a signpost declaring to all who wish to see and hear my commitment to my culture and to a spiritual, natural way of life . . . Because of my dreads, I cannot be ignored, thus my message cannot be ignored. Freedom, rebellion, love, nature: Dreads speak these truths from many people around the world. My message cannot be ignored.

—Chinna Smith, "My Dreads Cannot Be Ignored"

Hair is never a straightforward biological fact, because it is almost always groomed, prepared, cut, concealed and generally worked upon by human hands. Such practices socialize hair, making it the medium of significant statements about self and society. And the code of value that bonds them, or does not. In this way hair is merely a raw material, constantly processed by cultural practices which thus invest it with meaning and value.

—Kobena Mercer, *Welcome to the Jungle*

I saw women handling real business against a backdrop of music, gossip, steam and oil sheen. I encountered professional women, housewives, teachers and women from other walks of life . . . I discovered the latest news, saw the recent fashion trends, ate delicious home-cooked food, and heard grown folks' talk . . . I enjoyed this nurturing ritual and scarcely noticed the tugging and

twisting. I bonded with my grandmother and my mother and
flourished in the company of the women in the shop.
—Akkida McDowell, "The Art of the Ponytail"[1]

I remember the meaningfulness of going to the barbershop as a child.
Those experiences were mixed with dread and excitement. The dread concerned my father's tyranny about getting a haircut. The excitement was
the social context of the barbershop. In the Black barbershop of my childhood there were always old men sitting in the corner playing checkers and
reading magazines, and talking trash, talking community, and talking culture.[2] The difference and confluence of these three serve as the basis of
this chapter, signifying the ways in which the occasion of the Black barbershop is both about specified action and community building.[3]

While going to the barbershop is a practice of everyday life, I wish to
explore and comment on this practice so that, as de Certeau suggests, it
no longer appears as merely the obscure background of social activity.[4]
Barbershops and hair salons are integral and specific cultural sites within
the Black community. And while the word "salon" refers to a site of hair
care and comfort, it can also be defined as a constructed community for
social and intellectual talk on agreed issues. Within the barbershop of my
childhood, young boys observed and listened to elder-men engaging in
the ritualized act of cutting/fixing hair and community building. The
notion of community building also suggests that there were men who
hung out in the barbershop whom I never saw get their hair cut. Adults
used this space as a cultural thrift store of services and information. Barbershops in the Black community are discursive spaces. While this may be
true in most barbershops, crossing borders of race and ethnicity, my primary interest is in the Black barbershop, where the confluence of Black
hair care—for and by Black people—and small talk establishes a context
for cultural exchange.

This chapter looks at the barbershop in a Black community as a cultural
site for ethnographic exploration and description, but more specifically as
a site of cultural practice. I define a cultural site not only as the chosen
geosocial locale of the ethnographic gaze, but also a centralized occasion
within a cultural community that serves at the confluence of banal ritualized activity and the exchange of cultural currency. For me, *currency* refers

to the fact that cultural communities provide and circulate information in ways that add to the collective knowledge of what's happening, bringing members up to date—establishing relationships and orientations to people, space, and time.

This chapter capitalizes on the complex issues of cultural contestation explored in the previous chapters. In particular, the issue of hair and the confrontation of difference that prompted the reflections in chapter 1 (in China) are placed in a homeplace of familiarity in the Black barbershop/salon, where the materiality of presence is recognized and celebrated yet does not negate the potential of intracultural challenge. And like the notion of passing (explored in chapter 3), the racialized space of the Black barbershop/salon demands the necessity of particular performances that validate social membership and establish comforting, but always contestable notions of community (as explored in chapter 2).

IN SEARCH OF COMMUNITY SPACE

Over the years, in moving from state to state seeking employment or education, the test of establishing community for me has often been grounded in locating a barbershop. A place where I could not only get my hair cut or cared for but also achieve affinity in the assumption and desire that the hair care professional and his community of clients were Black. I thumbed through the yellow pages looking for the racial signifiers of those who do Black hair—the literal words or African/Afrocentric symbols and images that signified blackness. I asked the Black men that I came into contact with for direction and counsel. I traveled the distance, crossing borders and boundaries between campus and location to find pockets of culture; Black communities that were often located far away from the university settings where I labored.

Such travel was both cost and reward; the cost was time and distance offset from those times when for convenience I chanced going to a chain salon like Super Cuts or the hair salons located in places like J.C. Penney or Sears. Places where I was often faced with phrases like, "I never tried to cut your kind of hair but I could try." These were kind and generous offers that were always accompanied with more than a twinge of hesitancy—on both our parts. In my act of traveling the distance to the Black barbershop, I sought the services of and communion with racial and cultural familiars in a geographical site that was unfamiliar.

In those spaces I imagined myself achieving a deep horizontal comrade-ship[5] with the Black folk that I encountered, a space where I would be greeted with the recognition of my embodied presence and where the materiality of my hair would be commonplace. Hence, the Black barber-shop is a cultural space marked by ritual and cultural enactments. These are performances of recognition that offer a sense of comfort—in hand-shakes, verbal greetings, language, the nature of talk, social play, and the acknowledged awareness and concern of issues relative to "the Black com-munity." Knowing of course that such a collectivizing construct has already been problematized in chapter 2.

In their book, *Stylin': African American Expressive Culture from Its Beginnings to the Zoot Suit*, Shane and Graham White state: "In African cultures, the grooming and styling of hair have long been important social rituals" (1998, 41). These social rituals have not been limited to issues of aesthetics or reductively thought of as vanity. In fact, hair and the moment of grooming hair become discursive and signify meaning within culture. Hence the discursive quality of cultural spaces also produce cultural arti-facts, shape the materiality of embodied presences, and initiate perform-ances of recognition that signal cultural affiliation. In essence, culture responds to space, and space is a practiced arena for culture.[6] Hence a cultural space is a discursive site. It is both a call and a response; it is both a geographical location and conceptual nexus of need, desire, and expres-sion.

These cultural spaces serve as a register of cultural identity denoting but not delimiting bodies distinguished by race, practices, and stylistics that signal cultural membership. It is these features of the barbershop that attract me both as a cultural member and as a researcher. Kenneth R. Olwig reminds me that "the contested, tensive, meaning of place, caught between being a substantial, historically constituted domain and being reduced to an insubstantial location in space, has a long epistemic history" (2001, 95). That history is grounded in the significance of geography, the ownership and claiming of land, and how location affects space. Olwig asks, "Is place to be defined in areal terms as the field defined historically by a people (its 'land or country'), or is it a location within the topograph-ical coordinates of an absolute and atemporal space? Place can mean both, depending on context" (97). The situatedness of Black barbershops in predominately Black communities marks territories as much as it signals location, sociality, and commerce.

ETHNOGRAPHY, ENGAGEMENT, AND ENQUIRY

"Ethnographies are documents that pose questions at the margins between two cultures. They necessarily decode one culture while re-coding it for another" (Van Maanen 1988, 4). Yet the process of decoding assumes an understanding of the lexicons that shape and define culture, which lexicons are often lacking in intercultural encounters (as explored in chapter 1). Hence ethnography is a representational act fraught with the danger of imperialism, colonialism, academic puffery, and self-aggrandizement. The process and ego investment in ethnography risks foregrounding individual insights over the meaningfulness of actual collective cultural experience. As Judith Hamera suggests, ethnography is a very specific technology of translation, rebounding between two differently framed experiences into language.[7] While Hamera is concerned with a kind of ethnography of the body in dance and specifically virtuosity in performance—it seems that ethnography is always and already interested in documenting the fantastical and meaningfulness of cultural performance and cultural impressions of experience.

While ethnography has often been interested in and used to report on the cultural other—other, in relation to the ethnographer's reporting body and the body to which the ethnographer reports—I am continually interested in using ethnography as a tool to excavate the meaningfulness of familiar cultural sites. In which case the reporter (ethnographer) holds a dual membership—in both the cultural community that he reports on and the cultural communities that he reports to—the intricacies of which offer greater opportunities for interpretation, translation, and transference. This dual membership positions the reporter in the study as an indigenous ethnographer, one who claims membership in the cultural communities being written about.[8]

I struggle with my representational positionality as an indigenous ethnographer claiming membership in the cultural communities that I explore—but held at arm's length, distanced at (by) the academic impasse of documenting experience. While I want to resist being Caliban, I want to engage the utilitarian and elusive act of capturing cultural images and practices in words. This task is difficult not because the cultural performances are ephemeral, since the repetition of the practices is sedimented in the collective consciousness of many Black folk and of those others who recognize these descriptions as meaningful to their experience. The images are slippery not because they are not qualifiable or even quantifiable, which are sometimes interests of ethnography—in terms of capturing articulated experiences of people in the shifting-location social positioning.[9] The slipperiness comes in my own hands. In my ability to always focus my eyes, ears, and senses to denote moments of flex and flux. The slipperiness comes in my own facility with language to carefully articulate the nuanced nomenclature of human experience and cultural practice. It happens between my roles as participant and observer and the negotiation between my own lived experience and my observation of experience.

In some very palpable ways my position as an indigenous ethnography evidences that the ethnographic researcher engaged in qualitative methods cannot stand outside of the politics of cultural criticism. I am always and already implicated in the cultural practices that I seek to critique. And it is because I am so embedded in the storied histories of these sacred places[10] that the slippage occurs. The slippage often occurs within my own desire to represent without reducing culture. To simultaneously capture and release, to celebrate but not exoticize, to signal and signify without "reading" culture—in that Black cultural tradition of calling others to task and engaging in some reifying struggle over cultural authenticity.

This chapter locates the Black barbershop as a specific cultural space where Black people convene and commune for cultural exchange. The ethnographic descriptions in this chapter work in a confluence between my own childhood memories of going to the barbershop and my participation-observation at Luke Walker's Beauty Care Center in Pasadena, California.

RECALLS, REFLECTIONS, AND REMEMBRANCES

I am the fourth of five boys, but my childhood memories of going to the barbershop related here really begin and end with me being the youngest of the first four boys in my family. There is nearly a ten-year difference between my younger brother and myself. People in the neighborhood used to describe us as "steps on a ladder." We were roughly two years apart with two inches' difference in our height.

My father had a rule about hair when we were growing up. He would say, "Comb it or lose it!" To test and apply his rule we were given a small black comb. For young Black boys with natural hair untouched with chemical relaxers or perms, this was a part of a charge and a signal. When we could no longer easily comb our hair with this comb, or if there were teeth missing from the comb (evidence of the difficulty of combing) it was time to get a haircut. The variation in growth patterns of the four boys served as the least common denominator. The need for one signaled a need for all.

Mr. Brown's barbershop was located one block away from our house (fig. 5.1).[11] It was a white, freestanding building about the size of our living room with an attached bathroom. It had the obligatory barber's cane, the red and blue twirling pole that was turned on when the shop was open and off when it was closed. In going to the barbershop we were charged to hold each other's hands as we crossed the street. Trailing along the one block we would look back to the house only to see my dad standing on

FIGURE 5.1
Brown's Barbershop as it currently stands. Mr. Brown passed away in the early 1990s. His shop was taken over by a younger guy; the business is now called "Robert's Ultimate Cuts."

the porch making sure that we went there directly. Come to think about it, I cannot remember my dad ever going with us to get his hair cut. It was something that we were forced to do that he never engaged in, at least not with us. But I do remember over the years hearing my mother tell him that it was time for him to get a haircut. He too would moan and groan, then disappear in the car. Somehow going to Mr. Brown to get a haircut was good enough for us kids but not for him. Yet he would return looking trimmed and neat.

In the barbershop Mr. Brown had a partner, Mr. Francis, who seemed much older than he. We always assumed that they were father and son, but as kids we could not quite figure out about the difference in their names. While Mr. Brown seemed young, at least the age of our dad, Mr. Francis was old. He was the kind of old that you could never picture yourself being—with gray hair, folds of wrinkles, hands that perpetually trembled and that old-man smell partially covered over with the aroma of Old Spice or Aqua Velva. And either his hearing was bad, which was signaled by how loud he spoke—or he just didn't listen when you said, "Just a little off the top."

But of course we knew that our father had already spoken to them about what he wanted for our heads. He always requested what they used to call an *ivory lee*. The haircut consisted of cutting the hair down to the scalp leaving only a shadow of its existence. What remained on the head was not enough to comb and not enough to cushion the bristles on the brush. If you were lucky enough you could also get a *bald fade*, a gradual reduction of hair in the back of the head and the sides that would eventually trail to baldness closer to the ears and the hairline. The contrast between the actual baldness on the sides and back, and the shadow of hair on the top—gave the illusion that you had much more hair than you actually did. Yet, if you were unlucky enough to get Mr. Francis, he would leave a *gop* in your head; an uneven removal of hair that looked like a hole or a patch. So, blaming our dad, we always politely resisted Mr. Francis's offers to cut our hair and waited for Mr. Brown.

Mr. Brown was a gentle man, who also drove the school bus that picked us up right in front of his shop and took us at varying ages to Vermilion Elementary School. Though he saw us constantly because of our frequent haircuts, driving us to school, and the fact that our grandmother lived right across the street—I am not sure if he ever knew our individual

names. We were just called by our last name, "Alexander!" This said less
about his memory and more about the categorizing of kids and house-
holds in my neighborhood. All of the older people just seemed to say,
"Aren't you Velma's boy?" or "Aren't you one of Joseph's sons?"

Mr. Brown would call us one by one to his chair and we would fall in
line. We always went in reverse order the youngest to the oldest. This was
primarily because my older brothers always used me as the warm-up head.
The hope was that once he got to them his bald fade would be tight, meaning gradual, smooth, and clean. They would also hope that Mr. Brown
would be more willing to listen to their pleas when they said, "Just a little
off the top, please." But he never was.

Walking to or waiting at the barbershop, there was always a sense of
dread; the confusion between choice and voice—knowing that, until we
were fifteen years old, no matter what haircut we said we wanted, Mr.
Brown would give us the haircut my father wanted. But there was also
some anticipation in going to the barbershop. I liked walking through the
door. There was a screen door, the kind that always appears on old Southern houses, the kind that we had on our house. The screen door, while
functional for the climate, also signaled a kind of domesticity—suggesting
that the shop was more home or social arena than business. Also, before I
walked into the shop, the aroma of hair oils and pomades and the sound
of talk rushed into my head, signaling arrival. Today whenever I smell
those aromas I think about that shop and the men who talked their way
into my memories.

SIGNIFYING, SOCIAL EXCHANGE, AND ENCULTURATION

The old men's talk in the barbershop served both as a functional component of social exchange, and as a way of perpetuating culture and community. In the process of their talk I came to understand that they were not
just spinning their wheels but promoting the cultural community in ways
that were based in talk. Hence the barbershop becomes framed as an occasion for developing and maintaining culture.[12] The act of cutting hair
seemingly became secondary in this occasion of performance. Like wordworkers[13] it was through talk that they recreated the world that existed
in between Carmel Avenue and Surrey Street in Lafayette, Louisiana, the
geographical markers of our neighborhood.

And while they often seemed to be in conflict over the facts of the story, these old men were enacting the spirit of community; a spirit that is both about collectivizing practices and the types of dissension that regulate social behavior.[14] Michael Oakeshott's notion of community also depicts an aggregate of people who recognize that they are attending to ongoing social arrangements, where it is the recognition itself that makes them a community, not some particular bonds, common goals, or even geographical borders. The salience of this definitional construction of community features the elements that we choose to focus on (and why we focus on them) as opposed to a reduction to those corporeal features that would link members of certain racial or ethnic sects, or the geographical borders of particular locations. Thereby, community is built on and around communicative and discursive strategies that mark shared interests and desires.

But even in their conflict these old men engaged in a playful exchange—testing the borders of conversation, friendship, and community. As they played checkers or cards, the old men in Mr. Brown's barbershop spoke a whole lot of trash.[15] Their banter back and forth reflected the kind of trash talking that the younger boys did in the athletic arena, even when it came to girls and their sexual prowess. Yet these were not just moments of observation in the barbershop; unwittingly we often became objects of their playful teasing. The old men would tease us about the growing fuzz on our faces—a first mustache and the shadowy presence of side burns. They teased us about having girlfriends or not having girlfriends.

In the barbershop these old men played a verbal game with us that was clearly designed to both tease and make fun while engaging in a social and cultural process of sense-making. Their ability to engage each other on this level spoke to the nature of building community and perpetuating culture. Their inclusion of us was a form of enculturation, a type of training, equipping us with the tools of living within the cultural community.[16] Sitting there and listening to their stories, I heard who was sleeping with whom in the neighborhood. I heard who missed church that Sunday or the meeting of the Knights of St. Peter Claver. I heard about whose child was born, whose mother died, who was sick or ailing, and the latest shenanigans in city government. I heard about the cultural politics of our community and sometimes what it meant to "talk the talk," both to share meaningful information or just to be engaged in social and cultural exchange. David Guss suggests that when exploring cultural ethnography and the specificity of cultural performance "what is important is that cultural performance be recognized as sites of social action where identities and relations are continually being reconfigured" (2000, 12).

LOCUS, LOCATION, AND LUKE'S

Unlike Mr. Brown's barbershop, which was a small stand-alone structure located on a residential street in a predominately residential Black neighborhood, Luke Walker's Beauty Care Center is located in a strip mall at the intersection of two major thoroughfares in what is becoming an increasingly commercialized Black and Hispanic community (fig. 5.2). The shop sits in the center of The Fair Oaks Renaissance Plaza between Tastee Donuts and Burgers, Chinese Food, and Sally's Beauty Supply, Stewart Plus Women's Fashion, and Pansy's Dry Cleaners.

The product-service advertisement component of these shop names is accompanied by what could be considered the given name of the owner—like "Luke's" or "Sally's"[17]—and thereby personalizes the service. The

FIGURE 5.2
Luke Walker's Beauty Care Center.

other linguistic accompaniments include a descriptive adjective like "tas-tee" or an Asian symbol that signals authenticity of the product—as if to say, "real" Chinese Food. These small shops are pressed between a Subway (sandwich shop) and Vons (a large grocery store). The positioning of these large chain stores further establishes the strip mall as a commercial zone of one-stop shopping, similar to those that stretch across the cultural land-scape of the country.

In the far end of the parking lot there is a Starbuck's coffeehouse and a Footlocker shoe store. The presence of these businesses confirms the growing intervention of pop-cultural commercial industry in this com-munity even when there is an incongruency in the class issues that these businesses suggest and the communities that they invade. The strip mall as a whole is a site of confused geographies, a site that inhabits the displaced structures of imagined and remembered locales, like the mom-and-pop grocery store, the hometown barbershop, and maybe the drive-in restau-rant, and replaces them with corporately owned chain stores. Culture and landscape have always been intricately interwoven. The strip mall is a commercial convenience that penetrates communities, often with a steril-ity of presence that reconfigures notions of neighborhood.[18] Thus, the location of Luke's in this strip mall does not immediately say "hometown" barbershop, but once again maybe it is not about structure or location, but engagement.

The main entrance to Luke's is a small foyer flanked with a glassed-in reception counter. Luke's daughter, an attractive peanut-colored woman with blond hair, often sits behind the glass and offers assistance. She greets me by name. Most people know that she is his daughter, which signals that this is a family-operated business. If I turn to the left and walk forward I enter the general seating area for the barbershop. The flooring throughout the shop is those black-and-white intermingling blocks that give the impression of a checkerboard, like in those nouveau Art Deco centers where the flooring is a feature of the room competing against the furni-ture.

A quick right turn leads down a long corridor to a back hallway, rest-rooms, and a newly installed massage and aromatherapy center. In the barbershop there is seating for ten waiting customers. The chairs are placed against the glass wall of the front of the building, facing the com-munal space of the shop. There are a total of six barber chairs with individual sinks and workstations. There are six barbers—five males and one female. Six elevated televisions are positioned in such a way that from any barber's station the customers have a view of a television. The channels vary but move between sporting events and the local news. I attended this shop for two years while wearing and maintaining my hair in a short flat top with a bald fade on the sides and back.

Luke Walker, the owner and operator, is a charming, bald headed, caramel colored, middle-aged man. He claims the first station as you walk in. His friendly demeanor reminds me of Mr. Brown, and there is that moment of familiar recognition when he greets me, saying, "Hey man." Then consciously or unconsciously he glances at my head to see the condition of my do (as in hairdo). If the shop is busy, as it usually is, he will tell me to take a number and find a seat. The pull-tab numbering system is a reminder that this is a business that does volume. Bodies translate into heads, heads into numbers, and numbers into money. When possible I sit in the far back chair, from which I can see the expanse of the room and listen to the exchange of men talking. The conversations that range from sports, music, local and national politics, and more are not unlike my experiences in Mr. Brown's shop. But my adult status offers me greater access to coded messages and meanings that are often encrypted from the immediate understanding of young listeners.

Young boys get special treatment in this shop—both in that playful way in which older men tease and in that meaningful way in which young Black boys are socialized. It is not uncommon to see a young boy sweeping hair from the floor as a part-time job. But unlike Mr. Brown, when I enter the chair Luke asks, "What are we doing today?" It is in these moments, like when he is shaving my beard and mustache, that I gleefully feel that I am a man—no longer living in the shadow of my father's desire and no longer under the critique of older men, at least not because of my hair.

If at the main entrance of Luke's I take a right turn instead of a left, I enter the salon. To my immediate right is a manicurist's station. The entrance to the salon requires a sharp left turn, and then the room flows into an open space. There are five chairs for waiting customers. Flanking the north wall of the room are four workstations with four female stylists. On the south side of the room there is a series of four dome-shaped hair dryers, two large throne-like pedicure chairs, and a hair-washing station with two sinks. At each workstation the women have individual televisions that also serve as viewing monitors. The televisions are equipped with small video cameras that can be stretched out and pointed so that the customer can see an image of the back of her (or his) head.

The floor throughout this section of the shop is covered with large ceramic tiles. While a cleaning lady will pass with a broom and dust pan, the floors are often covered with bits of multicolored hair; some of this is cut human hair, the rest is synthetic hair used in weaving and extensions. This is a space marked by the work that the women do. But while the physicality of the location marks the space as a salon, it is the presence of people caught in the act of cultural performance that gives this location its life.

The aromas in the salon remind me of my mother's kitchen—but not her food. The kitchen in my childhood home was also the place where my mother would press my sisters' hair. My mother would sit on a chair near the stove with one of my sisters sitting on the floor between her legs facing in the opposite direction. To the left of her, the iron comb would sit in the fire on the gas stove. To her right she would have her supplies—often a large towel, a large- and a small-toothed comb, a brush, and a jar of Sulfur 8 scalp and hair conditioning grease. She would detangle and section off my sisters' hair and then reach for the hot iron and methodically pass it through their hair. Under the heat of the comb, the short and kinky hair would be straightened, leaving long and silky hair. The skill of my mother's hands would position the hot comb near but never on the scalp, pulling the hair up from its roots to its ends. But this would never stop my sisters from flinching from the fear of being burned.

I would watch in amazement and curiosity at the process of pressing hair and the talk that came out of it. While it was the smell—the combination of heated metal, hair, and grease—that triggered my memory, the smell only punctuated the talk between my mother and sisters. These conversations seemed like coded messages; secret exchanges that only they really understood. When I would ask them questions my mother would say, "Stay out of this—this is women's talk." She intentionally used the plural possessive of "women's talk" common to Black vernacular.

She used the phrase "women's talk" to claim both a privacy of her conversation with my sisters (as it related to subject matter) and also a specified gendered relational exchange. She claimed this to be unique to women—the type of exchange that I only noticed during the process of doing hair. And yet, the Black vernacular use of this phrase does not simply emphasize the distinction between women's and men's talk.[19] It claims a specified discursive space that is influenced by gender and race. Hence it is not only women talking, but Black women talking, which from my lived experience has the potential to turn the world.

I was a customer in the salon. I started by wearing my hair in what my stylist calls twists. Twists are tightly strewn curls that lay close to the head. The process of transforming my growing kinky hair into an average of eighty or so spirals takes about two hours. The twists were a precursor for developing what are popularly called "dreadlocks" or what many progressive African Americans seeking to subvert oppressive systems now call "brother and sister locks."[20] In making the transition, the twisting technique is simply continued on a long-term basis until the hair is locked (entangled). Every three to five weeks I returned to the shop to have my hair washed and tightened. In that time, like the boy I was in my mother's kitchen, I was privy to the women talking. They engaged each other on issues that range from family (children and child rearing), church (religion and spirituality), food, fashion, media (television and film), news (local and national), racial and sexual politics, and what my mother might refer to as the untranslatable intimacies of "women's talk."

On any given day and especially on the weekends, spaces like Luke Walker's Beauty Care Center in Black neighborhoods are filled with the hustle and bustle of activity, where the traffic between talk and trade signals cultural performance.

STANDING AT THE BORDER

When I enter Luke's—before his daughter greets me by name and either directs me to the barbershop, where I still get a shave, or confirms my appointment with Deanne, my stylist—there is a moment when I am just standing. I am standing at a threshold of a cultural site, a space that is inscribed by social practice and divided by gender difference. Yet the two are bridged together by the cultural performance of an imagined and assumed community. In that moment I am standing at two borders. First, I am entering a space that is marked by the performance of Black culture and Black people; and while I am Black, the everydayness of my experiences are not performed exclusively, or primarily in their company. As a university professor I walk out of the ivory tower into this culturally marked space knowing that culture is performance and my performances must shift.[21] The facticity of my race serves as a visible recognition of similarity but not familiarity in the barbershop. So in my process I engage in an intentional shift, an adjustment in my presentation of self. I assume a cultural performance that I hope will be accepted and recognized, one that affords me (re)entrance each time—knowing that I still carry some of the residual traces and the stench of my academic culture and training in my verbiage, logic, and manner.

Second, as a Black gay man I am standing "betwixt and between" a site designated for men and one designated for women. And though my desire is specific and my manner is determined, to enter either of these spaces means that I must acknowledge the politics of gender performance that cross borders of neighborhood, race, and culture. I must also resolve myself to understand that the social antistructure of these spaces is gendered between definite and determinate identities.[22] While my identity is gendered, it does not always fit comfortably within conversational spaces marked by heterosexual discourse, which is often the case in the barbershop/salon. [23]

While I am standing at this threshold I am once again engulfed in the aroma of hair oils and pomades. The sound of talk rushes into my head and I am transported, not back to Mr. Brown's barbershop, or even to my mother's kitchen, but to a place of comfort and familiarity that is exclusive not to the site but to the occasion. I hear people engaging each other through laughter and the telling of tall tales. I hear the politics of the community unfolding as people tell their version of what happened or what did not happen. I hear people arguing over issues and engaging in the negotiation of culture and community. The protean ritual and cultural act of manipulating hair occasions the nature of their engagement.[24] So I enter what Alicia Arrizón calls the discursive spatiality of the barbershop—seeking services, desiring company, and engaging in the active performance of culture that defines all social spaces.[25]

In the following sections I continue with an interpretive ethnographic analysis of the articulated experiences of being in a Black barbershop and a Black salon. I describe the sensate sounds and unspecified voices that emerge and present themselves in the cultural milieu of the shop. I also try to articulate my own experience as researcher and customer, participant and observer, and someone negotiating the tensiveness of the out-sider/insider role within a cultural community.

ETHNOGRAPHY OF A "MANLY" EXPERIENCE

As an adult I have always enjoyed getting a haircut and getting my beard shaved. I must admit, though (and I am sure that other men may not want to admit it), it is one of those forbidden sensual experiences. As Mr. Brown used to do, the first thing Luke does is palm my head—rubbing his large hands over my head as if trying to sense what would be the most appropriate cut—like a phrenologist trying to read the bumps on my head for direction. Instinctively he then turns the chair counterclockwise. The chair is lowered and tilted backward as he leads my head to the bowl to wash my hair. Like a father preparing for the bath of his child, he tests the water then slowly angles the nozzle over my head. He moves his hand across my head, making sure that the water saturates the entirety. Then he applies shampoo to his hands and begins the process of massaging until I can hear the sounds of suds bubbling around my ears, smell the clean of the shampoo tickling my nose, and feel the worries of my day draining away.

He rinses my hair thoroughly and then towel dries it with a gentle mas-saging action. He moves expertly through this process while managing at the same to maintain a conversation, briefly with me—but I am not a big talker, I like to listen. Most often he is talking with a waiting customer or the barber across from him. The barber across from Luke is another older guy. Maybe through seniority, the two of them have claimed the front chairs in the shop, leaving the younger guys and the one woman to claim spaces in the back. They talk as old friends talk—overlapping their conver-sations and laughing at inside jokes that only they really know. I am always both tickled and disturbed by these conversations. They are entertaining in that way that you vicariously enjoy the pleasure of other people. But these are coded conversations; they reference familiar people and places, situations and occurrences; and shared histories.

There is a certain construction of Black masculinity in this barbershop. These images are unlike the stoic images of Black masculinity that we see on television, or the rough, mean, and aggressive images that we see in film. These images are not of the violent, sexualized, and sometimes inef-fectual images of Black men that we are expected to take as real. These are not the performances of "the angry Black man" that has become the iconic representation of Black masculinity—and that we sometimes shamelessly use to a/effect service (chapter 2). The images of Black masculinity in the barbershop are mostly of smiling faces, brothers engaged in friendly exchanges, negotiating space and intention. These are the performances that I find more reflective of my own experiences with other Black men. In the barbershop these are resistant performances; performances that work against the public consumption of our image. It is a performance that resists the negative public constructions of Black masculinity to affect the more privatized exposures of Black men to each other. The barbershop becomes a place where Black men find sustenance, supportive and empowering reflections of our own reality and possibility.[26] A place where context and contact are linked in ways that are both inclusive and exclusive, creating a contract of particular social relations.

Lest I construct some utopia of humanistic Black masculinity in the Black barbershop (whether specific to Luke's or in general), the Black barbershop is also a crucible for performative social mandates on Black masculinity. In conversation there is a certain level of talk about sports and women that clearly promotes a heterosexual agenda (see the discussion of a homosexual agenda in chapter 4). It is a conversation among heterosexual men that both reveals and promotes desire for women. Conversations that are spurred on in reference to celebrity females like Beyoncé or Halle Berry, or everyday women who pass by the window, or those who drop off their young sons for haircuts and then leave.

These women leave with the eyes of multiple men glued to them. That performative heterosexual-male-gaze surveys the terrain of the female body and then passes back to other men accompanied by a smile—as a confirmation of shared assessment and desire. It is a gaze that has always intrigued me as a gay man. A gaze that I studied and even tried as a young boy, though I could never quite muster or master the right interpretive frame in relation to the object of my desire and the appropriate audience for such performances. Yet it is a gaze that I still study in the barbershop and in daily life. Because while it is an individual expression of interest or desire, the result of the shared appreciation is actually translated as a carefully constructed performance of heterosexual homosociality; one which is of course constructed as divergently different from homosexual desire.

In the barbershop there are conversations about "family" and constructs related to marriage and children, with references to church and religious doctrine that dictate particular social and gendered affiliations. These discussed orientations are often subtle, but often buttressed against the sometimes-overt homophobic comments that question another man's (or boy's) orientation, based either on specific action and mannerisms or on politicized position on social issues. In these instances, the heterosexual-male-gaze is intensely fixed on other men looking for signifiers of masculinity or, more reductively, whether this is a "real man." As is the case when the object of the gaze is a woman, these glances return to each other as a confirmation of shared assessment. This too makes the Black barbershop a site where Black men can engage in an ethnography of our bodies, both the literal body and the ideological Black male body.[27] For me this is an opportunity to be in the company of other Black men, to see the resemblance of their presence, and to engage in talk that reveals our cultural selves. It is a site where the cultural and racial familiarity of Black male bodies is acknowledged as meaningful, but far from uncontested. Such is the case with any community.

The crafting of Black masculinity in this barbershop is done within community by and with other Black men. It is done through the buzz of clippers, the drone of televisions, or the smooth grooves of soft jazz. The construction is done in talking, laughing, joking, and engaging the intimate and not-so-intimate aspects of shared communities. The construction is done with delicate razors—controlling coifs, straightening hairlines, defining lips by shaping mustaches, jaw lines, and beards. Knowing of course that sometimes razors cut, which reminds us that Black masculinity is forged out of resistance against forces that are both internal and external, and the boundaries of sexual identity are limited and fixed (Harris-Lacewell 2004).

I am also reminded of how the Black barbershop has always been a particular locale where physical male contact often seemed mediated by necessity and convention. In particular, I juxtapose the ritual greeting of some Black men against the act of getting a shave. I have always been intrigued by Black male greeting rituals, whether the staid and rigid handshake, the performance brotherman handshake, playful hitting, or the more liberated greeting that includes a hug and a kiss (most often relegated to old men, young boys, or specific sibling/parental relationships). But here I am often taken aback by the hybrid greeting. The greeting that is both a handshake and a hug, but also suggests a contested if not contentious performance of sociality and resistance. It is a sign of greeting and also a performative challenge. My perception comes in reading the body of the Black man approaching you and of trying to detect the mechanism of his intention. It is seeing the signal, that wide outward swing of the right hand and arm that stretches out from the body first as it comes in with a force of contact—a contact that both stings and enlivens as you match your swing and synchronize the moment of contact. It is in the intensity of the grip, a modified clasp that seems like a test of strength and will. It is then sometimes accompanied by the hug; the hug that is mediated by the still clasped hands that crosses the body and prevents actual intimate contact but still gestures care.

On the other hand, after cutting my hair Luke without asking looks at my facial hair and makes a move toward trimming it. But unlike with Mr. Brown I need not say, "Don't cut that please." I am a man, not a boy; a cultural reality, a historical dilemma that has meaning in the Black barbershop—beyond the specificity of my age. Luke knows this. Before trimming, he places a hot towel on my face to loosen my beard. He removes it and then applies hot shaving foam. And then with expert care and a straight razor he begins to etch away excess. The trimming of a man's facial hair is an act of trust and intimacy. It requires close proximity. It requires unmediated contact.

Luke leans his body against mine when he is trimming my facial hair. I am not sexualizing Luke or the experience, for he is a father figure. But I find that it is one of those few moments when men, and for me Black men, come into an unacknowledged yet sanctioned intimate contact with each other. We understand the meaningfulness of the engagement not only in the functionality of the action but also in the knowing. The knowing that a Black man who knows and understands the growth pattern of Black hair and the sensitivity of Black skin is caring for another Black man. For many Black men with coarse facial hair are prone to severe razor burn and ingrown hairs if their face is not properly prepared before and cared for after shaving.

So I allow Luke to cut my facial hair and I enjoy the sanctioned trust of that engagement. And I know that for me, this act becomes a symbolic representation of the meaningfulness of the Black barbershop as a site for cultural exchange and personal maintenance.

A MAN IN WOMEN'S SPACE

I must admit that when I am sitting in the chair in the salon I feel out of place. I almost hear the phantom voice of my mother saying, "Stay out of this—this is women's talk." But now I am the one in the chair not my sister. And while I am not engaged in a lot of talk, other than the initial phatic communication of introductions and current events, I am a paying customer. In essence I have bought my way into women's space. Thus I am a welcomed but oddly misplaced member of this cultural community.

Lately I have had mixed feelings about being in this space. My feelings travel along three vectors of dis-ease. First is a struggle over the tendency to domesticate the work of these women. As Stewart Hall suggests, this would follow a long tradition of disavowing "the economic value of women's domestic labour." And like my perception of male barbers "the domestic is political [and] the political is gendered (1997, 280). For my first experience of watching my mother doing my sisters' hair lays the foundation for my viewing. My mother did this work in the kitchen, which is already a site that domesticates the lives of women. And while I know that many of these stylists also "do hair" in their homes, this is a business. Their skill is a marketable commodity that transcends pedestrian notions of just doing hair. There is an exchange of commerce and professionalism that occurs here.[28] And while there is also a cultural exchange and cultural reproduction that occurs in the process, it is the work—the skill and artistry that initiates the contact and reaps its own reward.

Second, the conversation that these women have is sometimes disarming. A discourse not intended for my ear, it is a world of talk established by the parameters of gender and experience. When they are talking about this guy or that guy, husbands or boyfriends, television actors or local-access men, the struggles of motherhood or being a wife, and so forth, I wonder if they acknowledge my presence. I wonder if they care. I wonder if, by sitting in this chair having my hair done, I have given up something—maybe my perceived masculinity. I wonder if, for the moment, I am considered a eunuch and hence no threat to their sex or to their revealed secrets; an honorary (wo)man. When they are talking about the immorality of the Showtime program "Queer as Folks," I wonder if they wonder what my thoughts are. I wonder if they assume that the ring on the middle finger of my left hand signifies a traditional marriage and assumed sexuality, and hence an assumed agreement. This is one of those

moments, an experience parallel to that in the barbershop in which I perform a compulsory heterosexuality through silence. And in that silence I
become complicit in promoting a particular brand of homophobia in the
Black community—which is as strongly present as any other empowering
cultural performance promoted in this location.

Third, I experience discomfort in the tensiveness between having my
hair done in this space and studying this cultural work-site. I am feeling
trapped in an ethical quandary, the ethnographer as eavesdropper or spy.
And while I have not secretly infiltrated this culture, nor have I entered
with pen and pad taking notes or asking them questions about this or that.
I am recording and documenting what is happening. I am trying to make
sense of it as an ethnographer and as a man, knowing that the sensed
observation of each influences the other. Ethnography is often about
infiltration and filtration, the entering of intimate spaces and the processing of substantive worth. I know that my intention is not to exploit these
women or this cultural site. I also know that this is as valued a cultural
space as is the barbershop.

Black women walk into this space with ease in the knowledge that their
needs will be met. They know that women who know Black hair will do
their hair and nails to their specifications. They also know that they will
engage in an exchange with other Black women on issues that are meaningful to their daily lives. And I sit in the chair as Deanna my stylist
engages in talk with these women. Like women engaged in a quilting cir-
cle, her hands seem to operate separately from her conversation, or maybe
it is in tandem. She grabs my hair (which is now locked) and pulls it
toward her. At the base of the hair she applies a protein styling gel and,
gripping the hair, she pulls and twists, extending and refreshing the lock.
She repeats this process for each lock as she spinstories[29] with the women
in the shop. And I know as I write about them now that many of those
stories have entered my head.

In these regular sessions it is clear to me that we are indexing time,
both on my head and also through collecting, categorizing, and comparing
experiences that are at the core of communal cultural performance—a
mirroring and reflecting of membership. My locks are slowly getting
longer, but more importantly through an intricate coiling of hair it has
formed knotted digits that enumerate my time in this space. Digits that
can neither be untangled nor delineated from the whole of the experience.

Stories have been twisted into my hair. These stories like my "brother locks" are not exotic; they signal an ancient history, a performative resistance of culture that like the salon itself is a localization of experience—in an organic unity they find their meaning.

Deanna comments on the growth each time that I am there. So do the other women in the shop, who always acknowledge my presence. I am the only man sitting and waiting. At first these women thought that I was waiting for my wife, but soon I became a familiar fixture and gained my own significance. Some now joke with me saying things like, "Now you understand what us women have to do for you men." Others say: "That looks really good. I have been trying to get my husband to get twists but he will not come into the shop." And still others make fun of me as I close my eyes during the process and fall asleep. In some ways I am gradually accepted into this community, but not as a member. The maleness of my body tells a different story. I am accepted. Yet I assume it is as the primates accepted Jane Goodall—certainly not as one of them but as a cultural familiar, for surely she had begun to acknowledge the accepted cultural performances and thus performed accordingly. And so do I.

LABORED REFLECTIONS

Like most ethnographies, this chapter is grounded in the labor of my reflection. But it also comments on the physical labor of work, care, and cultural communion that occurs within the space of the barbershop/salon. I have entered these spaces as a cultural member and client as well as an academic and ethnographer. My motivation to enter and make commentary has not been to mark uncharted territory, but in fact to engage familiar territory in ways that magnify the meaningfulness of this cultural location and the itinerant practices that give it cultural significance. I have entered this space both to seek the services and the familiarity of these cultural spaces and to explicate the significance of this cultural site. Traditional ethnography, as a representational act, would require the separation between locality and positionality, the relationship between where I am and who I am, and the distinction between why I am and what I am in order to articulate when I see and what I experience within a cultural field.[30] Yet as an indigenous ethnographer, I understand that the very confluence of these binaries greatly informs my appreciation for these spaces and the nature of the cultural exchanges that occur within them. It is the joint care of my cultural membership and my academic intentions that allows the reader a particular access to cultural practices.

The Black barbershop/salon is a physically and acoustically sensual cultural site. A site where Black people come in contact with each other through touch, the manipulation of hair (length, shape, texture, and form), through the sounds of talk, information sharing, and the deep penetration of cultural memory. The doing of Black hair in the specific contexts that I have discussed is both cultural activity and cultural practice; the difference between activity and practice separates the meaningfulness of doing and levels of commitment to culture. The Black barbershop/salon is a site where through the act of socializing hair people also socialize themselves in community.[31]

In momentarily closing this aspect of my documentation of experience, I wonder if other Black folk will confirm the nature of my observations. I wonder this both as a nervous academic and in the desire to be a loyal cultural member being true to a meaningful cultural ritual. In writing that, I also realize the slippage and reordering of my desire from Black cultural member to member of academic culture. Certainly the written medium of this articulation engenders its own influence. But I also come to believe that my location as a Black academic and a Black cultural member might in fact operate on a single social surface that is the sedimentation of historical facts and probabilities from which I operate. I am the consistent element in my travels across social and cultural borders. And while I make political allowances and performative shifts in my behavior I am fully present in each moment. My observations are filtered through a consciousness of those multiple factors in/of my identity.[32]

So maybe my ethnographic description can work both as an isolated and subjective experience, as well as a generalizable and collective experience that is marked in the singularity of my being and an accumulation of cultural knowledge over time. In other words, my description is both singular and plural as it speaks of my own experience and my description of others—which is the very nature of ethnography.[33] And while I respond to my own concern the impulse to question and the desire to continue to explore culturally familiar sites still remains. What also remains is my need to engage in the reflexive act of critiquing how I am implicated in these cultural sites—as participant and observer.

I do not romanticize the barbershop as some idealized cultural space, because I know that culture is essentially contestatory.[34] Culture is an accumulation of practices, attitudes, beliefs, and social orientations that are sometimes perceptually incongruent and fractious, yet held in place by the desire of those who seek to build community. Within culture forces of change and conformity often do symbolic battle to determine the land-scape of social practice. In the process it is not only performances that are regulated, but bodies.

CODA: REPLAY AND REVISION

I remember the meaningfulness of going to the barbershop as a child. Those experiences were mixed with dread and excitement. The dread con-cerned my father's tyranny about getting a haircut. The excitement was the social context of the barbershop. In the Black barbershop of my child-hood and the Black barbershop of my adult life, the experience has served as a marker and reminder of community.

These cultural spaces are infused with the past and are enlivened in the present with those who carry those histories of experience.[35] Black people enter these spaces for cultural maintenance and cultural proliferation. And as I sit in the barber's chair my body, like my history, is in relation to other Black bodies, we are relative bodies—bodies conjoined by history and proximity.[36] Mr. Brown, Luke, Deanna, and those who came before and those who will follow are simultaneously present. The fading, twist-ing, and weaving of hair, of voices, and of life stories are a part of the process, a part of the experience, a part of me. But these are my stories. My hair tells its own story.

6

"Were/Are, Fort/Da"

The Eulogy as Constitutive (Auto)biography (or, Traveling to Coalesce a Public Memory)

The black men in my family died of too much hope, perished from the absence of opportunities. The black men who have disappeared from my family could not save themselves or their sons in all too many instances. But, I—and so many others like me—have refused to stand in mute witness.

—Houston A. Baker Jr., *Critical Memory*

Long ago, a father or fathers would take sons into dark trackless woods and ruff them up a bit, teach them laws of Society and Universe, teach them Mysteries of Manhood. I remember no such night journey, yet I know the years I have undergone silent powerful initiation with you, Father. For in your example I have found seeds of mysteries.

—Omar McRoberts, "Song for Father"

Although eulogies have been an easily recognizable and important rhetorical genre since the time of the ancient Greeks, there have been surprisingly few studies by communication scholars. . . . George Kennedy stated that the funeral orations in ancient Greece had "highly formulaic quality" in which the speeches had a similar structure: praise, lament, and consolation with "some individual variation to give an illusion of novelty."

—Jensen, Burkholder, and Hammerback, "Martyrs for a Just Cause"

During mourning, the living and the deceased constitute a special group, situated between the world of the living and the world of the dead, and how soon living individuals leave that group depends on the closeness of their relationship with the dead person.

—Arnold Van Gennep, *The Rites of Passage*

I am on a Southwest Airlines flight traveling from Los Angeles to New Orleans. Once there I will acquire my Hertz rental car and drive toward my final destination to attend my father's funeral. I am sitting in the back of the plane in the midst of families that all seem fully present (parents and children) at a time when a member of my family is absent. On the plane I am struggling to pull words together for my father's obituary and what my church calls the tribute (the eulogy)—all of which I am expected to do. It is payment for my absence, my academic duty as the professor in the family, and my performance of exemplary son.[1]

Though I have written about him before, I am struggling for words to describe my father's life—for ultimately I will be describing my life with my father. The task of delivering my father's eulogy illuminates the politics of familial biography.[2] These politics allow me to pay tribute to my father, but doing so reveals how my father is implicated in my life and I in his. It is a kind of complicity that circulates in the blood, made manifest on my body in my resemblance to him. It is revealed in the effects of my social upbringing and becomes inescapably evident in this moment of both public tribute and personal confession. Hence familial biography in the form of the eulogy is really a contested construct and practice. For the acknowledged and unacknowledged levels of self-implicature in telling familial biographies resides in the context of the telling, the content of the told, and the level of reflexive self-appraisal of the teller.[3]

I am struggling.

I am struggling with the tensive relationship between telling his story and my story of his life.

I am struggling between the issues of time and circumstance, the relation between structure and process, and the tensiveness in the emotional and logically objectified conditions of this endeavor.

I am struggling to find the most useful and appropriate mechanisms of intellectual knowing and interpretive frames to engage what is a social responsibility that cuts at the core of mourning. Knowing that this process is about qualitative knowing and not a quantitative documentation of my father's life.[4] For this time I must also speak for others—my grieving mother, siblings, grandchildren, and friends—knowing the politics of telling someone else's story, but hoping that in the shared in-between-ness of this family figure that there is a cogent and consistent experience.[5]

I know that while the eulogy is about a person it is not the person, the place, or a thing. It is a time involving patterns of continuity and discontinuity, of both presence and absence.[6] In the Catholic belief system of my family we must operate in that imagined space of belief that death is a homecoming and that we will all meet again. I find that as the plane moves closer and closer to my destination I am suspended between *were/are, fort/ da* and what is to come. As through the yearn of nostalgia, I am being transported to another time, the product space of memory and not place; knowing at the same time that space and place become porous and unstable but still remain as a site of legacies of struggles yet to be fulfilled.[7] In the eulogy, memory and reality collide in the space of cultural performance. It is a performance about being and the being of nothingness, but also a space that necessitates making meaning of absence.

So in order to write this eulogy I must recall the text of my father's life. I must backtrack through my grief from the moment of his death, his illness, into the dailiness of his character—looking for those salient moments, traits, and fragments that signal his being—my private relationship with him, a public knowledge, and a collective social experience that others can recognize. And like many good stories, or by the very nature of narratology, the study of the process by which a story becomes a plot, my story must mix the facts of his life with the aesthetic and sometimes fictive features of narrative that enhance the telling while they illuminate the told.[8]

This chapter is less about my father than it is what Carolyn Ellis has referred to as an introspective case study in emotional sociology.[9] I too seek to connect lived experience to an archaeology of emotions to engage readers in topics that are sedimented in all of our lived experiences. By examining the relationship between the eulogy and the constitutive nature of (auto)biography through the frame of the emotionality associated with loss and specifically the tensive occasion of traveling to my father's funeral (writing and delivering his eulogy).[10] This is a story told both through the feelings of experience and through the thoughts of theory. It is a story about the telling of a story that interrogates the conditions of the experi-

ence and my own processes of sense-making. And like the chapters that
precede it—situations and circumstances of travel, confrontation, and the
turbulent confluence of cultures—this chapter takes up issues of text and
context, voice and culture, writing the self and writing the other in ways
that magnify self-implication in the social and cultural mechanisms that
shape lives.

In this chapter I am more than marginally interested in focusing on
the performative processes of the eulogy—the rigorous act of cultivating
memory, articulating thought in the face of theme, the moment of engagement, and reflection on the act. This is all in the presence of absence. I am
far from engaging what Peggy Phelan refers to as the futile act of trying to
preserve and represent the performance event of the funeral, and thereby
preserve an illustrative corpse, a pop-up anatomical drawing of my father.
Nor am I particularly interested in pursuing the ephemeral affective outline of what we've lost, though that is a purpose of the eulogy.[11] I am interested in exploring the occasion of a specialized performance—a complex,
contestable, and even convoluted performance that is not designed for the
entertainment of others. Yet the eulogy is designed to hold their attention
and have them hold, in their minds and hearts, thoughts and feelings of
the deceased. Indeed the eulogy is a *coiled performance*, one that folds and
envelops the living and the dead in a careful twisting of words, reverence,
and memory.

I am most interested in the power of performance and the writing
about performance to offer careful articulations and descriptions of
human engagement knowing that the act establishes a template of sociality
and remembrance for all who audience it.[12] For me *performance as template of sociality* and remembrance refers to the reflexive revelation and
the descriptive illumination of social practice, which is gathered through/
in performance and is the hallmark of ethnography and cultural studies.
The hope of/in this approach to describing human engagement is to coun-
teract the notion that performance has to refer to the broader aesthetic
event, which is so often invalidated as mere entertainment. But here a
focus on performance foregrounds the everyday struggles of social and
cultural interplay in which we are all expected to dramatize our own lives
and that of others. Thus performance operates within and as a rhetoric of
possibility, one that speaks to our individual and collective humanity.[13]

This chapter is structured around several movements. These movements track the difference between geographical location and psychic space, between an act of remembering and a sense of reliving, and between my disposition in the writing and my positionality in the telling. Knowing that there is nothing habitual about the act of writing your father's eulogy and that he and I will be located within a set of social relations that will mark us both. In other words, I first explore the divination of my process in writing what is tentatively to become my father's eulogy, while exploring the relationship between autobiographical and biographical writing/ performances. Second, I explore the structural considerations of the eulogy. Third, I engage in a reflexive pause before the delivery of the eulogy; this is then followed by the actual eulogy. Fourth, I offer a self-critique on the said and the not said, followed by implications of process and form as it relates to the eulogy and (auto)biographical writing/performance.

"WRITING THE SELF VERSUS WRITING THE OTHER"[14]

The constitutive nature of autobiography signals the design and desire of the eulogy to invoke a specific image of the deceased and concretize that memory for posterity. It is about a ritual of building and rebuilding relationships in time or in the moment of the delivery.[15] The use of the parenthesis in (auto)biography suggests that the eulogy includes both elements of self-storying or autobiography and the act of telling someone else's story that is signaled in biography. And if in biography you are placing yourself as the authority about another person's life, then the eulogy becomes a rhetorical form that typifies the intimate intersections of a life lived and a life described and the complications of claiming authority.[16] In writing this eulogy, I am struggling with the idea of whether I have the narrative authority to tell my father's life story, also knowing at the same time that I have been appointed to do so by my mother.

My mother's request that I do my father's eulogy is both a sign of her trust for my delicate care as well as being an assumption. The assumption is that as the professor in the family I would somehow find comfort or ease in this position of speaking for or speaking of. And, like most people, she assumes that what I do is who I am. She of all people should know better—for I was and am in many ways like my father; I am a loner in the family and if given the chance I would retreat.

I know that in writing this eulogy, in writing my father, that I am writing for the other who cannot write for himself. I know that writing my father into being is in fact my own method of detection and revelation that actually distances me from the reality of his death and the moment of the occasion; and in this moment it is as it has always been. It is me displacing myself out of the emotional and into the intellectual; reading a book to escape family conflict or doing homework to avoid other social pressures. In this process I find myself reveling in memory and not in reality, trying to find myself in relation to my dad. That is, by getting ever closer to myself as the subject of the study in terms of my relationship with my father, I am actually getting even further from my father, as he exists in the moment of the writing.

It is in this tensive predicament—the subjective role of son and the objectified process of writing—that I must negotiate the distance between occasion and relationship, lived experience and articulated memory. In performance terms, as Jill M. Carleton writes about her attempt to perform someone else's autobiography, maybe I am engaged in a mode of thematizing my father in a process of embodiment.[17] Yet in this case, I am not trying to translate his lived bodily experience in my own body. I am trying to articulate a relational and experiential reality with/of him for myself and for the others who will be present at the funeral service. So the act of reflecting on my father's life and my emotional response to his absent presence (his death and the presence of his body in the casket) will in fact reincorporate him into our family and community. It will make our knowledge of his death recessive and his life present in a moment when we might all surrender to memory and give faith to communion.[18]

But I am still sitting on the airplane, while others are laughing and priming themselves for the party that is New Orleans. It is their final destination, and I have miles to travel before I rest. I am trying to block out their sounds of joy as I struggle with this text. To say it sounds funny, "This text." A text is a written thing and in some ways it is a life. The eulogy is a text or maybe it displays the complex qualities of intertextuality; the overlapping of the actual and the imagined, a dialogue between the real and the reel—like imagined and projected images on the screens of our experience. In the eulogy we play the memories of the dead, like films, over and over again trying to capture the nuances of their character and our relations with them.[19]

There are on-going discussions that seek to define the nature of a "text"—from the fixed location of the page to a social accumulation of experiences and shared meanings or merely a site of meaning. I am interested in the basic derivation of the term from the Latin *textus*—meaning "a woven thing." I think that it is this etymology of *text* that serves as the fabric on which literary critics, as well as cultural and performance studies scholars focus attention in doing analytical study of found and created, written, performed, and social texts. It is a focused attention on how the fabric of the text is woven with diverse strands of information, life experiences, social mandates, and cultural practices that cannot be isolated in the conflict and confluence of cultural encounters.

There are necessary differences in reading a written text versus a performed or cultural text. The printed page is presented as a finished product, and we know that a close textual analysis will not stray too far from the author's intent.[20] A performance text like the eulogy is a dynamic text. It moves in space and time. While it offers the linguistic structures of a written text, the import is in the active engagement of the performative moment, or rather in the performance; the actual doing gives meaning to expression. It is through the performance that the mourners, the audience/reader/critics will find rationalization for taking their cue as an excuse for action.[21] The performance of the eulogy will help them to collate the fragments of a life lived from the story told of that life. It seems to me that the nature of the eulogy is grounded in the desire to coalesce a public memory. This is in opposition to the exclusive structural impetus of the actual performance text, which serves as the evidence of grammar and the articulate crafting of language to evoke images. I know of course that the accomplishment of that intent will only be made manifest in the delivery of the eulogy. Hence unlike the eulogy that I must write, my father is not a defined object, he is now a memory, a relational dynamic that has had its effect but does not take complete blame or authority of the experience.[22]

So in writing my father's eulogy maybe he is not a defined object, like the image of his body in the casket that I dread seeing. What I am working on in constructing this eulogy is not about his body, but his person—how he existed and exists within the stages, processes, and sinews of my life. I need to find language—words and signifiers that manifest into the images of my father's life. And maybe these linguistic images can become the imaginary tale that others can hold onto as narrative has a way of helping

to concretize and collectivize experience and language will help to textual-
ize my father's bodily presence.[23]

In writing my father's eulogy I must also think about the relationship
between the text, the performance of the text, and the intent of that
engagement. This is an issue of representation, and the eulogy like any
text is a site of interaction between the me that is writing the text, the man
that was my father's son, my father, and those who are present.[24] I find
that I am engaged in an archaeology of experience—excavating that which
might be meaningful but carefully examining the artifacts for cracks and
fissures that might suggest stress between me and him, in this make-shift
(auto)biography. For as Regina Gagnier tells me, "Autobiography is the
arena of empowerment to represent oneself in a discursive cultural field
as well as the arena of subjective disempowerment by the 'subjecting' discourses of others" (1990, 102). In other words, the eulogy for my father is
a site of contestation for the competing forces between what I want to say
and what I need to say for myself and my father, but also for family and
friends.

I find that I am also engaged in the reading of my life text with my
father—weaving experiences, memories, and occasions. It is a struggle to
construct a whole life out of fragments of a life lived within the constraints
of a temporal continuum. I am really engaged in constructing my autobiography, it is just that my father is the major character in the story of my
life that I wish to tell. Thus, I find autobiographical performance to be
what Kathleen Hall Jamieson and Karlyn Kohrs Campbell call a
"*dynamis*—a potential fusion of elements that may be energized or actualized as a strategic response to a situation" [original emphasis] (1982, 146).
In this sense autobiographical performance, like the eulogy, is often initiated as a response to trauma or a desire to excavate lived experience for
some meaningful conclusion, and to make public both the process and
products of sense-making. Like Denzin's description of the life history, "it
presents the experiences and definitions by one person" so others may
compare, contrast and critique the performance through the lens of their
own experience (1970, 220–221).

In this sense the eulogy creates the conditions for boundary disputes
with differing relationships rebounding around particular narratives.[25] It
is in this sense of implicating cultural others that might be my stumbling
block in writing this eulogy. Can personal narrative, and in this the eulogy,

privilege the individual over the community? How are we responsible to a community and responsible for a community as we engage in personal narrative?[26] Maybe this is the challenge of the eulogy, which is of course also its purpose.[27] Within the social context of the eulogy and in my role as family representative, the responsibility to community becomes paramount.

Like the reconstructive and recuperative politics of autobiography and the performance of personal narrative, the performance of eulogy is a response to a death and the need to articulate the life character and contributions of the deceased in a public forum. Yet while the eulogy may be described as biographical performance, it is a hybrid genre that demands the personalization of the "auto" in the telling of the "biography."[28] Hence the identity politics that operate in the eulogy are complicated by the relationship between the teller and the told, narration and narrated, who we were, who we are, and the constructional task of building bridges across time.

This is especially complex in the sometimes tensive relationship between fathers and sons. It is a prideful yet resistant narcissism that becomes a skewed embodiment of one in/for the other. The relationship is tied through the genetics of DNA and the regulatory practices that shape ways of knowing self and other. For in fact the birth of the son and the mortality of the father signal a beginning and end to which the time in between is a grand attempt to reflect and project the self into and onto the other. But unlike that Freudian notion that suggests that in order for a boy to become a man he must reject the mother and embrace the father—in the midst of being my father's son I remained a momma's boy. It was a reality that he accepted, but only in my adult life when he saw the man and not just the mannerisms. And now I stand in place for him who cannot stand for himself—the son for the father.

I acknowledge these things, as I sit on this plane realizing that I have not written anything on the page that lies bare before me. In my other performance work I have often found that beginnings and endings (like life and death) share the simultaneity of construction that signals the other. The project of constructing the narrative often lies in the in-between-ness, for we often know how and where we would like to begin, and the ending is always and already written. Autobiographical performance resides in the residue of experience and the impulse to tell; thus the past becomes the prologue of a story to be told. The challenge in this eulogy is how do I read backward? How do I detail experience bridging the gap between the beginning and the ending without losing the autobiographical construct,[29] my father—in relation to auto/scripting the moment of the telling and the audience to whom I will tell?[30]

In trying to articulate words of/for my father, I am truly trying to find the mode of production in his living that became his life. Leff and Sachs find the correlate to this process of constructing the autobiographical text: "Working from the evidence within the text, the critic proceeds to make inferences about what the work is designed to do, how it is designed to do it, and how well that design functions to structure and transmit meanings within the realm of public experience" (1990, 256). In this sense—to what degree in constructing this eulogy for my dad do I become a critic of his biographical text, of his life? Consequently the audience receives my critique of my dad, which potentially influences their critique of both him and me.

"STRUCTURAL PARAMETERS AND NEGOTIATED ORDERS"[31]

The eulogy as performance fits under the more expansive umbrella of performance as commemoration. In this medium, performance is engaged as a means of documenting the life and character of an absent other, an absent experience, or an absent construct of the self.[32] Specifically, commemoration is an act of remembrance and recovery.[33] Performance as commemoration can include eulogy, testimony, personal narrative, ethnography, biography, autobiography, autoethnography—and other performances of reflection, remembrance, remorse, and mourning. The eulogy for my father will be the result of the slippage between my emotional state, the clarity of memory, and the occasion of the telling.

Linda Park-Fuller states that "all performances, and indeed all arts give testimony to absences—even as they manifest presence" (2000, 20). Park-Fuller spends worthy time distinguishing and linking the autobiographical staged personal narrative and testimony. I would like to distinguish and link her notion of testimony with my discussion here of eulogies. Both make present that which is absent. But a eulogy also navigates the headwaters of emotions as a sign of remembrance, a means of recouping experience with a particular person and a way of saying goodbye. The eulogy is always in relation to an absent other, thus it is a referential (auto)biographical performance that recounts the life of another in relation to the self. It is a process of unreading a life text in order to recontextualize the life lived. But Della Pollock asks a series of questions that can appropriately be applied to the eulogy, for the conditions of the eulogy are always the same regardless of the timeliness of death or the particular situations of mourning:

> What happens when a story begins in absence? When it takes its momentum from a gap, a break, a border space, or element of difference that violates laws of repetition and re-presentation even in the act of repeating, retelling, and representing [a life]? What happens when "the boundary becomes the place from *which something begins its presencing*"? (original emphasis; 1999, 27)

The eulogy positions the teller in a liminal space, betwixt and between. The person offering the eulogy becomes a *stand between person*, helping others (and the self) to cross over, mediating and bridging the chasm either between life and death, presence and absence, or the social reconstructions of memory and desire.[34]

A eulogy is constructed as a commemoration of a life. It "responds to those human needs created when a community is sundered by the death of one of its members. In Western culture, at least, a eulogy will acknowledge the death, transform the relationship between the living and the dead from present to past tense, ease the mourners' terror at confronting their own mortality. Console them by arguing that the deceased lives on, and reknit the community"(Jamieson and Campbell 1982, 147).[35] When eulogies are given within family units, the intention is grounded in the desire to remember the meaningfulness of the life lived and to marshal the deceased to the next level of being complicated by the complicity of blood and inheritance of deceit.[36]

Hence eulogies are also rhetorical hybrids, a metaphor constructed by Jamieson and Campbell to emphasize the complexity of competing intentionalities in the performative act.[37] The authors ground their discussion in a detailed understanding and fusion of the traditional requirements of the eulogy and the elements of forensic, epideictic, and deliberative genres identified by Aristotle, as they reveal themselves in presidential eulogies. The influential nature of eulogy as rhetoric is within the manipulation of the complex set of requirements while striving for a particular effect.

For the purposes of this discussion, I would like to tease out and extend what are some of the eulogistic requirements as discussed in the previous definitional descriptions:

> A eulogy responds to those human needs created when a community is sundered by the death of one of its members.
>
> A eulogy will acknowledge the death.
>
> A eulogy will attempt to transform the relationship between the living and the dead from present to past tense.
>
> A eulogy establishes the relationship between the speaker and the deceased and those on whose behalf the speaker speaks.
>
> A eulogy may attempt to reconcile the interpersonal relationship between the speaker and the deceased.
>
> A eulogy may attempt to ease the mourners' terror at confronting their own mortality.
>
> A eulogy will console the mourners by arguing that the deceased lives on.
>
> A eulogy will signal shared cultural beliefs about death.
>
> A eulogy will attempt to reknit the community.

The complex of these requirements is to be accomplished in a manner fit for the solemnity of the occasion. In my church tradition there has also been a subtle encouragement to speak the truth and to keep it real.[38] This is to suggest that in the midst of addressing the primary eulogistic requirements, that the "true" character of the deceased is not lost. This is also to suggest that somewhere between the acknowledgment and the mourning—between the signaling of departure and living in the absence, between the recognition of nature's way and the embrasure of good memories—the eulogizer must also speak to the fullness of the character of the deceased. Maybe it is an allusion to how they lived or how they died. Maybe it is acknowledgment of their vices or virtues.

I find that this intention is designed to "speak the truth" in the house of the Lord and serves as a reminder of human fallibility. Like the funeral ceremony itself, it provides a catharsis for those with diverse and complicated relations to the deceased. In this manner a eulogy is *dynamis*, fusing multiple intensions and expectations both public and private. Speaking about the narration of traumatic historical events, Lea Wernick Fridman offers a perspective of viewing autobiographical narrative. She writes that the act is "caught on the warp of pressures both to tell and to disavow that telling, to integrate and to disintegrate, to establish factuality and, at the same time, to expose the fiction of that project, and in so doing to recover the experience in its fragmentary nature" (2000, 104). In fact the eulogy is this type of narrative event, one that attempts to make the moment of the telling seem natural, a tribute or salute that distracts from the immediacy of loss and celebrates the gain of lived experience.[39]

Within this vein, autobiographical performances, and the eulogy in particular, can also be seen as coy texts, teetering betwixt and between intentions as they respond to the desires of the occasion and the impulse to tell. Mae G. Henderson constructs the notion of *coy texts*, which divert or avert the reader's attention from one site or locus of meaning potentially risky or dangerous, to what appears to be a more comfortable and secure space, but in fact becomes a place of entrapment.[40] While the notion of textual coyness might suggest pretense or an annoying reluctance to write or say something into being, it is that very quality in the coy text that creates the openness that allows the listener/reader to enter.[41] Yet it traps the speaker/writer (and the subject) as an element of the rhetorical construction.

I apply Henderson's logics to autobiographical performances and to the eulogy as a specified performative text. Both are designed to illuminate and celebrate as well as to coyly situate the humanity of a life lived while acknowledging the tensiveness of the occasion. The place of entrapment might be considered the quagmire of representational politics that exists within the text itself as it speaks to multiple and varying audiences. Autobiographical performance and the eulogy both situate the performer/speaker in a public arena in which they have to engage in private talk. The success of the eulogy is sometimes in its ability to say what needs to be said without really saying it: to coyly signal a life lived as a form of respect and reverence. I find that Henderson's construct offers me not only an approach to writing the eulogy but also a performative mode. This is a performative mode that gives me the liberty to meet the criterial requirements of the eulogy, while also signifyin(g) my own feelings and negotiating the tensions between the life my father lived and the story of his life that I will tell.

So I begin to write. I jot down individual narrative fragments, *lexias* that I later hope to stitch together to create a biographical text.[42] In doing this I realize that these bits of knowing exist in particular places and occasions. I know that I am plucking them out of the contiguity of time to meet the needs in this particular moment. That is the nature of storytelling, and I am charged with telling my father's story.

I know that by doing this I am also challenging the laws of familial relations by foregrounding thoughts of my father over actual experiences with my father. It is the necessary equation of the eulogy that will result in a strategic and simultaneous form of telling and silencing stories, those that need to be heard in the moment of mourning and those that should not be spoken. It will establish a sighting of him while at the same time encouraging a selective blindness to the totality of his being. These are the challenges that we all face when we dare to tell our own stories and the stories of others. When we dare to make public private knowledges. When we dare to challenge the memories of others by buttressing our recollections against theirs. When we dare to delicately or indelicately pick at scabs long healed to reveal the residue scars of lived experiences.

As I am writing, there is this image of my father that I am holding dear, both in my hand and in my heart. The image is not some idealized family portrait that was and never was. It is not the Hallmark image of a father doting on his son—teaching him to ride a bicycle, playing baseball, or driving a car—for those are not parts of my memory book. It is not a heroic image that casts my father as more than he was in our family or in the community. It is the solitary image of a Black man (fig. 6.1). It is a picture of my father taken in a reception hall on one of his rare family outings a year before his death. It is the image of my father dressed in shades of brown, his jacket draped over the back of the chair, sleeves rolled up, sitting with his legs crossed, hat in his hand, with a beer almost outside of the frame but within arm's reach. I am standing behind the camera taking the picture. I have requested that my dad take off his signature dark shades so that I can see his eyes.

And I look at him.
And he is looking at me.

And through the magnification of the camera lens, in the stillness of that staged moment, in time and circumstance—

I am almost seeing him for the first time.
Maybe he is seeing me for the first time.

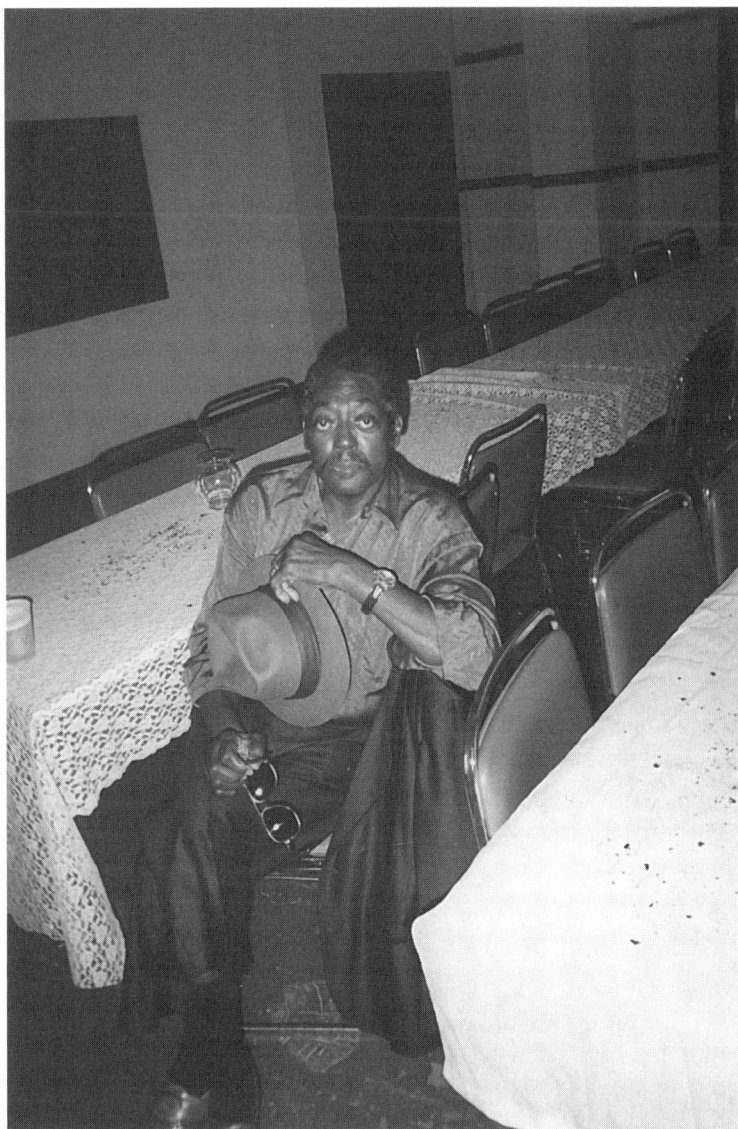

FIGURE 6.1
My father.

We are Black men looking into each other's eyes with a kind of knowing sense of the other, but with a mediated intimacy that often marks masculine desire and the expressed love between fathers and sons.

This is the image that I will be using to memorialize him. But not just the literal snapshot sent to the local newspaper and copied on so many programs for people to take home and press between the pages of their bibles as an act of prayer. This is the image that I wish to capture in words and thoughts, a father staring into his son's eyes wanting to be seen and a son wanting his father to be remembered. The eulogy may help me recover from the wounds of his death and our time together, though it will still take my lifetime to heal.

My plane is now arriving in New Orleans. I begin to negotiate the processes of crossing borders and customs. I secure my rental vehicle and begin the two-hour drive to my home. The drive seems longer than before. The bridges that stretch across Lake Pontchartrain and the Atchafalaya Basin seem longer. They seem narrower, forcing me to focus on what is ahead as I tell stories to myself. I arrive in town but instead of taking the direct route to the house I continue to drive. I drive to familiar places—the park where my dad used to fish when I was a kid; I hated to fish but enjoyed being with him. I see the little white grocery store on the edge of the neighborhood where my dad would send me with money saying, "Buy me a pack of KOOL (cigarettes), not the long ones. You know the ones dáddë likes. And buy something for yourself." I go and stand under the pecan tree in the center of my childhood yard. And in the moment I try to hold on to old memories without looking across the street to the funeral home where my father's body awaits.

Throughout my childhood the funeral home across the street was just a fixture. It was a place where other people enacted the ritual performance of death and saying goodbye. It wasn't until years later, when my brother died, that the relationship between beginnings and the location of endings became real, and the fact that we are all—always and already—standing at the crossroads of life and death became clear.[43]

"THE FAULTLINE OF CONSCIOUSNESS"[44]

In delivering my father's eulogy I stand on the faultline of consciousness—or is it Henderson's place of entrapment? Maybe, for now, I prefer

David Maines's heuristic metaphor to apply to this situation. It is a way of talking and a prevailing rhetoric that both reveals and conceals.[45] It is both an individual response to a death and also a response to an audience, who actively seeks and invites speech that performs and hopefully eases their stress and understanding of the loss.[46]

The faultline of consciousness that I speak of is also the knowing awareness of the tensive relationship between my articulated words of my father (for others and my deeply felt emotions that are presented), coyly muffled in the text and the moment of my delivery. In the eulogy the faultline is located in that precarious positionality between presence and absence. Between what is spoken and what is known. It is between our past and present experiences. The relationship between the telling and the told and between what we say and to whom we say it. It is the necessary political location of the performer in performance, who "struggles to recuperate the saying from the said, to put mobility, action, and agency back into play" for the self, and most notably for the absent other (Conquergood 1998, 31). In this eulogy I will be talking my way into my social role—both as speaker and as my father's son,[47] knowing that in his absent presence I will engage in my final negotiation with my dad.[48]

In my father's house there were things that we could not say or do. The host of those forbidden acts was concretized in saying "No" to my father. It was in the performative act of raising your voice above his—or worse yet, talking to him like a child or talking about him in his presence as if he were not there. My father, a man with a limited education, embodied a tensive relationship with his educated children, especially his teacher-professor-son. That relationship was one of both pride and resentment. For me to talk like a professor to him or in his company was for him to assume that I was talking down to him. Yet he would often command such performances in the company of his friends: "See, MY SON—The Professor." (I mention this dynamic in more detail in chapter 2.)

These performances also created another place of entrapment, situating me as the embodiment of my father's dreams while simultaneously marking me as other. I would do the formal greetings and try to politely escape before the inevitable series of questions about what I teach were posed. The questions and my responses to them tested my ability to navigate the landmines between language and culture, and to articulate my meaning and my positionality in two disparate locations at the same time; without alienating myself from either in the process. The performance required an appropriate academic tenor delivered through the racialized vehicle of being my father's son. The two had to coexist both for my academic and Black cultural credibility.

So here I stand in his absent presence, talking about him.

I know the basic axiom that language shapes perception. What I have to do in the moment of this eulogy is to make substance with rhetoric. And I know that this rhetorical performance that I must give will not completely change the memories of those in the audience as much as it will constitute an image in the moment of saying goodbye. So the faultline that I am standing on is sutured together with hopes, dreams, and good intentions. And my feet are firmly planted on either side, somehow willing them to stay in place.

HE FELL DOWN: A EULOGY

(Delivered from the pulpit of Immaculate Heart of Mary Catholic Church on April 18, 2001)

> On behalf of my mother, sisters, and brothers, I thank you for being here with us to share in our sorrow and in our joy. I am the fifth child of seven children and the fourth boy of five boys born to Joseph J. Alexander Sr. and Velma Ray Belle Alexander.
>
> Last Sunday, Easter Sunday, I attended church with my mother. The choir sang a song that is still resonating in my head. If you attended the 11:00 a.m. mass then you may know the song that I am talking about. The lyrics were simple yet prophetic. They said *(in performance this is sung)*: "We fall down, but we get up. We fall down, but we get up. We fall down, but we get up. For a saint is just a sinner who fell down, and got up."[49] Mr. Cotton, the commentator for the mass, spoke about how appropriate the song was for the season. He marked a symbolic parallel with the song lyrics and the persecution, crucifixion, death, and resurrection of Christ. But I was thinking about the death of my father. "He fell down, but he got up."
>
> I thought about the multiple and varying ways in which we all fall down in our lives. We fall either through what is commonly called sin; maybe it is through the things that we have done or not done, or the things said or not said. Maybe we fall in not fulfilling our potential or wasting our gifts, or not showing enough care for others.
>
> I thought about the many times that my father fell.

He fell when he drank a little too much.

He fell when he cursed and shouted a little too loud.

He fell when he did not go to public functions with his family.

He fell when he didn't go to church as much as he should have or could have.

He fell when he couldn't publicly display his affection toward his children.

He also fell when he did not take care of himself.

Yet I also remember how my father got up. I remember that with limited education he stood up—stood up so tall that his seven children could stand on his back and shoulders to reach their dreams and the dreams that he had for them.

He got up when working as a laborer he successfully supported his wife and children—resulting in his ability to retire, having two children who were college graduates and eleven grandchildren.

He stood tall as a father who developed a personal, albeit private, relationship with each of his children and grandchildren—letting them know in his own way, just how much he loved them and valued the adults that they became.

"He fell down, but he got up."

I love coming back to Immaculate Heart of Mary Church—for this is the place where most of our lives are documented. We bury my father today, as we buried my brother six years ago and as we have buried grandparents and relatives before. My parents were married in this church. My two brothers and my sister were married in this church. My siblings and I were all confirmed in this church, as we made our first communion in this church, and as many of you here today were baptized in this church. And the cycle of life continues.

"We fall down, but we get up."

But if these pews could talk they would tell all of our business.

I remember sitting in these first couple of pews (*pointing to the front right pews*)—because as kids we were forced to sit up front. I remember Mr. Rio. Do you remember Mr. Rio—that short and portly usher? (*pointing left to the choir loft*). I believe that it was his sister that was in the choir. They were like bookends in the front of the church, maybe pillars of the church (*suggestive laughter, using hand gestures to suggest movement*). I remember that Mr. Rio would tell us little boys when to sit down, when to stand up, and when to kneel. He would take away candy and gum from our hands, and even sometimes directly from our mouths. I remember that I didn't always like Mr. Rio. (*pause*)

As a teenager I remember that I did what most teenagers did *(using hand gestures to suggest movement)*. I moved to the back of the church and away from Mr. Rio as a form of resistance and independence. Later as a young adult I remember moving back to the front of church—because I had come to my own relationship with God. During mass I remember looking to my left and seeing Mr. Rio doing the same things with other little boys *(using hand gestures to suggest movement)*. He would tell them when to sit down, when to stand up, and when to kneel. He would take away candy and gum from their hands, and even sometimes from their mouths. And I remember in that moment—appreciating Mr. Rio.

"I fell down, but I got up."

I think that Mr. Rio symbolically represented most of our fathers—and mine in particular. Men, like most men of his generation, who did not show their affection as much as they could; gruff and sometimes mean men who were strict disciplinarians—who showed their care only in private. But somehow over time we came to understand their care in their actions. And I remember hoping that those little boys would travel the distance of their own independence and return to an understanding that Mr. Rio, like my father, was not just ushering bodies but directing lives by refocusing gaze.

"We fall down, but we get up."

My mother told me that in the days before my father passed he was looking good. She said that he was joking and picking at my sisters. She said that he commented on a blouse she was wearing, which in his words was "Too sexy to wear outside of the house." My dad was a protective and jealous man—even after forty-four and a half years of marriage. She said that he told my brother that he wanted to go fishing, his favorite pastime. And in the midst of his playfulness we mistakenly thought that he was preparing to come home to us. But in fact he was preparing to go home to our Lord Jesus Christ. And while we will miss his physical presence in our lives we know that he is in a better place. We will look forward to meeting with him again.

So, in reference to my father I believe that the song I heard on Easter Sunday was just in saying *(in performance this last verse is sung)*, "He fell down, but he got up. He fell down, but he got up. He fell down, but he got up. For a saint is just a sinner who fell down . . . *(extended pause)* . . . and got up."

SELECTIVE PATTERNS AND MIGRATING IDENTITIES[50]

In the moment of delivering the eulogy, as in the moments of constructing it, I saw the diverse faces and the relational connections of family and friends. Their nodding responses and teary eyes signaled a subtext that always signals another story. The subtext is a story that is not articulated but lingers in the shadows and in the telling of the told.[51] My words do not capture their experience with my father; the words only serve to signal their relationships. Like when I said my father fell down when he drank a little too much. The life of an alcoholic leaves residual traces, hence falling down becomes both literal act and metaphor for struggle.

As a child and through my teenage years, maybe because of insecurity or fixation, I sucked the two middle fingers of my right hand. The habit annoyed my father; it annoyed him probably because he thought it was a bad habit or something only a sissy would do, or maybe that it cast a poor reflection on his masculinity. On a day when he had been drinking and was outside with one his friends he caught me sucking my fingers. He yelled at me, grabbed my hand, and shoving it down a dirty metal trashcan he dragged my hand on the bottom. Maggots and refuse covered my fingers as the jagged edges of the rusting can bruised my knuckles. All the while he chastised me for sucking my fingers.

My father's act of pedagogical violence worked only in embarrassing me, leaving not-so-faint scarred memories of his drinking. In fact, as the adult man that I am, I am not embarrassed to confess that I still desire to suck my fingers when insecurity and anxiety takes over me—which is often. I may even do it. The fact that his drinking may have complicated his death lingers in my mind like a painful memory. I know that in the act of telling, then (in the eulogy) and now (in the writing about the eulogy) like Ellis and Bochner,[52] I am voicing experiences that are often shrouded in secrecy. The act of telling bridges the dominions of public and private, but also the chasm between presence and absence for me, and for those to whom I speak. It is that component of the eulogy that attempts to reconcile differences between the living and the dead, and helps to reconcile interpersonal relationships between the speaker and the deceased. So I tell these painful family secrets not as a passive aggressive act in the absence of my father, but in the presence of so many others (including my siblings and readers), who live in the ever-present moments of the past.

In the eulogy I said my father fell when he cursed and shouted a little too loud, or when he did not go to church as much as he should have or could have. This knowledge resonates in the memories of all who heard him—family and friends—and the presence of his absence in our com-

pany, in church, in death, and in that moment, rang with an irony that
we all had to face. But I choose not to articulate those realities in detail,
relegating them to the narrative gestalt of the eulogy. I spend time resur-
recting his character in the face of family and friends—foregrounding the
positive not the punitive, the peaceful not the painful, the proper parent
in the memory of a peeved yet polite child. It is my duty and it is my
responsibility to reknit the text of my father's life and his place in community.

In the eulogy I acknowledged the occasion of my father's death. In fore-
casting our meeting again I also acknowledge our collective community
beliefs about death and our own mortality. My comparative analogy to
Mr. Rio and my father attempts to suture the wounds of his disciplinary
impulse by foregrounding if not his intentions, then the effects of his
actions. It is my way of reconciling painful aspects of my relationship with
my dad and offering others a mechanism to negotiate their own differences without unduly chastising the dead.

As performative and rhetorical engagements eulogies, like the people
who give them, are trapped somewhere between the viscosity and vicissi-
tude of memory and the fixity of death. Which always creates a reference
to the verisimilitude of otherness, even their own otherness.[53] The eulogy
can cauterize a wound and help in the healing; both the wounds inflicted
during life and the pains of loss. In his book *Critical Memory*, Houston A.
Baker Jr. offers his hopes for Black fathers and sons. He writes: "If we
structure our commitments to accord critically and memorially with the
best of our past, there is just a chance that black fathers and sons may yet
gather again in legions, genuinely about the business of redeeming ourselves and bringing the majority out of the dread darkness" (2001, 73).
And while he speaks of the possibility of engagements in living, the eulogy
for my father, like all eulogies, seeks to embody the same spirit and possibility.

"BODIES AND SELVES"[54] (A CONCLUSION)

In this chapter I have been particularly interested in the ways in which we
construct eulogies as (auto)biographical scripts—not just the actual writing or descriptive qualities that dictate form and function, but also the
tormented process of excavating memory, aestheticizing experience, and
reshaping identity from the hubris and umbrage of lives lived—our own

and others' lives.[55] Critique, commentary, and celebration are essential elements of eulogies and autobiographies and serve as the vehicle in many ways, but also become the tenor of the study. Like the relationship between the teller and the told, meaning resides in a journey to the self in order to reach the other, both for the telling and retelling; the narrating and testimony of experience insinuates itself into being as a form of invisible presence, like the very act of invoking presence in absence. I know that the person who has documented this travel is not the person who actually experienced it. I am the man that I have become. And there are more than just residual traces of my father in me. I stand as evidence of his presence in the world.

AN UNTIMELY TRIBUTE TO A MOTHER

On October 3, 2003, when I was in the process of completing the rewrite of this chapter, a drunk driver tragically killed my mother, Velma Ray Belle Alexander (fig. 6.2). My mother was on her regular early-morning pilgrimage to church. I include her tribute here not only as a commemoration of her life but also as a reflexive, refractive, and reflective act on the eulogy—a process that was made evident in the actual eulogy. This tribute was delivered on Wednesday, October 8, 2003, at Immaculate Heart of Mary Church.

Good morning. And, on behalf of my brothers and sisters, I thank you for being here. I must begin by making two confessions. First, I am not ready to do this, to give a eulogy and tribute to my mother. I am not sure if I ever will be. At first I thought that maybe if, like my father or my brother, my mother had lingered in sickness—maybe somehow sickness would have signaled our need to be prepared for her death. But how do you reconcile the moments of a life so suddenly and tragically taken? I suspect that none of us is ever prepared to say good-bye to those we love, so we tie our hearts and we do what we must. This is an untimely tribute to my mother.

My second confession is that I have been struggling to find the words to give tribute to my mother. I have not been struggling with thoughts, for certainly my mind is swirling with memories of her—the kindness of her spirit, the gentleness of her care, the strength of her faith. I have not been struggling with feelings, though certainly my heart aches with the death of my mother. There is a lack of congruence between the image that I have of

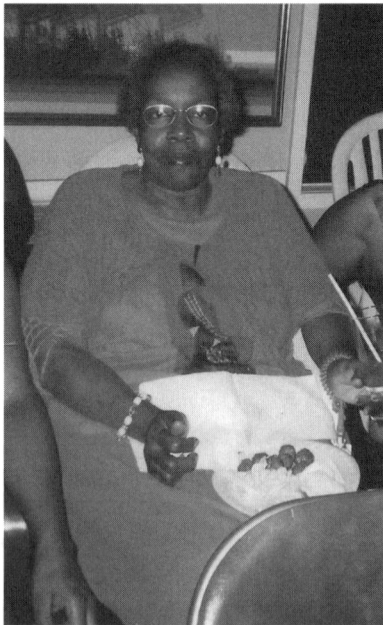

FIGURE 6.2
My mother.

her in my mind's eye and that of her in the casket. And my brothers and I will most certainly bear the weight of her absent presence as we carry her to her final resting-place.

I know what this tribute must do. I have been struggling with words, trying to find the right signifiers that signal my mother's life in a way that sincerely and publicly represents what I feel and that others will recognize. I have been struggling with articulating a life lived for this public forum, knowing and hoping that where my words fall short you will complete the thought, the feeling, and the impulse of my care, which is trapped for the moment in a teary haze of remembrance and responsibility.

In offering your condolences, many of you have assisted me in finding the words. Some of you said that in losing Ms. Velma, "it is like there is a hole in my heart." Some said, "I am losing my right hand." Some said, "I always knew she had my back," or "Your mother was always in my head. She always knew what I was thinking and feeling." One person said, "I can't stomach the thought of not seeing her every day." In reflecting on these sentiments I translate your references to my mother's thoughtfulness, her service, strength, care, and her substantive worth in your lives. I also see the manner in which you have written my mother into the script of your lives. I encourage you to continue reading her there. These embodied metaphors also suggest to me that maybe the tribute to my mother outside of these ceremonial words should really be the manifest results of her living.

Maybe the real tribute to my mother is in how people keep her memory and how we all translate our loss into the remembrance of her life.

Maybe the real tribute to my mother is the presence of her children as living evidence of her being here.

Maybe the real tribute to my mother is present in her grandchildren as a lineage of her legacy as a mother, grandmother, and great grandmother.

Maybe the real tribute to my mother is a challenge to her children to live the lives that she wanted for us.

Maybe our challenge is loving and supporting each other in her absent presence—for surely we know that she will be looking down on us, monitoring our actions, celebrating our choices, and secretly offering us ways of seeing ourselves with new eyes.

I remember as a kid growing up, and I am sure that my siblings do as well, that in the eyes of our mother the greatest sin that we could commit was to fight and be mean toward each other. My mother would say, "When Mámë and Dáddë are gone, all you will have is each other." And here we are—children living in the absence of our parents. Let us live our lives as brothers and sisters in tribute to our mother's care and love for us and for our family.[56]

There is an image of my mother that I hold dear to me. It is not in the pictures of her that I have chosen for the memorial program that many of you will place between the pages of your bible as an act of prayer. The image of her that I have in my mind and heart is not easily captured but it is felt. It is the image of her saying goodbye to me at the end of my many visits in the nearly twenty years that I have been away from home. The image is of her standing outside of the door, leaning against the wall, watching me as my car pulled out of the driveway. It is a cinematic scene of movement, distance, of saying goodbye, with the image growing smaller and smaller. There was always such a sad beauty in those moments—the look of pride and sadness in my mother's eyes.

The sadness was always so great that each time I would stop my car at the end of the driveway and run back to hug her. She would call me silly and we would laugh. And that too had become a part of our ritual negotiations in saying good-bye. It was a joyous mixture of crying and giggling; my mother taught me how to do both. We would stand there beneath the carport holding on as long as we could. She was always the first to let go, as she has for one last time.

That image is clear in my head and the feeling of her hug is still with me.

I am still holding on.

CODA: "CULTURE AND TEMPORALITY"[57]

In the days after my father's funeral and later after my mother's funeral I drove my Hertz rental car back to the airport. I boarded another Southwest Airlines flight that traveled from New Orleans back to Los Angeles. Once there I resumed the dailiness of my life. I greeted my partner, who had returned home early from the funerals and was waiting for me at the airport. He wore a tentative smile that spoke of his joy in seeing me as well as his concern for me. We then traveled the distance through the decadence of downtown to the quiet of our residential life. I greeted the cat, who like clockwork dropped and rolled on the carpet in front of the door—a signal for me to scratch her belly. I greeted the dog, who also dropped and rolled on the carpet—a signal for me to scratch her belly as well. Knowing that it was not business as usual, in each case, I returned to classes the next morning and tried to resume my life in that practiced place.

I will continue to write the presence of my parents into being, knowing that the time in which I write and what I write is not wholly equal to what I lived and who they were. And I will continue mixing the facts of their lives with the aesthetic and sometimes fictive features of narrative that enhances the telling, while it illuminates the told, and brings me comfort in their absence.

Notes

INTRODUCTION

1. Raymond Williams writes:

A culture has two aspects: the known meanings and directions, which its members are trained to; the new observations and meanings, which are offered and tested. These are the ordinary processes of human societies and human minds, and we see through them the nature of a culture: that it is always both traditional and creative; that it is both the most ordinary common meanings and the finest individual meanings. (2002, 93)

2. In *Striking Performances*, Kirk Fuoss begins to define *contestation* when he says:

Contestation occurs as a struggle over scarce resources enacted between competing agents or interests attempting to simultaneously realize mutually exclusive goals. The term refers to the struggle among individuals or groups endowed with variable amounts of economic, cultural, and symbolic capital to pursue their interests and secure their aims. (1997, 175n3)

In W. B. Gallie's notion of *contested terms*, the

recognition of a given concept as essentially contested implies recognition of rival uses of it (such as oneself repudiates) as not only logically possible and humanly "likely," but as of permanent potential critical value to one's own use or interpretation of the concept in question. (1964, 187–188)

3. In writing on a feminist methodology Dorothy E. Smith writes: "It does not transform subjects into the objects of study or make use of conceptual devices for eliminating the active presence of subjects. Its methods of thinking and its analytic procedures must preserve the presence of the active and experiencing subject" (2002, 272). I apply these logics to my general orientation to how this overall book is structured and engaged.

4. See how Joe Roach discusses the partisan nature of culture issue (1992, 10).

5. See Carlson (1996); Pelias (1999); and Stern and Henderson (1993) for basic texts in performance/performance studies.

6. Kirk Fuoss offers scholars studying performance contestation an important "topoi for their analysis of specific performance practices" grounded in the notion that all performance is essentially contestatory (1993, 347), later expanded in Fuoss (1997).

7. I expand on Judith Hamera's construction of "template of sociality" in chapter 1.

8. See Shelley Mallett's discussion on the authors of reflexive texts in ethnography (2003, 28–30).

9. See Madison (2005, 3–4).

10. I outline Denzin's (1997) six levels of reflexive engagement in chapter 4.

11. See Mostern (1999, 32).

12. Phillip Brian Harper uses this construct (1999, 150).

13. See Blau (1992, 440).

CHAPTER 1

1. Anscombe and von Wright translated fragments from Wittgenstein found in a box-file (1967, 40e).

2. The authors are citing Michel Foucault, *Discipline and Punish* (1979).

3. See how Dwight Conquergood engages this logic (2002, 150).

4. Herbert Blau uses the term *ideology* "to deploy a term that may, with its risks of reification, bear upon the materialities of performance, particularly in their resemblance" as people causally and callously encounter cultural difference in tourism (1992, 430).

5. See Alexander (2001).

6. In offering this construction Franklin attributes this investigative move in tourism to the work of Urry (1990); MacCannell (1976); and Graburn (1989).

7. See S. Pollock (2001, 43).

8. Ellen Strain uses the term "exoticized" to "reference the active process of seeing out, recognizing, and fetishizing difference" (2003, 17).

9. Urry states: "This is a book about pleasure, about holidays, tourism and travel, about how and why for short periods people leave their normal place of work and residence" (2002, 1).

10. This is also the critique and lack that Ellen Strain finds in the work of Urry (2003, 15).

11. See bell hooks (1996) for an example of how this is applied to Black female spectators in/of film.

12. Michael Bowman writes: "Like good cultural critics everywhere, tourists often proceed by staring long and hard at the people, places, objects, and activities they encounter, and not infrequently they become absorbed in or enchanted by the sights they see. But tourism also permits the possibility of rejecting what is

seen; it includes moments of sharpened focus, narrowed gaze—of skeptical assess-ment as well as wide-eyed wonder" (1998, 155).

13. See Wald (1998, 210).

14. Here I particularly note Jane Desmond's work related to the tourism in Hawaii. In the introduction she notes: "Many, many people are willing to pay a lot of money to see bodies which are different from their own, to purchase the right to look, and to believe that through that visual consumption they have come to know something that they didn't know before" (1999, xiii).

15. In writing on international tourism Harry G. Matthews writes:

> Besides the international relations of tourism brought by a visitor-to-host relation-ship, there is also the interaction of groups, national and transnational, involved in the tourist industry. . . . First, international tourism hinges to a large extent upon a et of government-to-government relations . . . A second . . . interaction[s] of national governments with foreign private enterprise . . . A third . . . the continuous contact between parent corporations and their subsidiaries around the world . . . Finally, there is at least a fourth set of international relations identified with the growth of international tourism. International organizations are increasingly being used by governments, especially in developing nations, for planning and development of tourism. (1978, 10–11)

16. Dann outlines four major theoretical perspectives on tourism and their sociolinguistic correlates: the authenticity perspective, the strangerhood perspec-tive, the play perspective, and the conflict perspective. Heavily theorized by Erik Cohen (1972), this perspective argues that "novelty and strangeness constituted essential elements in the touristic experience" (1996, 12).

17. See Mair (1965, 190) for one such discussion.

18. Ellen Strain writes: "At the heart of the fetishization is the basic presump-tion that the confrontation of difference involves a negotiation of boundaries in order to bolster a sense of self" (2003, 17).

19. John Urry offers nine principles that he describes as "a baseline for the historical, sociological, and global analyses" that he develops in the book. These are brief descriptions of his principles: 1) Tourism is a leisure activity that presup-poses its opposite. 2) Tourist relationships arise from a movement of people to, and their stay in, various destinations. 3) The journey and stay are to, and in, sites outside the normal places of residence and work. 4) The tourist gazes on these places for purposes not directly connected with paid work. 5) A substantial por-tion of the population of modern societies engages in such tourist practices. 6) Places are chosen to be gazed on because there is anticipation, especially through daydreaming and fantasy, and the anticipation of intense pleasure. 7) The tourist gaze is directed to features of landscape and townscape that separate them off from everyday experience. 8) The gaze is constructed through signs, and tour-ism involves the collection of signs. 9) An array of tourist professionals attempt

to reproduce ever-new objects of the tourist gaze (2–3). Urry also uses the specific construct of the "organizing power of vision" (2002, 146).

20. Ellen Strain puts it this way: "When one's own culture becomes denaturalized through the experience of the wide range of diversity possible among cultures [races, ethnicities, embodied presences], boundaries of self appear disturbingly diffuse as one tries to separate self from the arbitrarily formed armature of culture" and humanity (2003, 180).

21. Ellen Strain has a good description of this practice with an extensive bibliography in her chapter "Tourist Births: Placing the Tourist" (2003, 37–73).

22. The basic distinction between individual and collective cultures is based on how cultures promote independence or interdependency among group members. See the work of Geert Hofstede (1980) as a representative theorist on components of "individualistic and collective" cultures.

23. Mae G. Henderson offers a description that helps in establishing the context for border crossing and cultural politics. She writes: "Forever on the periphery of the possible, the border, the boundary, and the frame are always at issue— and their location and status inevitably raise the problematic of inside and outside and how to distinguish one from the other" (1995, 2).

24. This construction of *performativity* is contained in a binary between Judith Butler's (1990a, 1990b, 1995) constructions of performativity as stylized repetition of acts that are socially validated and discursively established, Lyotard's (1984) construction of performativity as it relates to maximizing efficiency by controlling outcomes and creating a culture of accountability, and J. L. Austin's (1962) speech-act theory whereby words in their embodied presentations of identity *do things.*

25. Mieke Bal uses the phrase "the gesture of exposing connects these two aspects" (1996, 2).

26. Here I am making an allusion to Jill Dolan. While Dolan is addressing the efficacy of representing gay/lesbian sex in performance as a resurgently political act, I am interested in the manner in which the presence of materiality—in places and spaces where it might be "unimaged, unimagined, invisible" in the everydayness of experience, might be perceived as a "transgressive act" and as a representation of excess (1992, 272).

27. In reflexive ethnographies the researcher/writer/observer engages in critical reflection of their own experience in a particular cultural context to understand the social and political implications of cultural contact (see Ellis and Bochner 2000).

28. See Bauman (1977).

29. In particular, Joseph Roach is commenting and explicating a citation from

John Fiske, the crux of which states: "Culture is not, then, the aesthetic products of the human spirit acting as a bulwark against the tide of grubby industrial materialism and vulgarity, but rather a way of living with an industrial society that encompasses all the meaning of that social experience" (1987, 254).

30. See Michel Foucault's (1975) discussions on surveillance and his particular discussion on the relationship between the watcher and the watched.

31. In particular, Kaplan references such films as Tracy Moffatt's *Nice Coloured Girls*, Fatimah Tobing Rony's *On Cannibalism*, Balvinder Dhenjan's *What Are Women Like in America?* and others.

32. This is the key question that E. A. Kaplan (1997) addresses in "Afterword, Reversing the Gaze, Yes: But Is Racial Inter-Subjective Looking Possible?"

33. See hooks (1996, 197).

34. An element of this logic was confirmed with another tour guide that I became friendly with. Raymond apologetically asked, "When you wash your hair—does it all come out?"—meaning do my dreadlocks untangle when I wash them. I answered, "No," and the conversation turned to other subjects, though from time to time I would catch him staring at my hair.

35. Yasmin Gunaratnam uses a similar construction (2003, 136).

36. Bruno writes:

> The lust to find out leads to a fascination with seeing, a perceptual attraction for sites, and consequently the formation of spectacle. This type of lust may lead the traveler-spectator astray, for as Tom Gunning shows, an aesthetic of attraction, with its perceptual shocks, implies distraction. And this very *curiositas* may also draw the viewer toward unbeautiful sights, for this noncontemplative mode entails an attraction for the dark sides of the visible. The lust of the eyes may turn into a panoramic-anatomic lust, leading our traveler-spectator into a curiosity for such things as mangled corpses. (1993, 59)

37. I am drawing here on Sue Thornham's analysis of Bhabha's colonial stereotypes and the manner in which she invokes Laplanche and Pontalis's definition of fantasy as "the setting rather than the object of desire" (1998, 151).

38. See how D. Soyini Madison discusses positionality in critical ethnography, especially how she lays out the issues in the introduction of her book (2005, i–xvi).

39. Lynch (2001).

40. Jane Desmond makes an important argument, which I apply here, when she states: "I am not suggesting that complicated subjectivities are reducible to bodily evidence, although this is precisely what the epistemological structures of these industries [meaning tourism] imply" (1999, xxiv). In particular there is a way in which the materiality of bodies, especially in this extreme example, might in fact reduce complex subjectivities in touristic encounters.

41. See how Rosemarie Garland Thomson (2005) introduces an argument for "staring from a distinctly social model" (p. 32).

42. Kirshenblatt-Gimblett and Bruner write:

> The issue is therefore less one of authenticity and more one of authentication: who has the power to represent whom and to determine which representation is authoritative? The representation of culture, what Richard Handler calls cultural objectification, is a complex ideological and political process. Edward Said, Michel Foucault, James Clifford, George Marcus and others have noted the relationship between knowledge and power and have suggested that the power to represent or to consume other cultures is a form of domination. (1992, 304)

43. In writing about ethnography, George W. Noblit, Y. Flores, and Enrique G. Murillo Jr. write:

> Critical ethnographers must explicitly consider how their own acts of studying and representing people and situations are acts of domination even as critical ethnographers reveal the same in what they study." (2004, 3)

Stuart Hall writes:

> What is particularly interesting from the point of view of the history of the modern subject is that, though Foucault's disciplinary power is the product of the new large-scale regulating collective institutions of late-modernity, its techniques and application of power and knowledge which further "individualizes" the subject and bear down more intensely on his/her body. (1997, 610)

44. See Deborah Gordon's (1990) insightful essay on the politics of ethnographic authority.

45. Here I am making an illusion to Ralph Ellison:

> It is sometimes advantageous to be unseen, although it is most often rather wearing on the nerves. Then too, you're constantly being bumped against by those of poor vision. Or again, you often doubt if you really exist. You wonder whether you aren't simply a phantom in other people's minds. Say, a figure in a nightmare that the sleeper tries with all his strength to destroy. It's when you feel like this that, out of resentment, you begin to bump people back. (1995, 3)

See also Foucault's discussions (1975).

46. The next day after my failed performance of passing or disguising myself, I approached a student, a young Black man traveling with the band. I had been told that he too was garnering a lot of attention from Chinese people—stares and requests to take pictures. He confirmed similar experiences and found them more funny than disturbing. The young Black man was heavyset and wore his hair in straight-lined corn-rolls that led to the back of his head.

47. Dann states: "The tourism industry knows that the visitor will feel isolated and that there will be communication gaps between tourist and 'native.' That is why it attempts to fill that void with language that it shares with the tourist. In so doing, it sells rather than informs" (1996, 15).

48. See Shields (1996, 279).

49. José Esteban Muñoz (1999) argues, among many things, that queer artists of color are always and already under excessive visibility as a function of dominant discourses.

50. This is an allusion to the title of Shields's article (1996).

51. See Bauman (1977, 28).

52. See Manning (1992, 296).

53. Brameld and Matsuyama (1978) engaged this possibility in what they presumed to be "two controversial case studies in educational anthropology."

54. See the edited volume by Ivan Karp and Steven D. Lavine (1991).

55. Here I am making an allusion to a written utterance by Mieke Bal. He writes: "Telling, showing, showing off in which the threshold between two worlds is more telling than the division between the two sides of New York's Central Park, and words expose images exposing words" (1996, 13).

56. See Wenshu Lee's important essay (2003), which reflects on the tonal variations and implications of the Chinese language.

57. Kenneth Burke argues that "we must use terministic screens, since we can't say anything without the use of terms; whatever terms we use, they necessarily constitute a corresponding kind of screen, and any such screen necessarily directs the attention to one field rather than another" (1945, 121).

58. See Kaplan (1997, 299).

59. Sue Thornham signals me to Bhabha's construct (1998, 150).

60. Bhabha writes:

> It is an apparatus that turns on the recognition and disavowal of racial/cultural/historical differences. Its predominant strategic function is the creation of a space for a "subject peoples" through the production of knowledges in terms of which surveillance is exercised and a complex form of pleasure/unpleasure is incited. It seeks authorisation for its strategies by the production of knowledges of colonizer and colonised which are stereotypical by antithetically evaluated. The objective of colonial discourse is to construe the colonised as a population of degenerate types on the basis of racial origin, in order to justify conquest and to establish systems of administration and instruction. (1994, 70)

61. See Foucault (1972).

62. Phillip Brian Harper writes that in many ways the project is his own "personal reckoning with the psychic dimensions of transnationalism" (1999, 150).

63. Rob Shields (June 2004) used the term *visualicity* to refer to aspects of the visual gaze, in particular "the glance" as a structure of surveillance that results in

an incomprehensible impenetrability of knowing; hence the glance becomes not what you see, but what you don't see, a flash shot of a reality whose meaning is not known. He offered six variables of analysis as the construct of *visualicity*— glance, gaze, focus, depth of field, representation, and exposure. The construct as a whole links his interests with visuality in the specific location of "the city" and pedestrian traffic.

64. Fuoss defines *the direction of effectivity* as "whether the cultural perform- ance maintains or subverts status-quo relations of power" and *the mode of effecti- vity* as "the strategies through which the maintenance of subversion is transacted" (1997, xiv).

65. Donal Carbaugh outlines several of these features as elements of intercul- tural communication (1990, 157–174). Yet while I invoke the specificity of inter- cultural communication as linked with tourism, this chapter is not designed to do the tough work to infuse literature on tourism with that of intercultural commu- nication. Yet I do want to invoke Wenshu Lee's important query as applied to tourism: "What will a concrete intercultural communication project look like if intersectionality is deeply integrated rather than given lip service?" (quoted in Collier et al. 2001, 273). In this sense I believe that the chapter begins to query these possibilities in order to illuminate new ways of seeing the intercultural implications of tourism.

66. I am drawing this construction from Matthew Spangler, who writes that "the very absence of authenticity is one of authenticity's pleasures" (2003, 125).

CHAPTER 2

1. Willie (2003) situates the personal stories of her own experience and those of her interviewees within a review of university policies regarding race and with suggestions for improvement for both White and Black universities seeking to make their campuses truly multicultural.

2. See Howes (2003, 9).

3. See Austin (1962).

4. See Eagleton (1993, 7).

5. See Butler (1993, 1990a, 1990b).

6. In addition, and in anticipation of my discussion of "passing as cultural performance" in chapter 3, see how the following theorists have shaped the dis- course on cultural performance: Conquergood (1994); Fine and Speer (1992); Fuoss (1997); Guss (2000).

7. See Bhabha (1994); Certeau (1984); and Goffman (1959) for further elabo- rations on the performance of culture in everyday life. Aspects of these logics are used throughout this book project.

8. See the work of Edward Said (1994) and Paulo Freire (1998) as a germinal introduction to these logics along with the critical volume edited by Leistyna, Woodrum, and Sherblom (1996).

9. Harper uses this construction (1996, 51).

10. Here I am using the term *endemic* to refer to the confinement of particularity—organisms, humans, or cultures relegated to geographical regions like ecospheres, the suburbs, the ghetto, uptown/downtown, or the figurative "other side of the tracks."

11. This is a term used by Raymond Williams (1980).

12. Stanley Fish is particularly talking about interpretive communities as related to literary texts. I am expanding this construct to foreground the ways in which cultural performance and cultural membership is always determined through the interpretive processes of those who claim membership and who will then validate or critique the performance of member/membership of others.

13. See Charisse Jones and Kumera Shorter-Gooden's (2003) project, which explores the metaphor of shifting, specifically focusing on the lives of Black women.

14. See Cohen (1982).

15. Miles defines the term racialization as "any process or situation wherein the idea of 'race' is introduced to define and give meaning to some particular population, its characterizations and actions" (1988, 246).

16. I believe that this construction is informed by a similar construction in the April 12, 2004, *Newsweek.*

17. Clella Iles Jaffe outlines these as functions of narrative (1995, 297–303).

18. See Cole and Omari (2003).

19. In this report I am using pseudonyms for my conversational partners—an act of protecting their identity that is both professional necessity and personal consideration.

20. In their work on Black students and their families, Michael K. Herndon and Joan B. Hirt reinforce and extend the significance of the Black family to the relative success of Black students when they write:

> The family is a conduit for educational attainment for several reasons. First, families are primary sources of academic potential. That is, the family is the first unit to develop and nurture the student's capacity for learning. Second, families set the parameters of community standards within the home environment. Such boundaries affect a student's outlook on the larger social order. Third, parents are influential in creating the context in which events and phenomena are evaluated. In this case, families provided the background for explaining meaning in life and the world. (2004, 491)

21. Also see the manner in which White and White (1998) address these issues.

22. This is a reconstruction of Anderson's construct of the "imagined community" (1991, 6).

23. See Charles Nero's (1997) examination of constructions and orientations to/of home.

24. This concept is also discussed in Cole and Omari (2003, 790).

25. See Nancy Fraser's (1994) reworking of Habermas.

26. For me this was particularly apparent in the media coverage of the 2004 presidential campaign, in which states are characterized as Blue or Red (Democratic or Republican) and in which people and candidates claim territories of space as politicized and ideological practice.

27. See Lusane (1996, 2).

28. Posnock (1998) attributes the phrase "Rather, it stands in reciprocal relation to the particular" to Naomi Wolf's blurb for Michael Eric Dyson's *Between God and Gangsta Rap* (1996).

29. See Dubois (1982), in particular chapter 1: "Of Our Spiritual Strivings" in *The Souls of Black Folks*.

30. "Always" is Zora's reference to a brand-name commercial feminine hygiene product.

31. In using the word *normative*, I am not referencing Jacobs's (1994, ch. 6) "normative code models of discourse analysis," but more linking the identification and identity management issues associated with "social identity theory" (Burgoon 1994, 245).

32. Of course here, I am using the scare quotes to suggest the particularity of my experience and not to generalize to broader constructions of a monolithic "Black community," which may or may not exist in the everyday life of most Black people.

33. Here I am also making casual reference to the work of Matthew Spangler (2002).

34. See Randall Kennedy (2002); and, for a more decisive explication of the term *nigger* and for its more colloquial intracommunal use ("nigga") by Black people, Fong and McKewen (2004).

35. See hooks (1994b).

36. See the work of Kirshenblatt-Gimblett and Bruner (1992) and E. P. Johnson (2003a) for examples.

CHAPTER 3

1. "The sardony of it: Mocking bitterness; scornful, cynical humor; Larsen creates a noun form of the adjective 'sardonic.'" This is an actual endnote included in the 1997 edition of Larsen's *Passing* (118).

2. "Passing and the fictions of identity" also serves as the title of a project by Ginsberg (1996).

3. While using Larsen's novel to explore the notion of *passing* in the specific context of Black masculinity, I am aware of the fact that Larsen is in fact using this novel to explore the intersections of race and femininity. As Thadious M. Davis writes about Larsen's efforts in "demystifying the racialized female" in *Passing*: "The novel depends upon an acceptance of diversity and complexity as the textures of African-American female life and rejects any totalizing gender or race view, even though it explores the cultural conditions and proscriptions that shape, but do not determine, the life of a female of color" (1994, 309).

4. Dreama Moon writes: "Which ever definition of passing you ascribe to, it is clear that passing as a social practice problematizes ideas about identity and offers itself as an adaptive tactic, particularly for those socially situated in the margins of a society" (1998, 324).

5. Elaine K. Ginsberg offers the following definitional genealogy of passing:

> The genealogy of the term passing in American history associates it with the discourse of racial difference and especially with the assumption of a fraudulent "white" identity by an individual culturally and legally defined as "Negro" or black by virtue of a percentage of African ancestry. As the term metaphorically implies, such an individual crossed or passed through a racial line or boundary—indeed trespassed—to assume a new identity and access the privileges and status of the others. Enabled by a physical appearance emphasizing "white" features, this metaphysical passing necessarily involved geographical movement as well; the individual had to leave an environment where his or her "true identity"—that is, parentage, legal status, and the like—was known to find a place where it was unknown. By extension, "passing" has been applied discursively to disguises of other elements of an individual's presumed "natural" or "essential" identity, including class, ethnicity, and sexuality, as well as gender, the latter usually effected by deliberate alternations of physical appearance and behavior, including crossing dressing. (1996, 2–3)

6. See J. Taylor (1987) and Park-Fuller and Olsen (1983).

7. Turner (1988) and Stern and Henderson (1993).

8. There is a growing body of literature that investigates the notion of cultural performance ranging from the disciplines of anthropology to performance studies. For more information see the following sources, just to name a few: James Clifford (1988); Ervin Goffman (1959); James MacAloon (1984); Milton Singer (1992); Victor Turner (1988); David M. Guss (2000); R. Bauman (1992); and of course the extensive body of work by Dwight Conquergood (1983, 1986, 1988, 1989, 1991, 1992a, 1992b, 1994, 1998, 2002) that I list here in brief.

9. Deborah Britzman et al. suggest that cultural performance is a process of delineation, performative practices used to mark membership and association:

NOTES TO CHAPTER 3

Much of this delineation also depends upon the privileging of one social marker, such as race, at the cost of another, such as sex. While such categories are always social constructions, their persuasiveness derives from their seeming factuality and from the deep investments individuals and communities have in setting themselves off from the "other" that they must then simultaneously and imaginatively construct. (1993, 192–193)

10. Victor Turner argues that "cultural performances are active agencies of social change, representing the eye by which culture sees itself and the drawing board on which creative actors sketch out what they believe to be more effective or ethical 'designs for living'" (1988, 24).

11. In particular, see Singer (1992) and Guss (2000).

12. See the above citation (n. 10) from Turner.

13. Linda Williams suggests that the performer suppresses the more obvious artifice of performance with the particular necessity of not "overacting" (2001, 176).

14. For a further discussion on liminality see Turner (1988).

15. The questions framed in this essay, concerning the performance, are reconstructed comments made after a presentation at the National Communication Association performance.

16. A student actually said this to me when I was teaching at Moorhead State University, in Moorhead, Minnesota, between 1989–1994. In that particular moment, I had to carefully negotiate the balance between what I "presumed to be" her good intentions, and what was undoubtedly a "teachable moment."

17. I explore the accusation of "acting White" and the politics of "whiteness" in further detail in Alexander (2004c).

18. See West (1991) and Banks (1996).

19. Majors and Billson remind us:

Many black men have learned to live up to a harsh standard: real men are not involved with anyone or anything that is not cool. Adhering to this standard means that black men may have a hard time being down to earth with each other; they have to be cool, especially with the "fellas." Their behavior must follow an unyielding code of coolness in order to gain acceptance. If a black man does not act in these prescribed ways [good man] others are quick to ostracize and label him as corny, lame, square [Bad man]. (1992, 45)

20. See West (1993, 129).

21. Herb Green states: "The parameters of my identity are not constrained by a single static border—my identity is fluid and flexible. In fact, sometimes the very essentializing and reductive nationalistic ideas that are supposed to unite us and

make us identifiable to ourselves and others often render us silent about significant realities about ourselves and our individual desires" (1996, 253).

22. It is the "general anxiety about black men's assumption of such masculinity as has been deemed socially proper [, expected,] and normative, as evidence of
its problem notwithstanding" (Harper 1996, 119).

23. Judith Butler states: "According to the understanding of identification as
an enacted fantasy or incorporation, however, it is clear that coherence is desired,
wished for, and idealized, and that this idealization is an effect of a corporeal signification. In other words, acts, gestures, and desire produce the effect of an internal core or substance, but produce this *on the surface* of the body, through the
play of signifying absences that suggest, but never reveal, the organizing principle
of identity as a cause" (1990a, 136).

24. Linda Williams states: "For blacks to adopt the heritage of minstrelsy is to
collude in their fetishization. But to not adopt (and adapt) this heritage is to lose
the very means with which to engage with an important part of the cultural past"
(2001, 140).

25. See Wallace (2002, 154).

26. Larsen (1997, 103–104).

27. In this section Whitehead (2002) is referencing Foucault (1978).

28. See Whitehead's discussion on this point (2002, 209).

29. I contrast Martha Cutter's description of Clare's racial passing in Nella
Larsen's novel that "passing" becomes a mechanism to get what she [Clare]
wants—which is not a singular identity, an identity that corresponds to a theoretical inner self, but an identity that can escape the enclosures of race, class, and
sexuality, enclosures that would limit her "having ways" (1996, 84).

30. Here I am capitalizing on Judith Hamera's argument when she writes
about "the conflation of the body and identity and, in turn, fore-grounding the
'impossibility of obliterating the "difference" that comprises representation'—
specifically here, the difference between the 'me' (my body/identity), the 'not/me'
(*not* my identity), and the 'not–not *me*' (*may*be my body/identity and maybe
not)" (1993, 55). In this instance Hamera is riffing off of Margulies (1993, 58)
and Schechner (1985, 112).

31. Here I am signaling back to Whitehead's "positive moment of (self)-
creation" (2002, 101).

32. Mallett signals and extends this important insight (2003, 94). See also
Pierre Bourdieu and Loïc Wacquant (1992).

33. Henry Louis Gates Jr. directs me to this citation (1988, 50).

34. See Cutter (1996, 75).

35. See Crang's discussion on the notion of palimpsest (1998, 22).

36. See Whitehead (2002, 209).

37. See Moon (1999).

38. See Woods (2003, 167–171).

39. See Phillip Brian Harper (1994) and Julia Woods, who uses the construct of "self-as-object" to refer to our "ability to self-reflect, enabl[ing] us to define ourselves and exercise some choice over who we will become" (2003, 154).

40. Richmond and McCrosky outline five basic types of power: 1) Reward power, based on the ability to mediate rewards; 2) Coercive power, based on the ability to mediate punishments; 3) Legitimate power, grounded in position and status; 4) Referent power, based on allocated authority through identification; and 5) Expert power, based on perceived knowledge or expertness (1992, 4–5).

41. This construction about the forces of singularity in relation to the event horizon is loosely drawn from my understanding of Einstein's general theory of relativity—specifically referencing black holes. See Dirac (1996).

42. I know that I am not "a resistant transcriber of my stage work," because the work is intricately interwoven into the very contested nature of my being as a Black-gay-male-teacher-scholar-performer (Pineau 2000, 1). Hence, "I understand the intellectual and political necessities of recasting my staged work in print" (2).

43. I say *irony* in this case because most will agree, as in the often cited work by Peggy McIntosh (1997), that privilege, whether in terms of resources, opportunity, or even the social construction of worth, is unearned.

44. Here I am mostly signaling the significant ways in which D. Soyini Madison (1993) engages discussion of "theories of the flesh" linked to performance and Black feminist thought.

45. In his use of the phrase "the gray zone," Primo Levi (1988) is describing the relational ambiguity involved in a soccer match in a Nazi extermination camp between SS guards and Jewish prisoners in charge of running the crematorium.

46. bell hooks (1994a, 248) offers me a method of understanding the process of decolonization. She states:

> Whenever those of us who are members of exploited and oppressed groups dare to critically interrogate our locations, the identities and allegiances that inform how we live our lives, we begin the process of decolonization. If we discover in ourselves self-hatred, low self-esteem, or internalized white supremacist thinking and we face it, we can begin to heal. Acknowledging the truth of our reality, both individual and collective, is a necessary stage for personal and political growth.

47. I explore this construction further in Alexander (2004a).

48. For further readings that explore issues of blackness, race, and representation, see the following: hooks (1992); Steel (1990); Madhubuti (1991); Hutchinson (1994); Johnson (2003a, 2003b).

49. See the following as points of reference: Morrison (1992); hooks (1990); Dyson (1993).

50. See the following as an introduction to writings about Black masculinity and Black gay identity: Belton (1995); Boykin (1996); Morrow and Rowell (1996); Ruff (1996); Hemphill (1991); Longress (1996).

51. In this conclusion I make allusions to a section of Jennifer Esposito's essay "The Performance of White Masculinity in *Boys Don't Cry*" entitled "No Border Crossing Allowed." I am arguing here, and maybe throughout this chapter, about the tension and tensiveness between the nature of racial, cultural, and gender borders, and the will or desire to cross. Like Esposito, here "I offer only my partial (re)presentation of the issues around identity, difference, [and] performance, imagination that haunt me, and I ask that we (I, you, they) continue to be haunted, for ghosts are one place of remembrance" (2003, 240).

52. See Moon (1999).

53. Like Bob Shacochis (2001), I am not writing with malicious intent so much as writing to out particular logics that are not always addressed in the social construct of polite talk.

54. See how Ginsberg (1996) plays through the logics of passing as crossing both racial/cultural borders and sexual/gender boundaries.

55. See Ginsberg, who develops this last point to some degree (1996, 2–3).

56. In a supportive sense Sanyal (2002, 11) writes:

At the intersection of these . . . claims—that history is a structure of displacement and repetition, and that history is a structure of entanglements—lies an ethical investment in the unrepresentability of both history and subjectivity. For it is the gap both within the event and the experiencing subject that opens up selfhood to otherness. What trauma reveals, then is a lack, a difference, a departure from oneself that is the condition of all subjects positing themselves as "I."

57. Gilroy uses this construction (1995, 16).

CHAPTER 4

1. Caughie goes on to write:

The purpose of pedagogy is to make things clear. . . . Even if, following John Dewey, we conceive pedagogy as teaching inquiry, not knowledge, as process-oriented rather than content-centered, and even if we resist its reduction to a set of rules or methodology, still pedagogy is largely conceived in humanist terms; it is supposed to be comforting by providing guidance, enabling students to become part of an academic community and to see themselves as members of a broader social community, responsive and responsible to it. (1999, 64)

2. Throughout this excursion I use the slash (/) to both disrupt and illuminate the gender roles being enacted in this scene. It is a visual cue and reminder to the reader of the subversive nature of gender performance being enacted. I maintain this technique even when the latent personal pronoun seems inappropriate— because of course, drag performance calls into question notions of what is and what is not "appropriate" in the social construction of meaning and identity.

3. I attribute the construction of this phrase to Teresa Carilli (1997) in a presentation made at the National Communication Conference.

4. Volcano and Halberstam (1999, 60) describe the drag king Justing Kase, a female Elvis impersonator, as having "a kind of organic Drag King aura; he wears very little facial hair (maybe slightly exaggerated sideburns) and he builds on a sturdy butch image." Halberstam (1998) explores the notion of organic masculinity further.

5. Carter writes: "Story has become more than a rhetorical device for expressing sentiments about teachers or candidates for the teaching profession. It is now, rather, a central focus for conducting research in the field" (1993, 5).

6. See Crary (1999, 7).

7. Norman K. Denzin states:

A theory of writing is also a theory of interpretive (ethnographic) work. Theory, writing, and ethnography are inseparable material practices. Together they create the conditions that locate the social inside the text. Hence, those who write culture also write theory. Also those who write theory write culture . . . [T]here is a need for a reflexive form of writing that turns ethnographic and theoretical texts back "onto each other." (1997, xii)

8. Denzin (1997, 217–224).

9. See "When Teaching Works: Stories of Communication in Education," Special Issue of *Communication Education* 42.4 (1993).

10. Caftanzoglou writes that "approaching place as a socially constructed, 'meaningfully constituted in relation to human agency and activity' may offer a way of overcoming the methodological and conceptual tensions between totally 'unhooking' identity and culture from place and constructing them as placebound" (2001, 21). In context she cites Tilley (1994, 10).

11. This narrative appears in Bryant Alexander (2005) "Embracing the Teachable Moment: The Black Gay Body in the Classroom as Embodied Text," in E. Patrick Johnson and Mae G. Henderson (Eds.), *Black Queer Studies: A Critical Anthology* from Duke University Press.

12. His cutting is from chapter 10, "Donning a Dress, Do Real Men Do Drag?" (Cohn 1995). Sergio's (the student in this performance) drag name is Sabrina. I thank Sergio for reading this description and allowing me to include it in my work.

13. See Gallop (1992).

14. See Roy's use of this construct (1995, 119).

15. Tony Morrison uses the construction of "genderized, sexualized and racialized" to describe the world context in which she writes—"unencumbered by dreams of subversion or rallying gestures at fortress walls" (1972, 4–5).

16. According to Leistyna, Woodrum, and Sherblom, technocratic models

> conceptualize teaching as a discrete and scientific understanding, embrace depersonalized solutions for education that often translate into the regulation and standardization of teacher practices and curricula, and rote memorization of selected "facts" that can easily be measured through standardized testing. As such the role of the teacher is reduced to that of an uncritical, "objective," and "efficient" distributor of information. (1996, 1)

17. Roger Baker cites Eric Partridge's *Dictionary of Slang and Unconventional English*, which says, "['drag'] describes 'the petticoat or skirt used by actors when playing female parts' and suggest that the word derives from 'the drag of the dress (on the grounds), as distinct from the non-dragginess of trousers'" (1994, 17).

18. I am drawing here from Epstein and Sears (1999).

19. See Lipman, Sharp, and Oscanyan (1980).

20. And in this way, capitalizing on the teachings of Paulo Freire, Marguerite and Michael Rivage-Seul state: "For in its transcendental form imagination places critical human subjectivity rather than institutional preservation at the center of the possible. In Freire's terms it is the drive to humanization, and is comprehensively historical because the process treats human beings as subjects who relativize or historicize their institutional reality, not as objects relegated simply to fulfilling ahistorical institutional requirements" (1994, 47).

21. Scott Dillard also tells me "we often, if not exclusively, equate the masculine in men with heterosexuality and the feminine in men with homosexuality" (1997, 1).

22. In relation to reference in his text Barthes states: "What comes from books and from friends occasionally appears in the margins of the text, in the form of names (for the books) and initials (for friends). The references supplied in this fashion are not authoritative but amical. I am not invoking guarantees, merely recalling, by a kind of salute given in passing, what has seduced, convinced, or what has momentarily given the delights of understanding (of being understood?) (1979, 8–9). Hence, he offers no direct citations for his particular invocation of Lacan.

23. Please note that in making this comment Brown (2000) is referencing the arguments of D. Bell et al. (1994) and the volume edited by Andrew Parker and Eve Kosofsky Sedgwick (1992).

24. I am honored to be written up in an article entitled, "Know Your Feminist Faculty: Bryant Alexander" in *LOUDMOUTH*, a publication produced by the Women's Resource Center at California State University Los Angeles (2004, 5). The article is written by Edahrline Salas.

25. See hooks (1992) and Frey (1983).

26. See Schacht (2000).

27. In constructing these logics I am placing myself both in relation to and in resistance to how Schacht's (2000) positions himself as a straight white man engaging feminist pedagogy.

28. Schacht (2000, 4) discusses a similar point.

29. See Kenway and Modra (1992); Loughlin (1993); hooks (1994b).

30. I link consciousness-raising in the practical ways hooks discusses the "process of decolonization" (1994a, 248).

31. See Gitlin (1994).

32. See the rather premeditated manner in which Schacht (2000) attempts to combat his positionality as a straight White man.

33. See Ajwang' and Edmondson (2003); Aoki (2004); Gallop (1992); hooks (1994b, 1994c).

34. In particular bell hooks states: "Teachers are not performers in the traditional sense of the word in that our work is not meant to be a spectacle. Yet it is meant to serve as a catalyst that calls everyone to become more engaged, to become active participants in learning" (1994b, 11). See also Pineau (1994).

35. See how hooks discusses this construct (1994b, 15).

36. Morris (1972).

37. Martin (1998, 193).

38. Denzin (1997, 34).

39. Azevedo states:

Not only are the form and the content of maps interest-related, so too are the methods used to produce each map. These methods are also affected by background assumptions about the nature of the area being mapped. A map is a formal representation of selected features and relations in the world that preserves relationships of particular interest. Each man, then, can be seen as a model. Models have a relationship not only to their subject (the territory, in the case of geographic maps) but to their source. The source for a three-dimensional replica of the Earth is a sphere. (1997, 109)

40. Del LaGrace Volcano and Judith "Jack" Halberstam state:

The Drag King, in a way, does not simply expose so-called abnormal desires or abnormal genders, rather he revels in what is already perverse in the normal. The Drag King gives us insight into the vagaries of normal masculinity, its own set of peculiarities, its own way of making those peculiarities seem mundane. We can call this the drag effect and take it out of the drag club and into everyday life as a strategy for restaging everyday life. (1999, 152)

41. See how these authors write about the essence of drag king performance: Halberstam (1998); Volcano and Halberstam (1999).

42. Norman Denzin describes messy texts as "texts that are aware of their own narrative apparatuses, that are sensitive to how reality is socially constructed, and that understanding that writing is a way of 'framing' reality. Messy texts are many cited, intertextual, always open ended, and resistant to theoretical holism, but are always committed to cultural criticism" (1997, 224). Within the original quote Denzin cites Marcus (1994, 567).

CHAPTER 5

1. Chinna Smith is quoted in Mastalia and Pagano (1999, 45). The quote from Akkida McDowell is from her essay "The Art of the Ponytail," as cited by Byrd and Tharps (2001, 151).

2. See Melissa Harris-Lacewell's important examination of Black talk in the barbershop (2004, 162–203).

3. The title of this chapter, "Fading, Twisting, and Weaving," makes reference to specific Black hairstyles. *Fading* is "a male hairstyle, high on top and very short or completely shaved on the sides and back; the top can be natural or dreaded" (Smitherman 1994, 106). *Twisting* is a style akin to dreadlocks in which the hair is twisted together, but is not entangled. *Weaving* is a "female hairdo with synthetic or human hair braided into the natural hair at the roots, with the rest left loose for a long full-looking hairstyle" (234). While these are hairstyles, these names are used as metaphorical descriptions of the relational and interactive patterns of people, conversations, and lives that intermingle in the barbershop.

4. Certeau (1984, xi).

5. Benedict Anderson uses this construct when talking about "imagined communities" (1991, 7).

6. Wendell Berry offers the notion that "our culture must be our response to our place, our culture and our place are images of each other and inseparable from each other" (1977, 22).

7. See Hamera (2000, 147).

8. See how Michael Quinn Patton (2001) and Lewis-Beck, Bryman, and Liao (2003) outline information on indigenous ethnography.

9. See Denzin (1997, 247).

10. Norman Denzin states:

"An interpretive ethnography for the next century is one that is simultaneously minimal, existential, autoethnographic, vulnerable, performative, and critical. This ethnography seeks to ground the self in a sense of the sacred, to dialogically connect the ethical, respectful self to nature and the worldly environment. In so doing, it recognizes the ethical unity of mind and nature" (Bateson and Bateson, 1987, p. 8–9, 11). It seeks to embed the self in storied histories of sacred spaces. This epistemology presumes a feminist moral ethic, stressing the sacredness of human life, dignity, truthtelling and nonviolence (Christians, 1998, p. 3). (1999, 510)

11. This is the primary site of my childhood memories in the barbershop. Depending on the relationship he had with the barber, my dad would often shift us back and forth between different barbers (Mr. Johnson or Mr. "Slim"), but most often we went to Mr. Brown.

12. Referencing his work in India, Milton Singer writes:

Indians, and perhaps all peoples, think of their culture as encapsulated in such discrete performances, which they can exhibit to outsiders as well as to themselves. For the outsider these can conveniently be taken as the most concrete observable units of the cultural structure, for each performance has a definitely limited time span, a beginning and end, an organized program of activity, a set of performers, an audience, and a place and occasion of performance. (1959, xii)

13. In using the term *wordworkers*, I am referencing a science fiction short story by Carolyn Ives Gilman (1991), in which "wordworkers," through language and storytelling, retell the story of their village every night in a literal attempt at reconstruction and cultural maintenance.

14. In this way, I use Eric Freedman's notion of *community* as a term "under which we can speak of collective involvement, or even unified resistance, while at the same time respect (and expect) difference (1998, 251). This is in relation to the ways that I addressed community in chapter 2.

15. Geneva Smitherman defines "talkin trash" as:

the art of dissin one's opponent during competitive play (as in basketball, Nintendo, Bid [or in this case checkers]) so as to erode their confidence, get them rattled or distracted so they'll make poor plays and lose the game. . . . [or it is] the art of using strong rhythmic, clever talk and forms in the African American Verbal tradition—e.g., signifyin, woofin—to entertain, to promote one's ego, to establish leadership in a group, or to project an image of BADness. (1994, 221)

16. Berry et al. write: "As the term suggests [enculturation], there is an encompassing or surrounding of the individual by one's culture; the individual acquires, by learning, what the culture deems to be necessary. There is not necessarily anything deliberate or didactic about this process; often there is learning without specific teaching" (1992, 18–19).

NOTES TO CHAPTER 5

17. Sally's Beauty Supply is a national chain, but maintains a sort of hometown feel. The stores are often located in strip malls. In my experience they are also most often located in predominantly Black neighborhoods.

18. In writing on cultural geography Edward Relph offers a meaningful way to perceive this point. He says, "Cultures, landscapes, and styles are being mixed up and redeposited like detritus in a terminal moraine" (2001, 150).

19. See Langellier and Peterson who speak of gendered language in the context of their discussion on personal narrative (1992, 157).

20. Evans writes: "Dreads/Dreadlocks: A misnomer for locks carries over two traditions. Firstly is the Rastafarian way of life, which refers to the uncut, unmanicured locks as Dreadlocks because of the fear they instilled in the White man. Secondly, the Eurocentric tradition of England referred to locked hair as dreadful, as they have historically slandered and disempowered any cultural feature that is not theirs. Today Africans perpetuate this slander by referring to their locks as 'dreads.' The most accurate description of this hair form is Locks, or African Locks which denotes its place of origin" (1992, 86). For a different history of "dread locks" see Mastalia and Pagano (1999). "Sisterlocks/brotherlocks" also refer to a specific technique of locking. See www.sisterlocks.com.

21. See for example some of the work by Dwight Conquergood in which he espouses the performance/culture link (1988, 1989).

22. See Turner's discussion of *communitas* (1977, 46).

23. See how Harris-Lacewell (2004, 187–188) discusses the "boundaries of sexual identity"; also see Harris (1979).

24. See Ingrid Banks (2000); Byrd and Tharps (2001); and Harris and Johnson (2001).

25. See Arrizón (2000, 27).

26. See Wilson (1995, xii).

27. See how Jackson discusses the concept of ethnophysicality (1998, 172).

28. See the two *New York Times* articles by Williams (2001) and Tannen (2001) on the popularity and politics of hair and the commerce of doing braids.

29. Langellier and Peterson use the term *spinstorying* to "emphasize the strategic dimensions of this storytelling, which, while not exclusive to women or characteristic of all women, does emerge most clearly in studies of women's personal narratives" (1992, 157–158).

30. In this way I am also linking the experience of doing ethnography with Kenneth Burke's (1945) construction of the pentad or dramatistic analysis that includes act, scene, agent, agency, and purpose.

31. See how Mercer engages these logics (1994, 99–100).

32. Jonathan Crary tells me:

Whether perception or vision actually changes is irrelevant for they have no autonomous history. What changes are the plural forces and rules composing the field in which perception occurs. And what determines vision at any given historical moment is not some deep structure, economic base, or worldview, but rather the functioning of a collective assemblage of disparate parts on a single social surface. It may even be necessary to consider the observer as a distribution of events located in many different places. (1999, 6)

33. Michel de Certeau writes: "Analysis shows that a relation (always social) determines its terms, and not the reverse, and that each individual is a locus in which an incoherent (and often contradictory) plurality of such relational determinations interact. Moreover, the question at hand concerns modes of operation or schemata of action, and not directly the subjects (or persons) who are their authors or vehicles" (1984, ix).

34. See Fuoss, who is specifically writing about cultural performance (1993, 347).

35. See Cooks (1998, 230).

36. See Jackson (1998, 179).

CHAPTER 6

1. The phrase "Were/Are, Fort/Da" is used by Dorothy Chansky to suggest the intimate relationship between the past and the present (the then and there, the here and now) in the sharing of personal histories and fond memories (1999, 345).

2. In writing about her parents, Pineau states that "familial biography allows [her] to pay tribute to [her] parents' lives without going through too many contortions of self-critique. Narrated from the sidelines, so to speak, the familial biography allows [her] to show [her] roots without being unduly implicated in them" (2001, 68). While I find her articulation extremely useful, in my application of her construct I am arguing for the meaningfulness of self-implication in what is always and already a performance of (auto)biography. I am a result of who my parents were. I accept the fullness of their legacy in me.

3. Richard Bauman cites Roman Jakobson (1971) to address "the special nature of narrative as doubly achored in human events. That is, narratives are keyed both to the events in which they are told and to the events that they recount, toward narrative events and narrated events" (1988, 2).

4. See Maines (2001c, 109).

5. Linda Park-Fuller (2000) speaks about the difficulties involved in speaking for others in the representational politics of solo performance. But I am also interested in the notion that no two children (biologically linked or otherwise) experi-

ence their parents in the same way. Maybe this is due to the individual nature of their relationship, or the point of entry of the child at the varying developmental stages of the parents. I appreciate the manner in which these issues are explored in the rich stories and theorizing that Mara Loeb (1996) offers, when she talks about the ownership of family narratives, the complicatedness of point-of-view, perception, and the slippage that takes place when differing family members attempt to tell their rendition of the same family story.

David Maines (1993, 21–22) outlines ten propositions in support of a narrative sociology. Numbers three and four are particularly pertinent to the concern of variability in accounting shared experience:

1) Since all socialized humans are storytellers, they are always in a potential story-telling situation when interacting with or encountering others.

2) The vast majority of all speech acts and self-representations contain at least some elements of narratives.

3) Variation in situation, audience, individual perspective, and power/authority relations will produce the universal condition of multiple versions of narrative events.

4) Narratives and narrative occasions are always potential sites of conflict and competition as well as cooperation and consensus.

5) All narratives are potentially rational accounts, but because of inherent human ambiguity and variation in linguistic competence, all narratives are ultimately incomplete.

6) Narratives exit at various levels of scale, ranging from the person to the institutional to the cultural, they exist for varying lengths of time, and they inevitably change.

7) All social science data are already interpreted data; the uninterpreted datum does not exist.

8) All sociological facts are narrated facts insofar as they have been processed through some form of story structure that renders events as factual.

9) The act of data collection is an act of entering respondents' lives that are partly formed by still unfolding stories. Therefore, in the name of honesty, research subjects will likely tell different stories about the same thing at different times and to different people.

10) A major implication of the above nine propositions is that sociology can only be a science of interpretations and to some extent must constitute itself as an interpretive science.

6. See Maines (1989, 107).

7. In writing about cultural studies Henry Giroux writes: "At the same time

space and place do not disappear as markers of memory, history, and lived experience; they become more porous, and unstable, but still bare the weight of history
and the legacies of struggles yet to be fulfilled" (2001, 6).

8. Or as Anna K. Kuhn says, "in writing lives, (self)-representation entails
various degrees of (self)-invention, that in writing we create (our)selves" (1990,
14).

9. See Ellis (1993, 724).

10. Ellis (1993, 724).

11. See Phelan (1997, 3).

12. And in the process, I extend Hamera's articulation to concretize her significant contribution to the categories of approaches to performance by framing
it—"performance as template of sociality." Kirk Fuoss does a good job in outlining these as he builds the foundation for the "agonistic" approach to performance.

> The proliferation of approaches to performance has led scholars to attempt to cata-
> logue these competing or complementary views. Conquergood for example, has
> argued that performance can be studied as communicative act, aesthetic event,
> method of literary study, and therapeutic resource. Finally, String, Long, and Hop-
> kins have argued that performance can be explored as a site of aesthetic enjoyment,
> intellectual inquiry, affective play, cultural memory, participatory ritual, social com-
> mentary political action or psychological probe (181–204). (1995, xi)

13. While a number of people work with the construction "rhetoric of possibility," my thoughts are informed here by the work of Kirkwood (1992) and Madison (1998).

14. The title of an essay by Maines (2001c).

15. See Cheal (1988, 83).

16. See Maines (2001c, 107).

17. See Carleton (1999, 75).

18. Jensen, Burkholder, and Hammerback state this in another way. They say:

> If mourners are to come to terms with the death, that if they are to understand the
> event and share in a renewed sense of community, transformation must be the key
> eulogistic element or strategy. Indeed two rhetorical transformations are essential
> for eulogies to achieve their purpose . . . the eulogy must first rhetorically alter the
> relationship by acknowledging the death in a straight forward, almost blunt, fashion
> . . . The eulogy must then rhetorically transform the deceased a second time, from
> physical death into spiritual life. (2003, 340)

19. See how Peggy Phelan discusses this (1997, 160).

20. See how McGee discusses this issue about textual analysis (1990, 279).

21. McGee (1990, 279).

22. In addition to this proposition Barthes also states:

(2) The text does not come to a stop with (good) literature; it cannot be appre-
hended as apart of a hierarchy or even as a simple division of genres. . . . (3) Whereas
the Text is approached and experienced in relation to the sign, the work closes itself
on a signified. . . . (4) The Text is plural. . . . (5) The work is caught up in a process
of filiation. . . . (6) The work is ordinarily an object of consumption. . . . (7) Pleasure
[is] associated with the work (at least with certain works). (1979, 75–81)

23. See Pineau (2000, 4).

24. See Hoey (2001, 11).

25. See Langellier (1999, 138).

26. Langellier poses these original questions (1999, 139). The author references
Carlin (1998), "I have to tell you. . . ."

27. In this sense, the shared world is the unitary whole of my family, the
moments of connection, and those moments that individuate and isolate all our
relationships with my father. Hence, the "[d]iscursive production [of writing the
eulogy] must be understood in terms of the multifarious purposes and projects of
specific individuals or groups in specific material circumstances" (Gagnier 1990,
101).

28. This dual orientation is similar to how Yalom references the notion of
"biography-cum-autobiography" and a "group of women who assumed authorial
worth vicariously and wrote from the ostensible position of biography" writing
their life story through the frame and or guise of writing the biographies of their
husbands and fathers (1990, 53). Caroline B. Brettell writes: "The boundaries
among various genres of life-writing and writing about culture are indeed blurred.
Paul Kendall (1965) once suggested that 'any biography uneasily shelters an autobiography within it; there are, perhaps, many ethnographies that shelter autoeth-
nographies within them'" (1997, 245).

29. See Pineau (1992, 97).

30. In reference to the character of "realist fiction," Terry Eagleton offers logic
for my curiosity in what might be an *unreading* of the text that is my father, in
order to entextualize his presence in this eulogy. But this is not a deconstruction
in that structuralist's way in which meaning is transient and arbitrary. Eagleton
states:

In some literary works, in particular realist fiction, our attention as readers is drawn
not to the "act of enunciating," to how something is said, from what kind of position
and with what end in view, but simply to what is said, to the enunciation itself . . .
part of the power of such tests thus lies in their suppression of what might be called
their modes of production, how they got to be what they are; in this sense, they have

a curious resemblance to the life of the human ego, which thrives by repressing the process of its own making. (1983, 170)

31. The title of an essay, Maines (1978a). Maines and Couch state: "The social acts that people produce through symbolically presenting and representing themselves and others must involve a level of conventionalization if there are to be any guarantees to society" (1998, 8).

32. Scott Dillard (2000) speaks to the notion of *performance as memorial* as he moves toward the building of a "useful queer mythology."

33. Eugene Vance defines *commemoration* as "any gesture, ritualized or not, whose end is to recover, in the name of collectivity, some being or even either anterior in time or outside of time in order to fecundate, animate, or make meaningful a moment in the present" (1979, 374–375).

34. In developing his notion of a useful queer mythology, Scott Dillard cites Andrew Ramer's (1998) construct of the "Stand Between People." Suggesting the social positionality of gay people, Ramer states: "We stand between genders. We stand between the living and the dead. We stand between night and day. We stand between matter and spirit. Our job is to scout that terrain for the main body of the tribe, and to bring back all that information for the main body of the tribe."

35. In a footnote Jamieson and Campbell (1982, 147) offer a reference to Jamieson (1978, 40–42).

36. Carl Cates suggests an alternative methodological approach to constructing a eulogy: The introduction acknowledges the occasion for the gathering, acknowledges family members by name and mentions friends. The main text has three considerations: memories, consolation, and the record or the reading of the official obituary. The conclusion seeks to focus on positive attributes of the deceased on which the audience can reflect and emulate (1992, 85–86).

37. See Jamieson and Campbell (1982, 147).

38. Here I am also making an allusion to Park-Fuller's discussion of "speaking the truth" as it relates to testimony and autobiographical performance (2000, 26–29).

39. For a practical comparison, as well as a means of extending these logics, I offer Park-Fuller's delineation of the varying levels of contestation in testimony of autobiographical performance. She states:

> As a performative speech act, the testimony of autobiographical performance involves numerous levels of contestation that, in turn, account for its dramatic power. Contention in autobiographical narrative includes: 1) the struggle to tell and the struggle to create one's self through telling; 2) the struggle to know one's own experience and the struggle to beget the truth of the past and influence the future; 3) the struggle to escape expert mediation (autonomy), the struggle of mediating

(accountability), and the struggle to balance the groups one represents; and 4) the struggle to participate and to distance oneself, and the struggle to embrace and to criticize. (2000, 38)

I find that Park-Fuller's levels of contestation directly parallel the tensiveness in the rhetorical task of performing/delivering a eulogy. It is a systematic and delicate telling and untelling in a public space with multiple mediating accountabilities. In reference to the eulogy, I apply Jamieson's link between a speaker/performer and the audience: "Because the speakers sometimes experience the same need as the audience, it is often impossible to separate the impact of human needs on a speech from the perceived options of the speaker. Nonetheless, it is important to stress the extent to which public address responds to and shapes the needs of the audience" (1978, 42).

40. These are excerpted and transcribed comments from a paper presented by Mae G. Henderson at the Black Queer Studies in the Millennium Conference. These excerpts are documented in the review essay of that conference (Alexander 2001, 1297).

41. In this sense I am also interested in the manner in which Richard Bauman signals discussions on metanarration—as "devices that index or comment on the narrative itself (such as its message, generic form or function, and discourse) or on the components or conduct of the storytelling event (including participants, organization, and action) (Babcock 1977 [1984])" (1988, 98).

42. See Gaggi (1997, 62).

43. I write about the death of my brother from AIDS in Alexander (2000b).

44. The title of a book by Maine (2001a).

45. See Maines (2001a, xv).

46. See Condit (1985, 288).

47. In "Narrative, Gender, and the Problematics of Role," in *The Faultline of Consciousness*, Maines suggests that men "talk their way into their social roles, and they search for authenticity in the identities that their stories contain" (2001a).

48. Here I am making an allusion to the book with the same title by Carolyn Ellis (1995).

49. The lyrics written throughout this eulogy are taken from the song entitled "We Fall Down" by Kyle Matthews, used here with the special permission of Marty Wheeler at Brentwood-Benson Music Publishing. Bob Carlisle, Donnie McClurkin, and Mark Lowry recorded the song, and McClurkin's recording earned Kyle a Dove Award for Traditional Gospel Recorded Song of the Year, Stellar Award for Song of the Year, and ASCAP's 2002 award for Gospel Song of the Year. In the reprise to the song as performed by Donnie McClurkin on his *Live in London and More . . .* CD, McClurkin references the significance of the song title and theme:

The Bible says in Proverbs 24:18, a just man, a just man falleth seven times, but rises back up again. Now what makes him just, we in the church would call him wicked. But he falls once, but seven times? What makes him just from the Bible's standpoint—is that he can get back up and not only just get back up, but get back in line. No matter where you've fallen from, no matter what you've done and no matter how many times you've done it, it's not too late . . . God is still faithful and just— even when we're unfaithful and unjust. He is so faithful and just that he would forgive of every single solitary sin.

50. This title is an allusion to ideas expressed in Maines (1978b).

51. Della Pollock (1999) uses this construction to describe a project in re-performing oral histories. I use variations of this construction throughout this essay.

52. Ellis and Bochner write that the act of telling "bridges the dominions of public and private . . . [and] become[s] a social process for making lived experience understandable and meaningful" for self and others (1992, 79–80).

53. I attribute aspects of this construction to Turner Steckline in a personal discussion exchange during our time in the doctoral program at Southern Illinois University, Carbondale.

54. The title of an essay by Maines (1978b).

55. Maybe, as Dwight Conquergood describes the work of Zora Neal Hurston, I have tried to "foreground the terrain of struggle, the field of power relations on which texts are written, exchanged, and read" (1998, 30).

56. In extending the logics of Condit (1985), and in building their argument for the eulogy as a tool for building martyrs, Jensen, Burkholder and Hammerback state: "In appealing for action the eulogist calls for the completion of tasks that the deceased had started or supported and asks the audience to accept beliefs or values that were held by the deceased" (2003, 340). Within the context of the eulogy for my mother, I call on this feature and on the strategy of epideictic speech to encourage, support, and challenge my siblings to live in ways worthy of our mother's wishes.

57. This is a title of a Maines (1989) essay.

References

Abler, R. F., Marcus, M. G. and Olson, J. M. (1992). *Geography's inner worlds: Pervasive themes in contemporary American geography.* New Brunswick, NJ: Rutgers University Press.

Adler, P. A. and Adler, P. (1998). Observational techniques. In N. K. Denzin and Y. S. Lincoln (Eds.), *Collecting and interpreting qualitative materials* (pp. 79–109). Thousand Oaks, CA: Sage.

Aerni, A. L. (1999). *Valuing us all: Feminist pedagogy and economics.* Ann Arbor: University of Michigan Press.

Ajwang', R. O. and Edmondson, L. (2003). Love in the time of dissertations: An ethnographic tale. *Qualitative Inquiry* 9.3: 466–480.

Alexander, B. K. (1998). Performing culture in the classroom: An instructional (auto)ethnography of black male teacher/student negotiations of culture. Unpublished dissertation, Southern Illinois University.

Alexander, B. K. (1999). Performing culture in the classroom: An instructional (auto)ethnography. *Text and Performance Quarterly* 19: 271–306.

Alexander, B. K. (2000a). Skin flint (or, The garbage man's kid): A generative autobiographical performance. *Text and Performance Quarterly* 20: 97–114.

Alexander, B. K. (2000b). Standing at the crossroads. In E. Danitcat (Ed.), *The Beacon best of 2000: Great writing by women and men of all colors and cultures* (pp. 172–176). Boston: Beacon.

Alexander, B. K. (2001). Reflections, riffs, and remembrances: The Black Queer Studies in the Millennium conference (2000). In *Callaloo: A Journal of African-American and African Arts and Letters* 23.4: 1283–1305.

Alexander, B. K. (2002). Performing culture and cultural performances in Japan: A critical (auto)ethnographic travelogue. *Theatre Annual: A Journal of Performance Studies* 55: 1–28.

Alexander, B. K. (2003a). Revisioning the ethnographic site: Interpretive ethnography as a method of pedagogical reflexivity and scholarly production. *Qualitative Inquiry* 9.3: 416–441.

Alexander, B. K. (2003b). Fading, twisting, and weaving: An interpretive ethnography of the black barbershop as cultural space. *Qualitative Inquiry* 9.1: 101–128.

Alexander, B. K. (2004a). Racializing identity: Performance, pedagogy, and regret. *Cultural Studies↔Critical Methodologies* 4.1: 12–27.

Alexander, B. K. (2004b). Passing, cultural performance, and individual agency: Performative reflections on black masculine identity. *Cultural Studies↔Critical Methodologies* 4.3: 377–404.

Alexander, B. K. (2004c). Black skin/white masks: The performative sustainability of whiteness (with apologies to Frantz Fanon). *Qualitative Inquiry* 10.5: 647–672.

Alexander, B. K. (2005). Embracing the teachable moment: The black gay body in the classroom as embodied text. In E. P. Johnson and M. G. Henderson (Eds.), *Black queer studies: A critical anthology* (pp. 249–265). Durham, NC: Duke University Press.

Altheide, D. L. and Johnson, J. M. (1998). Criteria for assessing interpretive validity in qualitative research. In N. K. Denzin and Y. S. Lincoln (Eds.), *Collecting and interpreting qualitative materials* (pp. 288–312). Thousand Oaks, CA: Sage.

Althusser, L. (1971). *Lenin and philosophy, and other essays*, tr. B. Brewester. London: New Left.

Anderson, B. (1991). *Imagined communities: Reflections on the origin and spread of nationalism.* New York: Verso.

Anderson, D. J. (1989). Deconstruction: Critical strategy/strategic criticism. In G. D. Atkins and L. Morrow (Eds.), *Contemporary literary theory* (pp. 137–157). Amherst: University of Massachusetts Press.

Anscombe, G. E. M. and von Wright, G. H. (1967, 1970). *Zettel: Ludwig Wittgenstein.* Berkeley: University of California Press.

Anzaldúa, G. (1987). *Borderlands/La frontera: The new mestiza.* San Francisco: Spinsters/Aunt Lute.

Aoki, D. S. (2004). True love stories. *Cultural Studies↔Critical Methodologies* 4.1: 97–111.

Aronowitz, S. and Giroux, H. (1991). *Postmodern education: Politics, culture, and social criticism.* Minneapolis: University of Minnesota Press.

Arrizón, A. (2000). Mythical performativity: Relocating Aztlán in Chicana feminist cultural production. *Theatre Journal* 52: 23–49.

Atkinson, P. and Hammersley, M. (1998). Ethnography and participant observation. In N. K. Denzin and Y. S. Lincoln (Eds.), *Strategies of qualitative inquiry* (pp. 110–136). Thousand Oaks, CA: Sage.

Augustine, Saint (1963). *The confessions.* New York: New American Library.

Austin, J. L. (1962). *How to do things with words.* New York: Oxford University Press.

Awkward, M. (1995). *Negotiating difference: Race, gender, and the politics of positionality.* Chicago: University of Chicago Press.

Azevedo, J. (1997). *Mapping reality: An evolutionary realist methodology for the natural and social sciences.* New York: State University of New York Press.

Babcock, B. (1984). The story in the story: Metanarration in folk narrative. In R. Bauman (Ed.), *Verbal art as performance* (pp. 61–79). Prospect Heights, IL: Waveland.

Bacon, W. A. (1979). *The art of interpretation,* 3rd edition. New York: Holt, Rinehart and Winston.

Bacon, W. A. (1996). The dangerous shore—one last time. *Text and Performance Quarterly* 16: 356–358.

Baker, H. (2001). *Critical memory: Public sphere, African American writing, and black fathers and sons in America.* Athens: University of Georgia Press.

Baker, R. (1994). *Drag: A history of female impersonation in the performing arts.* New York: New York University Press.

Bal, M. (1996). *Double exposures: The subject of cultural analysis.* New York: Routledge.

Baldwin, J. (1985). *Price of the ticket.* New York: St. Martin's.

Baldwin, J. (1993). The choices of Hercules. In W. J. Bennett (Ed.), *The book of virtues* (pp. 390–392). New York: Simon and Schuster.

Banks, I. (2000). *Hair matters: Beauty, power, and black women's consciousness.* New York: New York University Press.

Banks, W. M. (1996). *Black intellectuals.* New York: Norton.

Barry, P. (1987). *Issues in contemporary literary theory.* London: MacMillan.

Barthes, R. (1978). *A lover's discourse.* New York: Hill and Wang.

Barthes, R. (1979). From work to text. In J. V. Harari (Ed.), *Textual strategies: Perspectives in post-structuralist criticism* (pp. 73–81). Ithaca, NY: Cornell University Press.

Bateson, G. P. and Bateson, M. C. (1987). *Angel's fear: Towards an epistemology of the sacred.* New York: Macmillan.

Bauman, R. (1977). *Verbal art as performance.* Rowley, MA: Newbury House.

Bauman, R. (1988). *Story, performance, and event: Contextual studies or oral narrative.* Cambridge, UK: Cambridge University Press.

Bauman, R. (1992). Performance. In *Folklore, cultural performances, and popular entertainments: A communication-centered handbook* (pp. 41–49). New York: Oxford University Press.

Behar, R. (1996). *The vulnerable observer: Anthropology that breaks your heart.* Boston: Beacon.

Bell, D., Binne, J., Cream, J. and Valentine, G. (1994). All hyped up and no place to go. *Gender, Place, and Culture* 1: 31–37.

Bell, E. (1995). Toward a pleasure-centered economy: Wondering a feminist aesthetics of performance. *Text and Performance Quarterly* 15: 99–121.

Bell, E. (1999). Weddings and pornography: The cultural performance of sex. *Text and Performance Quarterly* 19.3: 173–195.

Belsey, C. (1980). *Critical practice.* New York: Routledge.

Belton, D. (1995). *Speak my name: Black men on masculinity and the American dream.* Boston: Beacon.

Berry, J. W., Poortinga, Y. H., Segall, M. H. and Dansen, P. R. (1992). *Cross-cultural psychology: Research and application.* New York: Cambridge University Press.

Berry, W. (1977). *The unsettling of America: Culture and agriculture.* New York: Avon.

Bhabha, H. K. (1994). *The location of culture.* New York: Routledge.

Bhabha, H. K. (1996). Aura and agora: On negotiating rapture and speaking between. In R. Francis (Ed.), *Negotiating rapture: The power of art to transform lives.* Chicago: Museum of Contemporary Art.

Blau, H. (1992). Ideology, performance, and the illusions of demystification. In J. G. Reinelt and J. R. Roach (Eds.), *Critical theory and performance* (pp. 430–445). Ann Arbor: University of Michigan Press.

Bliss, S. B. (2002). Needles and pins. *Camerawork* 229.2: 24–31.

Blocker, J. (1999). *Where is Ana Mendieta?* Durham, NC: Duke University Press.

Bly, R. (1990). *Iron John: A book about men.* Reading, MA: Addison Wesley.

Boal, A. (1985). *Theatre of the oppressed.* New York: Theatre Communication Group.

Bourdieu, P. (1977). *Outline of a theory of practice,* tr. R. Nice. Cambridge, UK: Cambridge University Press.

Bourdieu, P. (1994). A reflecting story. In M. S. Roth (Ed.), *Rediscovering history: Culture, politics, and the psyche* (pp. 371–377). Stanford, CA: Stanford University Press.

Bourdieu, P. and Passerson, J. (1992). *Reproduction in education, society, and culture.* London: Sage.

Bourdieu, P. and Wacquant, L. (1992). *An invitation to reflexive sociology.* Cambridge: Polity.

Bowman, G. (1997). Identifying versus identifying with "the other": Reflections on the siting of the subject in anthropological discourse. In A. James, J. Hockey and A. Dawson (Eds.), *After writing culture: Epistemology and praxis in contemporary anthropology* (pp. 34–50). London: Routledge.

Bowman, M. B. (1998). Performing southern history for the tourist gaze: Antebellum home tour guide performances. In D. Pollock (Ed.), *Exceptional spaces: Essays in performance and history* (pp. 142–158). Chapel Hill: University of North Carolina Press.

Boykin, K. (1996). *One more river to cross: Black and gay in America.* New York: Doubleday.

Brady, H. (1995). *Schooling young children: A feminist pedagogy for liberatory learning.* New York: State University of New York Press. Also available at www.net .library.com/reader.

Brameld, T. and Matsuyama, M. (1978). *Tourism as cultural learning: Two controversial case studies in educational anthropology.* Washington, DC: University Press of America.

Brettell, C. B. (Ed.). (1993). *When they read what we write.* Westport, CT: Bergin and Garvey.

Brettell, C. B. (1997). Blurred genres and blended voices: Life story, biography, autobiography, and the auto/ethnography of women's lives. In D. E. Reed-Danahay (Ed.), *Auto/ethnography: Rewriting the self and the social* (pp. 223–246). New York: Berg/Oxford International.

Britzman, D. P., Santiago-Válles, K., Jiménez-Múñoz, G. and Lamash, L. M. (1993). Slips that show and tell: Fashioning multicultural as a problem of representation. In C. McCarthy and W. Crichlow (Eds.), *Race, identity, and representation in education* (pp. 188–200). New York: Routledge.

Broadhurst, S. (1999). *Liminal acts: A critical overview of contemporary performance and theory.* London and New York: Cassell.

Brodkey, L. (1987). Writing critical ethnographic narratives. *Anthropology and Education Quarterly* 18.2: 67–76.

Brody, J. D. (1995). Hyphen-nations. In S. E. Case, P. Brett and S. L. Foster (Eds.), *Cruising the performative: Interventions into the representation of ethnicity, nationality, and sexuality* (pp. 149–162). Bloomington: Indiana University Press.

Brown, M. (2000). *Closet space: Geographies of metaphor from the body to the globe.* New York: Routledge.

Brubach, H. (1999). *Girlfriend: Men, women, and drag,* with photographs by M. J. O'Brien. New York: Random House.

Bruno, G. (1993). Spectatorial embodiment: Anatomies of the visible and the female Bodyscape. In *Streetwalking on a ruined map: Cultural theory and the city films of Elvira Notari* (pp. 58–76). Princeton, NJ: Princeton University Press.

Buraway, M., A. Burton, A. A. Ferguson, H. J. Fox, J. Gamson, N. Gatrell, L. Hurst, C. Hurzman, L. Salzinger, J. Schiffman and S. Ui (Eds.). (1991). *Ethnography unbound: Power and resistance in the modern metropolis.* Berkeley: University of California Press.

Burgoon, J. K. (1994). Nonverbal signals. In M. L. Knapp and G. R. Miller (Eds.), *Handbook of interpersonal communication,* 2nd edition (pp. 229–285). Thousand Oaks, CA: Sage.

Burke, K. (1945). *A grammar of motives.* New York: Prentice Hall.

Butler, J. (1990a). *Gender trouble: Feminism and the subversion of identity.* New York: Routledge.

Butler, J. (1990b). Performative acts and gender constitution: An essay in phenomenology and feminist theory. In S. E. Case (Ed.), *Performing feminisms: Feminist critical theory and theatre* (pp. 270–282). Baltimore: Johns Hopkins University Press.

Butler, J. (1993). *Bodies that matter: On the discursive limits of "sex."* New York: Routledge.

Butler, J. (1995). Contingent foundations. In S. Benhabib, J. Butler, D. Cornell and N. Fraser (Eds.), *Feminist contentions* (pp. 35–57). New York: Routledge.

Byrd, A. and Tharps, L. L. (2001). *Hair story: Untangling the roots of black hair in America.* New York: St. Martin's.

Caftanzoglou, R. (2001). The shadow of the sacred rock: Contrasting discourses of place under the Acropolis. In B. Bender and M. Winer (Eds.), *Contested landscapes: Movement, exile, and place* (pp. 21–35). New York: Berg.

Carbaugh, D. (1990). Intercultural communication. In D. Carbaugh (Ed.), *Cultural communication and intercultural contact* (pp. 151–175). Hillsdale, NJ: Erlbaum.

Carilli, T. (1997, November). Captivity, or the last time I saw Eileen. Paper presented at the meeting of the National Communication Association, Chicago, IL.

Carleton, J. M. (1999). Embodying autobiography: A Lesbian performance of gay male performance art. *Women and Performance: A Journal of Feminist Theory* 19.10: 1–2, 73–83.

Carlin, P. S. (1998). "I have to tell you . . .": The unfolding of personal stories in life performance. In S. J. Dailey (Ed.), *The future of performance studies: Visions and revisions* (pp. 226–231). Annandale, VA: National Communication Association.

Carlson, M. (1996). *Performance: A critical introduction.* New York: Routledge.

Carter, K. (1993). The place of story in the study of teaching and teacher education. *Educational Researcher* 22.1: 5–12.

Case, S. E., P. Brett and S. Foster (Eds.). (1995). *Cruising the performative.* Bloomington: Indiana University Press.

Casey, E. S. (2001). Body, self, and landscape: A geophilosophical inquiry into the place-world. In P. C. Adams, S. Hoelscher and K. E. Till (Eds.), *Textures of place: Exploring humanist geographies* (pp. 403–425). Minneapolis: University of Minnesota Press.

Cates, C. (1992). Eulogies as a special occasion speech. In S. E. Lucas (Ed.), *Selections from the speech communication teacher, 1994–1996* (pp. 85–86). Boston: McGraw-Hill.

Caughie, P. L. (1999). *Passing and pedagogy: The dynamics of responsibility.* Urbana: University of Illinois Press.

Certeau, M. (1984). *The practice of everyday life*, tr. S. Rendall. Berkeley: University of California Press.

Certeau, M., Giard, L. and Mayol, P. (1998). *The practice of everyday life.* Volume 2: *Living and cooking*, tr. T. J. Tomasik. Minneapolis: University of Minnesota Press.

Chansky, D. (1999). Memory, manhood, management, and "mentalities": The C.C.C. murder mystery and its audience. *Text and Performance Quarterly* 19: 332–354.

Cheal, D. J. (1988). Relationships in time: Ritual, social structure, and the life. *Studies in Symbolic Interaction* 9: 83–109.

Chesebro, J. W. (1998). Performance studies as paradox, culture, and manifesto: A future orientation. In S. J. Dailey (Ed.), *The future of performance studies: Visions and revisions* (pp. 310–319). Annandale, VA: National Communication Association.

Christian, K. (1997). *Show and tell: Identity as performance in US Latina/o fiction.* Albuquerque: University of New Mexico Press.

Christians, C. (1998). The sacredness of life. *Media Development* 2: 3–7.

Clark, A. H. (1962). Praemia geographiae: The incidental rewards of a professional career. *Annals of the Association of American Geographers* 52: 229–241.

Clifford, J. (1983). On ethnographic authority. *Representations* 1.2: 118–146.

Clifford, J. (1986). Introduction. In J. Clifford and G. E. Marcus (Eds.), *Writing culture: The poetics and politics of ethnography* (pp. 1–17). Berkeley: University of California Press.

Clifford, J. (1988). *The predicament of culture: Twentieth-century ethnography, literature, and art.* Cambridge, MA: Harvard University Press.

Clough, P. T. (1994). *Feminist thought: Desire, power, and academic discourse.* Cambridge, MA: Blackwell.

Coffey, A. and Delamont, S. (2000). *Feminism and the classroom teacher: Research, praxis, and pedagogy.* Philadelphia: Taylor and Francis.

Cohee, G. E., E. Daumen, T. D. Kemp, P. M. Krebs, S. A. Lafky and S. Runzo (Eds.). (1998). *The feminist teacher anthology: Pedagogic and classroom strategy*. New York: Teachers College Press.

Cohen, E. G. (1982). Expectation states and interracial interaction in school settings. *Annual Reviews of Sociology* 8: 209–235.

Cohn, M. (1995). *Do what I say: Ms. Behavior's guide to gay and lesbian etiquette*. New York: Houghton Mifflin.

Cole, E. R. and Omari, S. R. (2003). Race, class, and the dilemmas of upward mobility for African Americans. *Journal of Social Issues* 59.4: 785–802.

Collier, M. J., Hedge, R., Lee, W., Nakayama, T. and Yep, G. (2001). Dialogue on the edges: Ferment in communication and culture. *International and Intercultural Communication Annual* 24: 219–280.

Condit, C. M. (1985). The functions of epideictic: The Boston massacre orations as exemplar. *Communication Quarterly* 33: 284–299.

Conquergood, D. (1983). A sense of the other: Interpretation and ethnographic research. In I. Crouch and G. Owen (Eds.), *Proceedings of the Seminar/Conference on Oral Traditions* (pp. 148–155). Las Cruces: New Mexico University.

Conquergood, D. (1986). Performing cultures: Ethnography, epistemology, and ethics. In E. Siembeck (Ed.), *Miteinander Sprechen and Handelm: Festschrift fur Hellmut Geissner* (pp. 55–66). Frankfurt, Germany: Scriptor.

Conquergood, D. (1988). Health theatre in a Hmong refugee camp: Performance, communication, and culture. *TDR: A Journal of Performance Studies* 32.3: 174–208.

Conquergood, D. (1989). Poetics, play, process, and power: The performative turn in anthropology. *Text and Performance Quarterly* 9: 82–88.

Conquergood, D. (1991). Rethinking ethnography: Towards a critical cultural politics. *Communication Monographs* 58: 179–194.

Conquergood, D. (1992a). Ethnography, rhetoric, and performance. *Quarterly Journal of Speech* 78: 80–97.

Conquergood, D. (1992b). Fabricating culture: The textile art of Hmong refugee women. In E. C. Fine and J. H. Speer (Eds.), *Performance, culture, and identity* (pp. 207–248). Westport, CT: Praeger.

Conquergood, D. (1994). Gang communication and cultural space. In L. R. Frey (Ed.), *Group communication in context: Studies in natural groups* (pp. 23–55). Hillsdale, NJ: Erlbaum.

Conquergood, D. (1998). Beyond the text: Towards a performative cultural politics. In S. Dailey (Ed.), *The future of performance studies* (pp. 25–36). Annandale, VA: National Communication Association.

Conquergood, D. (2002). Performance studies: Interventions and radical research. *The Drama Review* 46.2: 145–156.

Cooks, L. M. (1998). Warriors, wampum, gaming, and glitter: Foxwoods Casino and the re-presentation of (post)modern native identity. In J. N. Martin, T. K. Nakayama and L. A. Flores (Eds.), *Readings in cultural contexts* (pp. 226–235). Mountain View, CA: Mayfield.

Corey, F. C. (Ed.). (1993). *HIV education: Performing personal narratives.* Proceedings of a conference funded by the U.S. Centers for Disease Control and Prevention and Arizona State University. Tempe, AZ.

Corey, F. C. (1998). The personal: Against the master narrative. In S. J. Dailey (Ed.), *The future of performance studies: Visions and revisions* (pp. 249–253). Annandale, VA: National Communication Association.

Corey, F. C. and Nakayama, T. K. (1997). Sextext. *Text and Performance Quarterly* 17: 58–68. Discussion of this essay archived at: www.natcom.org/Publications /CRTNET%20News/home.htm.

Couclelis, H. (1992). Location, place, region, and space. In R. F. Abler, M. G. Marcus and J. M. Olson (Eds.), *Geography's inner worlds: Pervasive themes in contemporary American geography* (pp. 215–233). New Brunswick, NJ: Rutgers University Press.

Crang, M. (1998). *Cultural geography.* New York: Routledge.

Crary, J. (1999). *Techniques of the observer: On vision and modernity in the nineteenth century.* Cambridge, MA: MIT Press.

Crouch, D. (Ed.). (1999). *Leisure/tourism geographies: Practices and geographical knowledge.* London: Routledge.

Culler, J. (1988). *Framing the sign: Criticism and its institutions.* Norman: University of Oklahoma Press.

Curry, M. (2001). The fragmented individual and the academic realm. In P. C. Adams, S. Hoelscher and K. E. Hill (Eds.), *Textures of place: Exploring humanist geographies* (pp. 207–220). Minneapolis: University of Minnesota Press.

Cutter, M. J. (1996). Sliding significations: Passing as a narrative and textual strategy in Nella Larsen's fiction. In E. K. Ginsberg (Ed.), *Passing and the fictions of identity* (pp. 75–100). Durham, NC: Duke University Press.

Dann, G. M. S. (1996). *The language of tourism: A sociolinguistic perspective.* Oxford: Cab International.

Darder, A. (1991). *Culture and power in the classroom: A critical foundation for bicultural education.* New York: Bergin and Garvey.

Davis, T. M. (1994). Succeeding with passing. In *Nella Larsen novelist of the Harlem renaissance: A woman's life unveiled* (pp. 287–330). Baton Rouge: Louisiana State University Press.

Deats, S. M. and Lenker, L. T. (1994). *Gender and academe: Feminist pedagogy and politics.* Lanham, MD: Rowman & Littlefield.

De Castell, M. and M. Bryson (Eds.). (1997). *Radical in(ter)ventions: Identity, politics, and differences in educational praxis.* New York: State University of New York Press.

Deloria, P. J. (1998). *Playing Indian.* New Haven, CT: Yale University Press.

Denzin, N. K. (1970). *The research act.* Chicago: Aldine.

Denzin, N. K. (1997). *Interpretive ethnography: Ethnographic practices for the 21st century.* Thousand Oaks, CA: Sage.

Denzin, N. K. (1999). Interpretive ethnography for the next century. *Journal of Contemporary Ethnography* 28.5: 510–519.

Denzin, N. K. and Lincoln, Y. S. (1998). Introduction: Entering the field of qualitative research. In N. K. Denzin and Y. S. Lincoln (Eds.), *Strategies of qualitative inquiry* (pp. 1–34). Thousand Oaks, CA: Sage.

Derrida, J. (1976). *Of grammatology,* tr. Gayatri Chakravorty Spivak. Baltimore: Johns Hopkins University Press.

Desmond, J. C. (1999). *Staging tourism: Bodies on display from Waikiki to Sea World.* Chicago: University of Chicago Press.

Diawara, M. (1993). Black studies, cultural studies: Performative acts. In C. McCarthy and W. Crichlow (Eds.), *Race, identity, and representation in education* (pp. 262–267). New York: Routledge.

Dillard, S. (1997). Pass, passing, and making passes. A paper presented at the Central States Communication Association.

Dillard, S. (2000). Breathing Darrell: Solo performance as a contribution to a useful queer mythology. *Text and Performance Quarterly* 20: 74–83.

Dirac, P. A. M. (1996). General theory of relativity. Princeton, NJ: Princeton University Press.

Dolan, J. (1991). *The feminist spectator as critic.* Ann Arbor: University of Michigan Press.

Dolan, J. (1992). Practicing cultural disruptions: Gay and lesbian representation and sexuality. In J. G. Reinelt and J. R. Roach (Eds.), *Critical theory and performance* (pp. 263–275). Ann Arbor: University of Michigan Press.

Dolan, J. (1993). Desire cloaked in a trenchcoat. In *Presence and desire: Essays on gender, sexuality, performance* (pp. 121–134). Ann Arbor: University of Michigan Press.

Douglass, F. (1845). *Narrative of the life of Frederick Douglass, an American slave,* ed. and intro. H. Baker, 1982. Harmondsworth, UK: Penguin.

Doxtader, E. (2001). Loving history's fate, perverting the beautiful soul: Scenes of felicity's potential. *Cultural Studies* 15: 206–221.

Dreyfus, H. and Rabinow, P. (1982). *Michel Foucault: Beyond structuralism and hermeneutics.* Brighton, UK: Harvester.

Dubois, W. E. B. (1903, 1982). *The souls of black folks.* New York: Signet/NAL Penguin.

Durkheim, E. (1984). *The division of labor in society*, tr. W. D. Halls. New York: Free Press.

Dyson, M. E. (1993). The plight of black men. In M. E. Dyson (Ed.), *Reflecting black: African-American cultural criticism* (pp. 182–194). Minneapolis: University of Minnesota Press.

Dyson, M. E. (1996). *Between God and gangsta rap: Bearing witness to black culture.* New York: Oxford University Press.

Dyson, M. E. (1996). The lives of black men. In M. E. Dyson (Ed.), *Between god and gansta rap: Bearing witness to black culture* (pp. 68–71). Oxford: Oxford University Press.

Dyson, M. E. (2003). *Open Mike: Reflections on philosophy, race, sex, culture, and religion.* New York: Basic.

Dyson, M. E. (2004). Between apocalypse and redemption: John Singleton's *Boyz N the Hood*. In *The Michael Eric Dyson reader* (pp. 327–334). New York: Basic Civitas.

Eagleton, T. (1983). *Literary theory.* Minneapolis: University of Minnesota Press.

Eagleton, T. (1993). It is not quite true that I have a body, and not quite true that I am one either. *London Review of Books* 15.10: 7–8.

Ellis, C. (1993). Telling a story of sudden death. *Sociological Quarterly* 34: 711–773.

Ellis, C. (1995). *Final negotiations.* Philadelphia: Temple University Press.

Ellis, C. (1996). Maternal connections. In C. Ellis and A. P. Bochner (Eds.), *Composing ethnography: Alternative forms of qualitative writing* (pp. 240–243). Walnut Creek, CA: Alta Mira.

Ellis, C. and Bochner, A. P. (1992). Telling and performing personal stories: The Constraints of choice in abortion. In C. Ellis and M. G. Flaherty (Eds.), *Investigating subjectivity: Research on lived experience* (pp. 79–101). Newbury Park, CA: Sage.

Ellis, C. and Bochner, A. P. (2000). Autoethnography, personal narrative, reflexivity: Researchers as subject. In N. K. Denzin and Y. S. Lincoln (Eds.), *Handbook of qualitative research*, 2nd edition (pp. 733–768). Thousand Oaks, CA: Sage.

Ellis, C. and A. P. Bochner (Eds.). (1996). *Composing ethnography: Alternative forms of qualitative writing.* Walnut Creek, CA: Alta Mira.

Ellis, C. and Bochner, A. P. (2002). *Ethnographically speaking: Autoethnography, literature, and aesthetics.* Walnut Creek, CA: Alta Mira.

Ellison, R. (1946, 1995). *Invisible man.* New York: Vintage.

Epstein, D. and Sears, J. T. (1999). *A dangerous knowing: Sexuality, pedagogy, and popular culture.* London: Cassell.

Erickson, F. (1986). Qualitative methods in research on teaching. In M. C. Wittrock (Ed.), *Handbook of research on teaching*, 3rd edition (pp. 119–161). New York: Macmillan.

Erickson, K. F. (1967). A comment on disguised observation in sociology. *Social Problems* 14: 366–373.

Esposito, J. (2003). The performance of white masculinity in *Boys Don't Cry*: Identity, desire, (mis)recognition. *Cultural Studies↔Critical Methodologies* 3.2: 229–241.

Evans, N. (1992). *Hairlocking: Everything you need to know, African, dreads and nubian locks*. New York: New Bein' Enterprises.

Fabien, J. (1983). *Time and the other: How anthropology makes it object*. New York: Columbia University Press.

Fabien, J. (1990). *Power and performance: Ethnographic explorations through proverbial wisdom and theater in Shaba, Zaire*. Madison: University of Wisconsin Press.

Fine, E. C. and J. H. Speer (Eds.). (1992). *Performance, culture, and identity*. Westport, CT: Praeger.

Fine, M. (1997). Witnessing whiteness. In M. Fine, L. Weis, L. C. Powell and L. M. Wong (Eds.), *Off white: Readings on race, power, and society* (pp. 57–65). New York: Routledge.

Fish, S. (1980). *Is there a text in this class?* Cambridge: Harvard University Press.

Fiske, J. (1987). British cultural studies and television. In R. C. Allen (Ed.), *Channels of discourse reassembled: Television and contemporary criticism* (pp. 284–326). Chapel Hill and London: University of North Carolina Press.

Fong, M. and McKewen, K. D. (2004). Cultural and intercultural speech uses and meanings of the term nigga. In M. Fong and R. Chuang (Eds.), *Communicating ethnic and cultural identity* (pp. 165–178). Lanham, MD: Rowman & Littlefield.

Foucault, M. (1972). *The archeology of knowledge*, tr. A. M. Sheridan Smith. London: Tavistock.

Foucault, M. (1975/1977/1979). *Discipline and punish: The birth of the prison*, tr. Alan Sheridan. New York: Vintage/Random.

Foucault, M. (1978). *The history of sexuality*. Volume 1: *An Introduction*, tr. R. Hurley. Harmondsworth, UK: Penguin.

Foucault, M. (1984). *The Foucault reader*, ed. P. Rabinow. New York: Pantheon.

Franklin, A. (2003). *Tourism*. Thousand Oaks, CA: Sage.

Fraser, N. (1994). Rethinking the public sphere: A contribution to the critique of actually existing democracy. In A. Giroux and P. McLaren (Eds.), *Between borders: Pedagogy and the politics of cultural* (pp. 74–98). New York: Routledge.

Freedman, E. (1998). Producing (queer) communities: Public access cable TV in the USA. In E. C. Geraghty and D. Lusted (Eds.), *The television studies book.* New York: St. Martin's.

Freire, P. (1998). *Teachers as cultural workers: Letter to those who dare teach.* Boulder, CO: Westview.

Frey, M. (1983). *The politics of reality: Essays in feminist theory.* New York: Crossing.

Fridman, L. W. (2000). *Words and witness: Narrative and aesthetic strategies in the representation of the holocaust.* New York: State University of New York Press.

Fuchs, C. T. (1995). Michael Jackson's penis. In S. Case, P. Brett, and S. L. Foster (Eds.), *Cruising the performative: Intervention into the representation of ethnicity, nationality, and sexuality* (pp. 13–33). Bloomington: Indiana University Press.

Fuoss, K. W. (1993). Performance as contestation: An agonistic perspective on the insurgent assembly. *Text and Performance Quarterly* 13: 331–349.

Fuoss, K. W. (1995). "Community" contested, imagined, and performed: Cultural performance, contestation, and community in an organized-labor social drama. *Text and Performance Quarterly* 15: 79–98.

Fuoss, K. (1997). *Striking performances/performing striking.* Jackson: University Press of Mississippi.

Gaggi, S. (1997). *From text to hypertext: Decentering the subject in fiction, film, the visual arts, and electronic media.* Philadelphia: University of Pennsylvania Press.

Gagnier, R. (1990). The literary standard, working-class autobiography, and gender. In S. Bell and M. Yalom (Eds.), *Revealing lives: Autobiography, biography, and gender* (pp. 93–114). New York: State University of New York Press.

Gallie, W. B. (1964). *Philosophy and the historical understanding.* New York: Schocken.

Gallop, J. (1992). Knot a love story. *Yale Journal of Criticism* 5: 209–218.

Gallop, J. (Ed.). (1995). *Pedagogy: The question of impersonation.* Bloomington: Indiana University Press.

Gardner, H. (1999). *Intelligence reframed: Multiple intelligence for the 21st century.* New York: Basic.

Gates, H. L., Jr. (1987). *Figures in black: Words, signs, and the "racial" self.* New York: Oxford University Press.

Gates, H. L., Jr. (1988). *The signifying monkey: A theory of African-American literary criticism.* Oxford: Oxford University Press.

Gathercole, P. (1989). The fetishism of artifacts. In S. M. Pearce (Ed.), *Museum studies in material culture* (pp. 73–81). London: Leicester University Press.

Geertz, C. (1973). *The interpretation of cultures.* New York: Basic.

Geertz, C. (1983). *Local knowledge.* New York: Basic.

Geertz, C. (1988). *Works and lives: The anthropologist as author.* Stanford, CA: Stanford University Press.

Geiger, D. (1973). Poetic realizing as knowing. *Quarterly Journal of Speech* 59: 311–318.

Gellner, E. (1979). *Spectacles and predicaments: Essays in social theory.* Cambridge, UK: Cambridge University Press.

Gersmehl, P. J. and Brown, D. A. (1992). Observation. In R. F. Abler, M. G. Marcus and J. M. Olson (Eds.), *Geography's inner worlds: Pervasive themes in contemporary American geography* (pp. 78–98). New Brunswick, NJ: Rutgers University Press.

Ghoussoub, M. and M. Sinclair-Webb (Eds.). (2000). *Imagined masculinities: Male identity and culture in the modern Middle East.* London: Saqi Books.

Gilman, C. I. (1991). Wordworld. *Fantasy and Science Fiction* June: 33–44.

Gilroy, P. (1995). ". . . To be real": The dissident forms of black expressive culture. In P. Gilroy (Ed.), *Let's get it on: The politics of black performance* (pp. 12–33). Seattle: Bay Press.

Ginsberg, E. K. (1996). *Passing and the fictions of identity.* Durham, NC: Duke University Press.

Giroux, H. A. (1996). Doing cultural studies: Youth and the challenge of pedagogy. In P. Leistyna, A. Woodrum and S. A. Sherblom (Eds.), *Breaking free: The transformative power of critical pedagogy* (pp. 83–108). Cambridge, MA: Harvard Education Review, Reprint Series no. 27.

Giroux, H. (2001). Cultural studies as a performative politics. *Cultural Studies ↔ Critical Methodologies* 1: 5–23.

Gitlin, A. (1994). *Power and method: Political activism and educational research.* New York: Routledge.

Goffman, E. (1959). *The presentation of self in everyday life.* New York: Overlook.

Goldberg, M. and Brown, C. (1999). Be to want I: A performance piece for print. *Women and Performance: A Journal of Feminist Theory* 19.10: 254–275.

Goodhall, H. L. (1994). *Casing a promised land: The autobiography of an organizational detective as cultural ethnographer.* Carbondale: Southern Illinois Press.

Goodhall, H. L. (2000). *Writing the new ethnography.* Boston Way, MD: Alta Mira.

Gordon, D. (1990). The politics of ethnographic authority: Race and writing in the ethnography of Margaret Mead and Zora Neale Hurston. In M. Manganaro (Ed.), *Modernist anthropology: From fieldwork to text* (pp. 146–126). Princeton, NJ: Princeton University Press.

Graburn, N. (1989). Tourism: The sacred journey. In V. Smith (Ed.), *Hosts and guests: The anthropology of tourism* (pp. 21–36). Philadelphia: University of Pennsylvania Press.

Green, H. (1996). Turning the myths of black masculinity inside/out. In B. Thompson and S. Tyagi (Eds.), *Names we call home: Autobiography on racial identity* (pp. 253–264). New York: Routledge.

Green, M. (1996). Cultural studies. In M. Payne (Ed.), *A dictionary of cultural and critical theory*. Oxford, UK: Blackwell.

Griffin, F. J. (1995). *Who set you flowin'? The African-American migration narrative*. Oxford: Oxford University Press.

Grillo, T. and Wildman, S. M. (1995). Obscuring the importance of race: The complication of making comparisons between racism and sexism (or other-isms). In R. Delgado (Ed.), *Critical race theory: The cutting edge* (pp. 564–572). Philadelphia: Temple University Press.

Grossberg, L. (1993). Cultural studies and/in new worlds. In C. McCarthy and W. Crichlow (Eds.), *Race, identity, and representation in education* (pp. 89–105). New York: Routledge.

Grossberg, L. (1994). Introduction. In H. A. Giroux and P. McLaren (Eds.), *Between borders: Pedagogy and the politics of cultural studies* (pp. 1–25). New York: Routledge.

Grossberg, L. (1996). Toward a genealogy of the state of cultural studies. In C. Nelson and D. Parameshwar (Eds.), *Disciplinarity and dissent in cultural studies* (pp. 87–107). New York: Routledge.

Grossberg, L., Nelson, C. and Treichler, P. (1992). *Cultural studies*. New York: Routledge.

Gunaratnam, Y. (2003). *Researching "race" and ethnicity*. London: Sage.

Gunny, T. (1983). An unseen energy swallows space: The space in early film and its relation to American avant-garde film. In J. Fell (Ed.), *Film before Griffith*. Berkeley: University of California Press.

Gunny, T. (1986). The cinema of attraction. *Wide Angle* 8.3–4: 63–70.

Gunny, T. (1989). An aesthetic of astonishment: Early film and the (in)credulous spectator. *Art and Text* 34: 31–45.

Guss, D. M. (2000). *The festive state: Race, ethnicity, and nationalism as cultural performance*. Los Angeles: University of California Press.

Halberstam, J. (1998). *Female masculinity*. Durham, NC: Duke University Press.

Hall, S. (1996). Introduction. In S. Hall, D. Held, D. Hubert and K. Thompson (Eds.), *Modernity and introduction to modern societies* (pp. 596–634). Oxford, UK: Blackwell.

Hall, S. (1997). *Representation: Cultural representations and signifying practice*. Thousand Oaks, CA: Sage.

Hall, S. (1998). Subjects in history: Making diasporic identities. In W. Lubiano, *The house that race built* (pp. 289–299). New York: Vintage.

Hamera, J. (1993). Emotional/theoretical response to HIV education through the performance of personal narratives. In F. C. Corey (Ed.), *HIV education: Performing personal narratives* (pp. 51–60). Proceedings of a conference funded by the U.S. Centers for Disease Control and Prevention and Arizona State University. Tempe, AZ.

Hamera, J. (1995, November). Bye bunheads, little feet and big red: Leaving le studio. Paper presented at the National Meeting of the Speech Communication Association.

Hamera, J. (1999). Editor's Note. *Text and Performance Quarterly* 19.3.

Hamera, J. (2000). The romance of monsters: Theorizing the virtuoso body. *Theatre Topics* 10.2: 145–153.

Haraway, D. (1988). Situated knowledges: The science question in feminism and the privilege of partial perspective. *Feminist Studies* 14.3: 575–599.

Harper, P. B. (1994). *Framing the margins: The social logic of postmodern culture.* Oxford: Oxford University Press.

Harper, P. B. (1996). *Are we not men?* Oxford: Oxford University Press.

Harper, P. B. (1999). *Private affairs: Critical ventures in the culture of social relations.* New York: New York University Press.

Harper, P. B. (1999). Take me home: Location, identity, transnational exchange. In *Private affairs: Critical venture in the culture of social relations* (pp. 125–154). New York: New York University Press.

Harris, J. and Johnson, P. (2001). *Tenderheaded: A comb-bending collection of hair stories.* New York: Washington Square.

Harris, T. (1979). The barbershop in black literature. *Black American Literature Forum* 13.3: 112–118.

Harris-Lacewell, M. V. (2004). Truth and soul: Black talk in the barbershop. In *Barbershops, bibles, and B.E.T.: Everyday talk and black political thought.* Princeton, NJ: Princeton University Press.

Hatab, L. (1992). *Ethics and finitude: Heideggarian contributions to moral philosophy.* Lanham, MD: Rowman & Littlefield.

Heath, S. (1992). Difference. In *The sexual subject.* New York: Routledge.

Heaton, D. (1998). Twenty fragments: The "other" gazing back. *Text and Performance Quarterly* 18.3: 248–261.

Heidegger, M. (1962). *Being and time,* tr. J. Macquarrie and E. Robinson. New York: Harper.

Hemphill, E. (Ed.). (1991). *Brother to brother: New writing by black gay men.* Boston: Alyson.

Hemphill, E. (1992). Tomb of sorrow. In *Ceremonies* (pp. 88–100). San Francisco: Cleis.

Henderson, M. G. (1995). *Borders, boundaries, and frames: Cultural criticism and cultural studies*. New York: Routledge.

Herndon, M. K. and Hirt, J. B. (2004). Black students and their families: What leads to success in college. *Journal of Black Studies* 34.4: 489–513.

Hesford, W. S. Storytelling and the dynamics of feminist teaching. *Feminist Teacher* 5.2: 1–6.

Hilliard, D. N. (2001). Knots of my existence: A One Man Show. An unpublished manuscript performed at the Kleinau Theatre, Southern Illinois University.

Hintzen, P. and J. M. Rahier (Eds.). (2003). *Problematizing blackness: Self-ethnographies by black immigrants to the United States*. New York: Routledge.

Hitchcock, P. (1994). Passing: Henry Green and working-class identity. *Modern Fiction Studies* 40.1: 1–31.

Hoey, M. (2001). *Textual interaction: An introduction to written discourse analysis*. London: Routledge.

Hofstede, G. (1980). *Culture's consequences: International differences in work-related values*. Beverly Hills, CA: Sage.

hooks, b. (1990). *Yearning: Race, gender, and cultural politics*. Boston: South End.

hooks, b. (1992). *Black looks: Race and representation*. New York: Routledge.

hooks, b. (1994a). *Outlaw culture: Resisting representation*. New York: Routledge.

hooks, b. (1994b). *Teaching to transgress: Education as the practice of freedom*. New York: Routledge.

hooks, b. (1994c). Eros, eroticism, and the pedagogical process. In H. A. Giroux and P. McLaren (Eds.), *Between borders: Pedagogy and the politics of cultural studies* (pp. 113–118). New York: Routledge.

hooks, b. (1995a). *Art on my mind*. New York: New Press.

hooks, b. (1995b). Performance practice as a site of opposition. In C. Ugwu (Ed.), *Let's get it on: The politics of black performance* (pp. 210–221). Seattle, WA: Bay.

hooks, b. (1996). The oppositional gaze: Black female spectators. In *Reel to real: Race, sex, and class at the movie* (pp. 197–213). New York: Routledge.

Horwitz, R. P. (1993). Just stories of ethnographic authority. In C. Brettell (Ed.), *When they read what we write* (pp. 132–143). Westport, CT: Bergin and Garvey.

Howes, D. (2003). *Sensual relations: Engaging the sense in culture and social theory*. Ann Arbor: University of Michigan Press.

Huggins, N. I., M. Kilson and D. M. Fox (Eds.). (1971). *Key issues in the African American experience*. Volume 1 (to 1877). San Diego: Harcourt Brace Jovanovich.

Humphreys, L. (1975). *Tearoom trade: Impersonal sex in public places*. New York: Aldine.

Hurston, Z. N. (1942). *Dust tracks on a road*. Philadelphia: Lippincott. (The restored text was published in 1995 by The Library of America. The Harper Perennial edition published 1996, New York: HarperCollins.)

Hurtado, A. and Stewart, A. J. (1997). Through the looking glass: Implication for studying whiteness for feminist methods. In M. Fine, L. Weiss, L. C. Powell and L. M. Wong (Eds.), *Off white: Readings on race, power, and society* (pp. 297–311). New York: Routledge.

Hutchinson, E. O. (1994). *The assassination of the black male*. Los Angeles: Middle Passage.

Ibanez, F. (1997). From confession to dialogue. In S. de Castell and M. Bryson (Eds.), *Radical interventions: Identity, politics, and difference/s in Educational Praxis* (pp. 107–130). New York: State University of New York Press.

Irigaray, L. (1985). *Speculum of the other woman*. Ithaca, NY: Cornell University Press.

Jackson, J. L. (1998). Ethnophysicality, or an ethnography of some body. In M. Guillory and R. C. Green (Eds.), *Soul: Black power, politics, and pleasure* (pp. 172–190). New York: New York University Press.

Jackson, S. (1998). White noises: On performing white, on writing performance. *The Drama Review* 42.1: 49–65.

Jacobs, S. (1994). Language and interpersonal communication. In M. L. Knapp and G. R. Miller (Eds.), *Handbook of interpersonal communication*, 2nd edition (pp. 199–228). Thousand Oaks, CA: Sage.

Jaffe, C. I. (1995). *Public speaking: A cultural perspective*. Belmont, CA: Wadsworth.

Jakobson, R. (1971). Shifters, verbal categories, and the Russian verb. In *Roman Jakobson: Selected Writings*, vol. 2 (pp. 130–147). The Hague: Mouton.

Jamieson, K. H. (1978). *Critical anthology of public speeches*. Chicago: Science Research Associates.

Jamieson, K. H. and Campbell, K. K. (1982). Rhetorical hybrids: Fusions of generic elements. *Quarterly Journal of Speech* 68: 146–157.

Jenkins, R. (1992). *Key sociologists: Pierre Bourdieu*. New York: Routledge.

Jensen, R. J., Burkholder, T. R. and Hammerback, J. C. (2003). Martyrs for a just cause: The eulogies of Cesar Chavez. *Western Journal of Communication* 67.4: 335–356.

Johnson, E. P. (2003a). *Appropriating blackness: Performance the politics of authenticity*. Durham, NC: Duke University Press.

Johnson, E. P. (2003b). Strange fruit: A performance about identity politics. *Theatre Drama Review* 47.2: 88–116.

Johnson, E. P. and Henderson, M. G. (2005). *Black queer studies: A critical anthology*. Durham, NC: Duke University Press.

Jones, C. and Shorter-Gooden, K. (2003). *Shifting: The double lives of Black women*. New York: Harper-Collins.

Kaplan, C. (1998). Resisting autobiography: Out-law genres and transnational feminist subjects. In S. Smith and J. Watson (Eds.), *Women, autobiography, theory: A reader* (pp. 208–216). Madison: University of Wisconsin Press.

Kaplan, E. A. (1997). Afterword: Reversing the gaze, yes: But is racial intersubjective looking possible? In *Looking for the other: Feminism, film, and the imperial gaze* (pp. 292–302). New York: Routledge.

Karamcheti, I. (1995). Caliban in the classroom. In J. Gallop (Ed.), *Pedagogy: The question of impersonation* (pp. 138–146). Bloomington: Indiana University Press.

Karp, I. and Lavine, S. D. (1991). *Exhibiting cultures: The poetics and politics of museum display*. Washington, DC: Smithsonian Institution Press.

Kirshenblatt-Gimblett, B. and Bruner, E. M. (1992). Tourism. In R. Bauman (Ed.), *Folklore, cultural performances, and popular entertainments: A communication-centered handbook* (pp. 300–307). Oxford: Oxford University Press.

Kemp, A. D. (1998). This black body in question. In P. Phelan and J. Lane (Eds.), *The ends of performance* (pp. 116–129). New York: New York University Press.

Kendall, P. M. (1965). *The art of biography*. London: George Allen and Unwin.

Kennedy, G. (1963). *The art of persuasion in ancient Greece*. Princeton, NJ: Princeton University Press.

Kennedy, R. (2002). *Nigger: The strange career of a troublesome word*. New York: Pantheon.

Kenway, J. and Modra, H. (1992). Feminist pedagogy and emancipatory possibilities. In C. Luke and J. Gore (Eds.), *Feminisms and critical pedagogy*. New York: Routledge.

King, M. L., Jr. (2001). I've been to the mountaintop. In C. Carson and K. Shepard (Eds.), *A call to conscience: The landmark speeches of Dr. Martin Luther King, Jr.* (pp. 207–223). New York: Warner.

Kirby, M. (1979). Autoperformance issue: An introduction. *The Drama Review* 23.1: 2.

Kirkwood, W. G. (1992). Narrative and the rhetoric of possibility. *Communication Monographs* 59: 30–47.

Knight, C. G. (1992). Geography's worlds. In R. F. Abler, M. G. Marcus and J. M. Olson (Eds.), *Geography's inner worlds: Pervasive themes in contemporary American geography* (pp. 2–26). New Brunswick, NJ: Rutgers University Press.

Kuhn, A. K. (1990). The "failure" of biography and the triumph of women writing: Bettina von Arnim's *Die Gunderode* and Christa Wolf's *The Quest for Christa T.* In S. G. Bell and M. Yalom (Eds.), *Revealing lives: Autobiography,*

biography, and gender (pp. 13–28). New York: State University of New York Press.

Kurup, S. (1995). In between space. In C. Ugwu (Ed.), *Let's get it on: The politics of black performance* (pp. 34–53). Seattle, WA: Bay.

Lacan, J. (1979). *The four fundamentals concepts of psychoanalysis.* Harmondsworth, UK: Penguin.

Laing, R. D. (1970). *Knots.* New York: Random House.

Landow, G. P. (1992). *Hypertext: The convergence of contemporary critical theory and technology.* Baltimore: Johns Hopkins University Press.

Langellier, K. M. (1989). Personal narrative: Perspectives on theory and research. *Text and Performance Quarterly* 9: 243–276.

Langellier, K. M. (1999). Personal narrative, performance, performativity: Two or three things I know for sure. *Text and Performance Quarterly* 19: 125–144.

Langellier, K. M. and Peterson, E. (1992). Spinstorying: An analysis of women storytelling. In E. Fine and J. H. Speer (Eds.), *Performance, culture, and identity* (pp. 157–180). Westport, CT: Praeger.

Lankshear, C. (1986). Foreword. In P. McLaren, *Schooling as a ritual performance: Towards a political economy of educational symbols and gestures* (pp. viii–xxii). New York: Routledge.

Larsen, N. (1997, 1929). *Passing.* New York: Penguin Books.

Leder, D. (1990). *The absent body.* Chicago: University of Chicago Press.

Lee, J. (1999). Disciplining theater and drama in the English department: Some reflections on "performance" and institutional history. *Text and Performance Quarterly* 19: 145–158.

Lee, W. (2003). Kuaering queer theory: My autocritography and a race conscious, womanist, transnational turn. In G. A. Yep, K. E. Lovaas, and J. P. Elia (Eds.), *Queer theory and communication: From disciplining queers to queering the discipline(s)* (pp. 147–170). Harrington Park, UK: Haworth.

Lefebvre, H. (1991). *Production of space,* tr. D. Nicholson Smith. Oxford: Blackwell.

Leff, M. and Sachs, A. (1990). Words the most like things: Iconicity and the rhetorical text. *Western Journal of Speech Communication* 54: 252–273.

Leistyna, P., A. Woodrum and S. Sherblom (Eds.). (1996). *Breaking free: The transformative power of critical pedagogy.* Cambridge, MA: Harvard Educational Review, Reprint Series no. 27.

Levi, P. (1988). *The drowned and the saved,* tr. R. Rosenthal. New York: Summit Books.

Lewis-Beck, M. S., A. E. Bryman and F. Liao (Eds.). (2003). *Sage encyclopedia of social science research methods.* Thousand Oaks, CA: Sage.

Lipman, M., A. M. Sharp and F. S. Oscanyan (Eds.). (1980). *Philosophy in the classroom*, 2nd edition. Philadelphia: Temple University Press.

Lockford, L. (2002). Performing the abject body: A feminist refusal of disempowerment. *The Theatre Annual* 55: 48–60.

Loeb, M. C. (1996). Family storytelling performances and the manifestation and maintenance of the family culture: Spinning the family fiber. Unpublished dissertation, Southern Illinois University, Carbondale.

Longress, J. F. (Ed.). (1996). *Men of color: A context for service to homosexually active men.* New York: Harrington Park.

Lott, E. (1996). Blackface and blackness: The minstrel show in American culture. In A. Bean, J. V. Hatch and B. McNamara (Eds.), *Inside the minstrel mask: Readings in nineteenth-century blackface minstrelsy* (pp. 1–32). Hanover, NH: University Press of New England.

Loughlin, K. A. (1993). *Women's perceptions of transformative learning within consciousness-raising.* San Francisco: Mellen Research University Press.

Lukerman, F. (1964). Geography as a formal intellectual discipline and the way in which it contributes to human knowledge. *Canadian Geographer* 8: 170.

Lusane, C. (1996). Foreword. In J. Anner (Ed.), *Beyond identity politics: Emerging social justice movements in communities of color* (pp. 1–4). Boston: South End.

Lynch, J. (2001). *Latin America between colony and nation: Selected essays.* Houndmills, UK, and New York: Palgrave.

Lyotard, J. (1984). *The postmodern condition: A report on knowledge*, tr. G. Bennington and B. Massouri. Minneapolis: University of Minnesota Press.

MacAloon, J. J. (1984). *Rite, drama, festival, spectacle: Rehearsals toward a theory of cultural performance.* Philadelphia: Institute for the Study of Human Issues.

MacCannell, D. (1976). *The tourist: A new theory of the leisure class.* New York: Schocken.

MacEachren, A. M., Butterfield, B. P., Campbell, J. B., DiBiase, D. W. and Monmonier, M. (1992). Visualization. In R. F. Abler, M. G. Marcus and J. M. Olson (Eds.), *Geography's inner worlds: Pervasive themes in contemporary American geography* (pp. 99–137). New Brunswick, NJ: Rutgers University Press.

Madhubuti, H. R. (1991). *Black men: Obsolete, single, dangerous? The Afrikan American family in transition: Essays in discovery, solution, and hope.* Chicago: Third World Press.

Madison, D. S. (1993). That was my occupation: Oral narrative, performance, and black feminist thought. *Text and Performance Quarterly* 13: 213–232.

Madison, D. S. (1998). Performance, personal narrative, and the politics of possibility. In S. J. Dailey (Ed.), *The future of performance studies: Visions and revisions* (pp. 276–286). Annandale, VA: National Communication Association.

Madison, D. S. (1999). Performing theory/embodied writing. *Text and Performance Quarterly* 19: 107–124.

Madison, D. S. (2005). *Critical ethnography: Method, ethics, and performance.* Thousand Oaks, CA: Sage.

Maher, F. A. and Tetreault, M. K. T. (1994). *The feminist classroom.* New York: Basic.

Maines, D. R. (1978a). Structural parameters and negotiated orders: Comments on Benson, Daly, and Day. *The Sociological Quarterly* 19.3: 491–496.

Maines, D. R. (1978b). Bodies and selves: Notes on a fundamental dilemma in demography. *Studies in Symbolic Interaction* 1: 241–265.

Maines, D. R. (1989). Culture and temporality. *Cultural Dynamics* 2.1: 107–123.

Maines, D. R. (1993). Narrative's moment and sociology's phenomena: Toward a narrative sociology. *The Sociological Quarterly* 34.1: 17–38.

Maines, D. R. (1999a). Information pools and racialized narrative structures. *The Sociological Quarterly* 40.2: 217–326.

Maines, D. R. (1999b). Interpreting the self: Two hundred years of American autobiography. *American Journal of Sociology* 105.3: 880–883.

Maines, D. R. (2000). The social construction of meaning. *Contemporary Sociology* 29.2: 577–584.

Maines, D. R. (2001a). *The faultline of consciousness: A view of interactionism in sociology.* New York: Aldine De Gruyter.

Maines, D. R. (2001a). Narrative, gender, and the problematics of role. In *The faultline of consciousness: A view of interactionism in sociology* (pp. 173–186). New York: Aldine De Gruyter.

Maines, D. R. (2001a). Narrative structures and incest. In *The faultline of consciousness: A view of interactionism in sociology* (pp. 187–204). New York: Aldine De Gruyter.

Maines, D. R. (2001b). Conceptual modeling as a toolbox for grounded theorists. *The Sociological Quarterly* 42.2: 253–269.

Maines, D. R. (2001c). Writing the self versus writing the other: Comparing autobiographical and life history data. *Symbolic Interaction* 24.2: 105–111.

Maines, D. R. and C. J. Couch (Eds.). (1998). On the indispensibility of communication for understanding social relationships and social structure. *Communication and social structure* (pp. 3–18). Springfield, IL: Thomas.

Maines, D. R. and McCallion, M. J., (2000). Urban inequality and the possibilities of church-based intervention. In N. K. Denzin (Ed.), *Studies in symbolic interaction* (pp. 43–53). Stamford, CT: JAI.

Mair, L. P. (1965). *An introduction to anthropology.* Oxford: Clarendon Press.

Majors, R. and Billson, J. M. (1992). *Cool pose: The dilemmas of black manhood in America.* New York: Simon and Schuster.

Mallett, S. (2003). Colonial impregnations. In *Conceiving cultures: Reproducing people and places on Nuakata, Papua New Guinea* (pp. 65–102). Ann Arbor: University of Michigan Press.

Manning, F. E. (1992). Spectacle. In R. Bauman (Ed.), *Folklore, cultural performances, and popular entertainments: A communications-centered handbook* (pp. 291–299). Oxford: Oxford University Press.

Marcus, G. E. (1994). What comes (just) after "Post"? The case of ethnography. In N. K. Denzin and Y. S. Lincoln (Eds.), *The handbook of qualitative research* (pp. 563–574). Thousand Oaks, CA: Sage.

Margulies, I. (1993). Delaying the cut: The space of performance in *Lightning over water*. *Screen* 34: 54–68.

Martin, A. (1993). Keynote address: "The power of performance." In F. C. Corey (Ed.), *HIV education: Performing personal narratives* (pp. xii–xvii). Proceedings of a conference funded by the U.S. Centers for Disease Control and Prevention and Arizona State University. Tempe, AZ.

Martin, R. (1998). Staging crisis: Twin tales in moving politics. In P. Phelan and J. Lane (Eds.), *The ends of performance* (pp. 186–196). New York: New York University Press.

Marx, K. (1954/1867). *Capital.* Volume 1: *A critical analysis of capital production.* Moscow: Progress.

Mastalia, F. and Pagano, A. (1999). *DREADS.* New York: Artisan Press.

Mathieson, A. and Wall, G. (1982). *Tourism: Economics, physical and social impacts.* London: Longman Chesire.

Matthews, H. G. (1978). *International tourism: A political and social analysis.* Cambridge, MA: Schienkman.

Matthews, K. (2000). We fall down. In *D. McClurkin: Live in London and More.* New York: Zomba Recording Corporation.

May, R. A. B. (2003). "Flirting with boundaries": A professor's narrative tale contemplating research of the wild side. *Qualitative Inquiry* 9.3: 442–465.

McArthur, T. (Ed.). (1992). *The Oxford companion to the English language.* Oxford: Oxford University Press.

McDowell, A. (1998). The art of the ponytail. In O. Edut (Ed.), *Adiós, Barbie: Young women write about body image and identity.* Seattle, WA: Seal.

McGee, M. C. (1990). Text, context, and the fragmentation of contemporary culture. *Western Journal of Speech Communication* 54: 274–289.

McGreevy, P. (2001). Attending to the void: Geography and madness. In P. C. Adams, S. Hoelscher and K. E. Till (Eds.), *Textures of place: Exploring humanist geographies* (pp. 246–256). Minneapolis: University of Minnesota Press.

McIntosh, P. (1997). White privilege and male privilege: A personal account of

coming to see correspondences through work in women's studies. In R. Delgado and J. Stefancic (Eds.), *Critical white studies: Looking behind the mirror*
(pp. 291–299). Philadelphia: Temple University Press.

McLaren, P. (1993). *Schooling as a ritual performance: Towards a political economy
of educational symbols and gestures*. New York: Routledge.

McLaren, P. (1998). *Life in school: An introduction to critical pedagogy in the foundations of education*, 3rd edition. New York: Longman.

McLaren, P. (1999). Unthinking whiteness, rethinking democracy: Critical citizenship in gringolandia. In C. Clark and J. O'Donnell (Eds.), *Becoming and
unbecoming white: Owning and disowning a racial identity* (pp. 10–55). Westport, CT: Bergin and Garvey.

McLaren, P. and Lankshear, C. (1994). *Politics of liberation: Paths from Freire.* New
York: Routledge.

McRoberts, O. (1996). Song for father. In D. J. Wideman and R. B. Preston (Eds.),
Soulfires: Young black men on love and violence (pp. 250–253). New York: Penguin.

Medina, C. (2002). A dialogue on the sublime: A conversation with Daniel J. Mar-
tinez. *Camerawork* 229.2: 18–23.

Mercer, K. (1992). "1968": Periodizing politics and identity. In L. Grossberg, C.
Nelson and P. Treichler (Eds.), *Cultural studies* (pp. 424–438). New York:
Routledge.

Mercer, K. (1994). *Welcome to the jungle: New positions in black cultural studies.*
New York: Routledge.

Meyer, M. (1994). *The politics and poetics of camp.* New York: Routledge.

Miles, R. (1988). "Racialization." In E. Cashmore (Ed.), *Dictionary of race and
ethnic relations*, 2nd edition (pp. 246–247). London: Routledge.

Miller, J. A. (1977–1978). Suture (Elements of the logic of the signifier). *Screen*
18.4: 24–34.

Miller, L. C. (2000). Gertrude Stein never enough. *Text and Performance Quarterly*
20: 43–57.

Miller, L. C. and Taylor, J. (1997). Introduction. *Text and Performance Quarterly*
17: v–vi.

Miller, L. C., Taylor, J. and Carver, M. H. (2003). *Voices made flesh: Performing
women's autobiography*. Madison: University of Wisconsin Press.

Miller, T. (2002). *Body blows: Six performance (Living out: Gay and lesbian autobiographies)*. Madison: University of Wisconsin Press.

Mitchell-Kernan, C. (1973). Signifying as a form of verbal. In A. Dundes (Ed.),
*Mother wit from the laughing barrel: Readings in the interpretation of Afro-
American folklore* (pp. 310–328). Englewood Cliffs, NJ: Prentice-Hall.

Mohanty, S. P. (1989). Us and them: On the philosophical bases of political criticism. *Yale Journal of Criticism* 2.2: 1–31.

Moon, D. G. (1998). Performed identities: "Passing" as an inter/cultural discourse. In J. N. Martin, T. K. Nakayama and L. A. Flores (Eds.), *Readings in cultural contexts*. Mt. View, CA: Mayfield.

Moon, D. G. (1999). White enculturation and bourgeois ideology: The discursive production of "Good (white) girls." In T. K. Nakayama and J. M. Martin (Eds.), *Whiteness: The communication of social identity* (pp. 177–197). Thousand Oaks, CA: Sage.

Moraga, C. and G. Anzaldúa (Eds.). (1981). *This bridge called my back: Writings by radical women of color*. New York: Kitchen Table—Women of Color.

Morner, K. and Rausch, R. (1992). *NTC's dictionary of literary terms*. Chicago, IL: National Textbook Company.

Morris, W. (Ed.). (1972). *New college edition: The American heritage dictionary of the English language*. Vol. 1. Boston: Houghton Mifflin.

Morrison, T. (1972). *Playing in the dark: Whiteness and the literary imagination*. Cambridge, MA: Harvard University Press.

Morrison, T. (1992). *Race-ing justice, engendering power: Essays on Anita Hill, Clarence Thomas, and the construction of social reality*. New York: Pantheon Books.

Morrow, B. and C. H. Rowell (Eds.). (1996). *Shade: An anthology of fiction by gay men of African descent*. New York: Avon.

Morson, G. S. (1981). *The boundaries of genre: Dostoevsky's "diary of a writer" and the traditions of literary utopia*. Austin: University of Texas Press.

Mostern, K. (1999). *Autobiography and black identity politics: Racialization in twentieth-century America*. Cambridge, UK: Cambridge University Press.

Muñoz, J. E. (1999). *Disidentifications: Queers of color and the performance of politics*. Minneapolis: University of Minnesota Press.

Munro, R. (1997). Introduction. In K. Hetherington and R. Munro (Eds.), *Ideas of difference* (pp. 3–24). Malden, MA: Blackwell.

Nakayama, T. K. and Corey, F. C. (2003). Nextext. In G. A. Yep, K. E. Lovaas and J. P. Elia (Eds.), *Queer theory and communication: From disciplining queers to queering the discipline(s)* (pp. 319–334). New York: Harrington Park.

Nast, H. J. and S. Pile (Eds.). (1998). *Places through the body*. New York: Routledge.

Neckerman, K. M., Carter, P. and Lee, J. (1999). Segmented assimilation and minority cultures of mobility. *Ethnic and Racial Studies* 22: 945–965.

Nero, C. I. (1992). Fixing ceremonies: An introduction. In E. Hemphill, *Ceremonies* (pp. xi–xiii). San Francisco: Cleis.

Nero, C. I. (1997). Black queer identity, imaginative rationality, and the language of home. In A. Gonzalez, M. Houston and V. Chen (Eds.), *Our voices: Essays in culture, ethnicity, and communication* (pp. 61–67). Los Angeles, CA: Roxbury.

Neumann, M. (1999). *On the rim: Looking for the grand canyon*. Minneapolis: University of Minnesota Press.

Newsweek, April 12, 2004.

Noblit, G. W., Flores, S. Y. and Murillo, E. G., Jr. (2004). Postcritical ethnography: An introduction. In G. W. Noblit, S. Y. Flores and E. G. Murillo Jr. (Eds.), *Postcritical ethnography: Reinscribing critique* (pp. 1–52). Cresskill, NJ: Hampton.

Norton, W. (2000). *Cultural geography: Themes, concepts, and analyses*. Ontario, Canada: Oxford University Press.

Oakeshott, M. (1962). *Rationalism in politics, and other essays*. New York: Basic.

Olwig, K. F. (1997). Cultural sites: Sustaining a home in a deterritorialized world. In K. F. Olwig and K. Hastrup (Eds.), *Siting culture: The shifting anthropological object* (pp. 17–38). New York: Routledge.

Olwig, K. R. (2001). Landscape as a contested topos of place, community, and self. In P. C. Adams, S. Hoelscher and K. E. Till (Eds.), *Textures of place: Exploring humanist geographies* (pp. 93–117). Minneapolis: University of Minnesota Press.

Park-Fuller, L. (1995). Narration and narratization of a cancer story: Composing and performing "A clean breast of it." *Text and Performance Quarterly* 15: 60–67.

Park-Fuller, L. (2000). Performing absence: The staged personal narrative as testimony. *Text and Performance Quarterly* 20.1: 20–42.

Park-Fuller, L. and Olsen, T. (1983). Understanding what we know: Yonnondio: From the thirties. *Literature in Performance* 4: 65–77.

Parker, A. and E. K. Sedgwick (Eds.). (1992). *Performativity and performance*. London: Routledge.

Patton, M. Q. (2001). *Qualitative research and evaluation methods*. Thousand Oaks, CA: Sage.

Pelias, R. (1999). *Performance studies: The interpretation of aesthetic texts*. Dubuque, IA: Kendal/Hunt.

Pelias, R. and VanOosting, J. (1987). A paradigm for performance studies. *Quarterly Journal of Speech* 73: 219–231.

Peters, M. and Lankshear, C. (1994). Education and hermeneutics: A Freirean interpretation. In P. McLaren and C. Lankshear (Eds.), *Politics of liberation: Paths from Freire* (pp. 172–193). New York: Routledge.

Phelan, P. (1993). *Unmarked: The politics of performance*. New York: Routledge.

Phelan, P. (1997). *Mourning sex: Performing public memories.* New York: Routledge.

Pinar, W. F. (1994). Autobiography and an architecture of self. In W. F. Pinar (Ed.), *Autobiography, politics and sexuality: Essays in curriculum theory 1972–1992* (pp. 201–222). New York: Lang.

Pineau, E. L. (1992). A Mirror of her own: Anaïs Nin's autobiographical performances. *Text and Performance Quarterly* 12: 97–112.

Pineau, E. L. (2000). Nursing mother and articulating absence. *Text and Performance Quarterly* 20.1: 1–19.

Pineau, E. L. (2001). Engraving the silver spoon: A critical calligraphy of privilege. In L. C. Miller and R. J. Pelias (Eds.), *The green window: Proceeding of the giant city conference on performative writing* (pp. 66–77). Carbondale: Southern Illinois University.

Pollock, D. (1990). Telling the told: Performing like a family. *Oral History* 18: 1–36.

Pollock, D. (Ed.). (1998a). *Exceptional Spaces: Essays in Performance and History.* Chapel Hill: University of North Carolina Press.

Pollock, D. (1998b). Performative writing. In P. Phelan and J. Lane (Eds.), *The ends of performance* (pp. 73–103). New York: New York University Press.

Pollock, D. (1999). *Telling bodies/performing birth.* New York: Columbia University Press.

Pollock, S. (2001). India in the vernacular millennium: Literary culture and polity. In S. N. Eisenstadt, W. Schluchter and B. Wittrock (Eds.), *Public spheres and collective identities* (pp. 41–74). New Brunswick, NJ: Transaction.

Posnock, R. (1998). *Color and culture: Black writers and the making of the modern intellectual.* Cambridge, MA: Harvard University Press.

Puwar, N. (2004). *Space invaders: Race, gender, and bodies out of place.* Oxford: Berg.

Rabinow, P. (1986). Representations are social facts: Modernity and post-modernity in anthropology. In J. Clifford and G. E. Marcus (Eds.), *Writing culture: The poetics and politics of ethnography* (pp. 234–261). Berkeley: University of California Press.

Ramer, A. (1998). Keynote address. First Annual Celebrating Gay Spirit Visions Conference. Highlands, NC. Available at www.mindspring.com/~gayspirit/key_1990.htmramer.

Reed-Danahay, D. E. (Ed.). (1997). *Auto/ethnography: Rewriting the self and the social.* Oxford: Berg.

Relph, E. (2001). The critical description of confused geographies. In P. C. Adams, S. Hoelscher, K. E. Till (Eds.), *Textures of place: Exploring humanist geographies* (pp. 150–166). Minneapolis: University of Minnesota Press.

Rich, A. (1994). If not with others. In J. Beaty and J. P. Hunter (Eds.), *New worlds of literature: Writings from America's many cultures* (pp. 786–791). New York: Norton.

Rich, M. (2001). Painful stories from camp Anuenue: Enactment and reenactment. *Text and Performance Quarterly* 21: 128–143.

Richmond, J. and McCroskey, J. C. (1992). *Power in the classroom: Communication, control, and concern.* Hillsdale, NJ: Erlbaum.

Rivage-Seul, M. K. and Rivage-Seul, D. M. (1994). Critical thought and moral imagination: Peace education in Freirean perspective. In P. L. McLaren and C. Lankshear (Eds.), *Politics of liberation: Paths from Freire* (pp. 41–61). New York: Routledge.

Roach, J. R. (1992). Introduction. In J. G. Reinelt and J. R. Roach (Eds.), *Critical theory and performance* (pp. 9–15). Ann Arbor: University of Michigan Press.

Román, D. (1998). *Acts of intervention: Performance, gay culture, and AIDS.* Bloomington: Indiana University Press.

Rose, D. (1990). *Living the ethnographic life.* Newbury Park, CA: Sage.

Roy, P. (1995). As the master saw her. In S. E. Case, P. Brett and S. Foster (Eds.), *Cruising the performative: Intervention into the representation of ethnicity, nationality, and sexuality* (pp. 112–129). Bloomington: Indiana University Press.

Ruff, S. S. (Ed.). (1996). *Go the way your blood beats: An anthology of lesbian and gay fiction by African-American writers.* New York: Henry Holt.

Said, E. W. (1994a). *Culture and imperialism.* New York: Vintage.

Said, E. W. (1994b). *Representation of the intellectual: The 1993 Reith lectures.* New York: Vintage.

Salas, E. (2004, Fall). Know your feminist faculty: Bryant Alexander. *LOUDMOUTH* 7: 5.

Sandelowski, M. (1994). The proof is in the pottery: Toward a poetic for qualitative inquiry. In J. M. Morse (Ed.), *Critical issues in qualitative research method* (pp. 46–63). Thousand Oaks, CA: Sage.

Sanyal, D. (2002). A Soccer match in Auschwitz: Passing culpability in holocaust criticism. *Representation* 79: 1–27.

Saukko, P. (2003). *Doing research in cultural studies.* Thousand Oaks, CA: Sage.

Schacht, S. P. (2000). Using a feminist pedagogy as a male teacher: The possibilities of a partial and situated perspective. *Radical Pedagogy*: 1–19 (an online journal), at radicalpedagogy.icaap.org/content/issue2_2/schacht.html.

Schechner, R. (1985). *Between theater and anthropology.* Philadelphia: University of Pennsylvania Press.

Schechner, R. (1988). *Performance theory: Revised and expanded edition.* New York: Routledge.

Schutzman, M. (1998). A fool's discourse: The buffoonery syndrome. In P. Phelan and J. Lane (Eds.), *The ends of performance* (pp. 131–148). New York: New York University Press.

Schutzman, M. (1999). *The real thing: Performance, hysteria, and advertising.* Hanover, NH: University Press of New England.

Schutzman, M. and J. Choen-Cruz (Eds.). (1994). *Playing Boal: Theatre, therapy, activism.* New York: Routledge.

Scott, J. U. (1963). *The art of being a girl.* Philadelphia: Macrae Smith.

Shacochis, S. B. (2001). Writing for revenge. In M. R. Waldman (Ed.), *The spirit of writing: Classic and contemporary essays celebrating the writing life* (pp. 14–16). New York: Penguin.

Shields, R. (1996). Meeting or mis-meeting? The dialogical challenge to Verstehen. *British Journal of Sociology* 47.2: 36–45.

Shields, R. (2004). Glimpsing the future: Articulating change and potential in the city. A paper presented at the 5th International Crossroads in Cultural Studies Conference, June 25–28. University of Illinois, Urbana-Champaign.

Sieg, K. (1995). Deviance and dissidence: Sexual subjects of the Cold War. In S. Case, P. Brett and S. L. Foster (Eds.),*Cruising the performative: Intervention into the representation of ethnicity, nationality and sexuality* (pp. 93–111). Bloomington: Indiana University Press.

Silverman, H. J. (Ed.). (1998). Introduction. *Cultural semiosis: Tracing the signifier* (pp. 1–19). New York: Routledge.

Silverman, K. (1992). *Male subjectivity at the margins.* New York: Routledge.

Simon, R. (1992). *Teaching against the grain: Texts for a pedagogy of possibility.* New York: Monthly Review.

Singer, M. (Ed.). (1959). *Traditional India: Structure and change.* Philadelphia: American Folklore Society.

Singer, M. (1992). *When a great tradition modernizes.* New York: Praeger.

Sisterlocks, at www.sisterlocks.com.

Smith, C. (1999). My dreads cannot be ignored. In F. Mastalia and A. Pagano (Eds.), *DREADS* (p. 45). New York: Artisan Press.

Smith, D. E. (2002). A feminist methodology. In B. Highmore (Ed.), *The everyday life reader* (pp. 271–281). London: Routledge.

Smitherman, G. (1994). *Black talk: Words and phrases from the hood to the amen corner.* Boston: Houghton Mifflin.

Snead, J. (1990). European pedigrees/African contagions: Nationality, narrative, and communality in Tutuola, Achebe, and Reed. In H. K. Bhabha (Ed.), *Nation and narration* (pp. 232–249). New York: Routledge.

Spangler, M. (2002). "A fadograph of a yestern scene": Performance promising authenticity in Dublin's Bloomsday. *Text and Performance Quarterly* 22.2: 120–137.

Sparke, M. (1998). Mapped bodies and disembodied maps: (Dis)placing cartographic struggle in colonial Canada. In H. J. Nast and S. Pile (Eds.), *Places through the body* (pp. 305–336). New York: Routledge.

Speer, J. H. (1992). Performance as meaning in a mountain folklore. In E. Fine and J. H. Speer (Eds.), *Performance, culture and identity* (pp. 117–134). Westport, CT: Praeger.

Spradley, J. P. and McCurdy, D. W. (1972). *The cultural experience: Ethnography in complex society.* Prospect Heights, IL: Waveland.

Spry, T. (1997). Skins: A daughter's (re)construction of cancer: A performative autobiography. *Text and Performance Quarterly* 17.4: 361–365.

Stecopoulos, H. and M. Uebel (Eds.). (1997). *Race and the subject of masculinity.* Durham, NC: Duke University Press.

Steel, S. (1990). *The content of our character: A new vision of race in America.* New York: St. Martin's.

Stern, C. S. and Henderson, B. (1993). *Performance: Texts and contexts.* New York: Longman.

Stocking, G. W. (Ed.). (1983). *Observers observed: Ethnographic fieldwork. History of anthropology.* Madison: University of Wisconsin Press.

Stone, L. (Ed.). (1994). *The education feminism reader.* New York: Routledge.

Strain, E. (2003). *Public places/private journeys: Ethnography, entertainment, and the tourist gaze.* New Brunswick, NJ: Rutgers University Press.

Strine, M., Long, B. and Hopkins, M. F. (1991). Research in interpretation and performance studies: Trends, issues, and practices. In G. Phillips and J. Wood (Eds.), *Speech communication: Essays to commemorate the 75th anniversary of the Speech Communication Association* (pp. 181–201). Carbondale: Southern Illinois University Press.

Tannen, M. (2001). The braided bunch: Identity politics or fashion? What does it matter? *The New York Times Magazine,* May 20, 76–77.

Taylor, D. (1994). Opening remarks. In D. Taylor and J. Villegas (Eds.), *Negotiating performance: Gender, sexuality, and theatricality in Latina/o America* (p. 14). Durham, NC: Duke University Press.

Taylor, J. (1987). Documenting performance knowledge: Two narrative techniques in Grace Paley's fiction. *Southern Speech Communication Journal* 53: 67–79.

Thayer-Bacon, B. (2002). *Relational epistemologies.* New York: Lang.

Thomson, R. G. (2005). Dares to stares: Disabled women performance artists and the dynamics of staring. In C. Sandahl and P. Auslander (Eds.), *Bodies in com-*

REFERENCES 247

motion: Disability and performance (pp. 30–41). Ann Arbor: University of
Michigan Press.

Thornham, S. (1998). Rereading difference(s) 2: Race, representation, and feminist theory. In *Passionate detachment: An introduction to feminist film theory* (pp. 137–157). New York: St. Martin's.

Tilley, C. A. (1994). *A phenomenology of landscape: Places, paths, and movements.* Oxford: Berg.

Tuan, Yi-Fu. (1974). Space and place: Humanistic perspective. *Progress in Geography* 6: 211–252.

Tuan, Yi-Fu. (1996). *Cosmos and hearth: A cosmopolite's viewpoint.* Minneapolis: University of Minnesota Press.

Turner, V. (1967). *The forest of symbols: Aspects of Ndembu ritual.* Ithaca, NY: Cornell University Press.

Turner, V. (1969). *The ritual process: Structure and anti-structure.* Chicago: Aldine.

Turner, V. (1977). Variations on a theme of liminality. In S. F. Moore and B. G. Myerhoff (Eds.), *Secular ritual* (pp. 36–52). Assen and Amsterdam: Van Gorcum.

Turner, V. (1982). *From ritual to theatre.* New York: PAJ.

Turner, V. (1988). Images and reflections: Ritual, drama, carnival, film, and spectacle in cultural performance. *The anthropology of performance* (pp. 65–88). New York: PAJ.

Turner, V. (1988). *The anthropology of performance.* New York: PAJ.

Tyler, S. (1987). *The unspeakable: Discourse, dialogue, and rhetoric in the postmodern world.* Madison: University of Wisconsin Press.

Urry, J. (1990, 2002). *The tourist gaze.* London: Sage.

Vance, E. (1979). Roland and the poetics of memory. In J. V. Harari (Ed.), *Textual strategies: Perspectives in post-structuralist criticism* (pp. 374–403). Ithaca: Cornell University Press.

Van Erven, E. (1993). *The playful revolution: Theatre and liberation in Asia.* Bloomington: Indiana University Press.

Van Gennep, A. (1960). *The rites of passage.* Chicago: University of Chicago Press.

Van Maanen, J. (1988). *Tales of the field: On writing ethnography.* Chicago: University of Chicago Press.

Van Maanen, J. (1990). Great moments in ethnography: An editor's introduction. *Journal of Contemporary Ethnography* 19: 3–7.

Van Maanen, J. (1995). *Representation in ethnography.* Thousand Oaks, CA: Sage.

Vélez-Ibáñez, C. G. (1996). *Border visions: Mexican cultures of the southwest United States.* Tucson: University of Arizona Press.

Volcano, D. L. and Halberstam, J. (1999). *The drag king.* London: Serpent's Tail.

Wald, P. (1998). Minefields and meeting grounds: Transnational analyses and American studies. *American Literary History* 10: 199–218.

Wallace, M. O. (2002). *Constructing the black masculine: Identity and ideality in African American men's literature and culture, 1775–1995.* Durham, NC: Duke University Press.

Weems, C. M. (1996). One million men committed to black families. In M. H. Cottman and D. Willis (Eds.), *The family of black America* (pp. 9–12). New York: Crown.

Wellman, D. (1999). Transforming received categories: Discovering cross-border identities and other subversive activities. In C. Clark and J. O'Donnell (Eds.), *Becoming and unbecoming white: Owning and disowning a racial identity* (pp. 78–91). Westport, CT: Bergin and Garvey.

West, C. (1991). The dilemma of the black intellectual. In b. hooks and C. West (Eds.), *Breaking bread: Insurgent black intellectual life* (pp. 131–146). Boston: South End.

West, C. (1993). *Race matters.* New York: Vintage.

"When Teaching Works: Stories of Communication in Education." Special Issue of *Communication Education* 42.4 (1993).

White, L. E. (2001). Autobiography as performative identity construction: The fragmented subjectivities of Charlotte Salmon. *Text and Performance Quarterly* 21.2: 77–94.

White, S. and White, G. (1998). *Stylin': African American expressive culture from its beginnings to the zoot suit.* Ithaca, NY: Cornell University Press.

Whitehead, S. M. (2002). *Men and masculinities.* Cambridge: Polity Press.

Wideman, J. E. (2001). Foreword. *Every tongue got to confess: Negro folk-tales from the gulf states* (pp. xi–xx). New York: HarperCollins.

Wiggens, D. (1967). *Identity and spatio-temporal continuity.* Oxford, UK: Black-well.

Williams, L. (2001). Posing as black, passing as white: The melos of black and white melodrama in the jazz age. *Playing the race card: Melodramas of black and white from Uncle Tom to O. J. Simpson* (pp. 136–186). Princeton, NJ: Princeton University Press.

Williams, M. (2001). Braids for a bargain in a battle for heads. *The New York Times,* May 19, A13.

Williams, R. (1973). Base and superstructure in Marxist cultural theory. *New Left Review* 82: 3–16.

Williams, R. (1980). *Problems in materialism and culture.* London: Verso.

Williams, R. (2002). Culture is ordinary. In B. Highmore (Ed.), *The everyday life reader* (pp. 91–100). London: Routledge.

Willie, S. S. (2003). *Acting black: College, identity, and the performance of race*. New York: Brunner-Routledge.

Wilson, A. (1995). Foreword. In D. Belton (Ed.), *Speak my name* (pp. xi-xii). Boston: Beacon.

Wolcott, H. F. (1999). *Ethnography: A way of seeing*. Walnut Creek, CA: Alta Mira Press.

Wolf, M. (1992). *A thrice told tale: Feminism, postmodernism, and ethnographic responsibility*. Stanford, CA: Stanford University Press.

Woodward, D. (1992). Representations of the world. In R. F. Abler, M. G. Marcus and J. M. Olson (Eds.), *Geography's inner worlds: Pervasive themes in contemporary American geography* (pp. 50–73). New Brunswick, NJ: Rutgers University Press.

Woods, J. T. (2003). *Gendered lives: Communication, gender, and culture*. 5th edition. Belmont, CA: Wadsworth.

Woodside, A. (2001). Territorial order and collective-identity tensions in Confucian Asia: China, Vietnam, Korea. In S. N. Eisenstadt, W. Schluchter and B. Wittrock (Eds.), *Public spheres and collective identities* (pp. 191–220). New Brunswick, NJ: Transaction.

Wright, M. M. (2004). *Becoming black: Creating identity in the African diaspora*. Durham, NC: Duke University Press.

Yalom, M. (1990). Biography as autobiography: Adele Hugo, witness of her husband's life. In S. G. Bell and M. Yalom (Eds.), *Revealing lives: Autobiography, biography, and gender* (pp. 53–64). New York: State University of New York Press.

Zarilli, P. B. (1992). For whom is the king king? Issues of intercultural production, perception, and reception in a Kathakali *King Lear*. In J. G. Reinelt and J. R. Roach (Eds.), *Critical theory and performance* (pp. 16–40). Ann Arbor: University of Michigan Press.

Index

ambition, 52
Anderson, Benedict, 33, 39
Anscombe, G. E. M., 1
Anzaldúa, Gloria, 51, 91
Aronowitz, Stanley, 96
Arrizon, Alicia, 150
asynchrony, xxi
Austin, J. L., 36
authenticity, 9, 31; and authentication, 194n42; as paradox, 65; as social construction, 66; as trap of, 65
autobiography, xx, 163, 164; autobiographical construct, 170; autobiographical performance, 168; performance of, 166 ; referential (auto)biographical performance, 170–71
autoethnography, xx; as interruption, 27; reflexive auto/ethnography, 2

Baker, Houston, 161, 182
Baker, Roger, 101
Baktin, Mikhail, 82
Barthe, Roland, 120
Bauman, Richard, 7
Bhabha, Homi, xiv, xx, 10, 27
blackness: performative agency, 48; as referential lexicon, 47

Blau, Herbert, xxi
Bly, Robert, 89
Bochner, Art, 181
Bourdieu, Pierre, 6, 25–26
Bowman, Glen, 23
Bowman, Michael, xiii, 190n12
Bryson, Mary, 102, 123
Butler, Judith, 10, 90, 99, 101, 119, 123, 201n23

Campbell, Karyln Kohrs, 168, 171
Carbaugh, Donal, xxi, 196n65
Carleton, Jill M., 166
Caughie, Pamela, 100, 203n1
Cohn, Meryl, 107
community: campus and, 35–38; interpretive, 37; knowable, 37; racialized, 48; views of, 40–67; confessional tale, 2
Conquergood, Dwight, 87, 177
contestation, xvii, 2; contested performance, xiv; cultural, 27; definition of, 189n2
coy texts, 173
Crary, Jonathan, 106
Culler, Jonathan, 65
cultural currency, 136
cultural performance, 22; cultural per-

Gates, Henry Louis, 47, 58
Gathercole, Peter, 24
Gellner, Ernest, 24–25
Gilroy, Paul, 45
Giroux, Henry, 37, 96
Green, Herb, 96
Green, Maxine, xviii, 72
Griffin, Farah Jasmine, 39
Grossberg, Lawrence, xvi, xvii
Guss, David, 144

hair: Black hairstyles, 207n3; dread-
    locks, 77, 135, 149, 193n34, 209n20;
    as sensuous component of human
    materiality, 20
Halberstam, Judith, 101, 117–18
Hall, Stuart, 46, 155
Hamera, Judith, xvi, 212n12
Harper, Phillip Brian, 78
Henderson, Mae G., 173
Hesford, W. S., 99
heterosexual homosociality, 152
heterotropes and homotropes, 119–20
historicity, 5
hooks, bell, 66, 75, 91, 123
Howes, David, 35
hybrid hyphenations, 10

identity: identity politics, xiv; perform-
    ative identities, 70; racialized identi-
    ties, 38
imagined community, 34
interpretive ethnography, 100, 102,
    105; in the classroom, 134; ethic of
    care, 116; subjective positioning,
    132–33; as theory of writing, 204n7

Jackson, Shannon, 87
Jamieson, Kathleen Hall, 168, 171

Kaplan, Ann, xxi, 13
Karamcheti, Indira, 74
Kemp, Amanda Denise, 87

Lacan, Jacques, 120
Larsen, Nella, xxiii, 70, 79
Levi, Primo, 87
liminality, 73, 200n14
looking, 12; in Chinese culture, 26; het-
    erosexual male gaze, 152; racial
    intersubjective looking, 13
Lott, Eric, xiii, 79
Lusane, Clarence, 60

Madison, D. Soyini, xv, 1
Maines, David, 177, 211n5
Manning, Frank, 22, 81
Marx, Karl, 6
masculinity: black masculinity, xv;
    masculine performativity, 75, 84;
    and performance , 76, 84; suspicion
    of black maleness, 78
materiality of bodies, xiv, 4, 5, 10; as
    evidence of difference, 15
McCurdy, David, 104
McDowell, Akkida, 136
McLaren, Peter, 93, 106
McRoberts, Omar, 161
meditated realities, 59
Mercer, Kobena, 36, 135
messy texts, 134
migration narrative, 38
Million Man March, 43
Moraga, Cherrie, 91
Morson, Gary Saul, 82
Myer, Moe, 120

narrative authority, 165
narrative sociology, 210–11n5
Nero, Charles, xx

About the Author

Bryant Keith Alexander received his BA (1985) and MS (1987) in interpersonal and public communication from the now University of Louisiana, Lafayette, and his PhD (1998) in speech communication with an emphasis in performance and pedagogical studies from Southern Illinois University, Carbondale. He is currently the associate dean of the College of Arts and Letters and professor of communication studies—teaching courses in pedagogy and performance cross-listed with the Department of Theatre Arts and Dance at California State University, Los Angeles. His commitment to interdisciplinary work also allowed him to serve as the chair of the Department of Liberal Studies. He has entries in *The Sage Handbook of Qualitative Research* and *The Sage Handbook of Performance Studies*. His publications have appeared in *Cultural Studies↔Critical Methodologies, Qualitative Inquiry, Text and Performance Quarterly, Theatre Topics, Theatre Annual, Communication Quarterly*, and others. He is the recipient of an American Communities Program Fellowship, a National Communication Association Ethnography Division Top Published Essay Award, and a Norman K. Denzin Qualitative Research Award, all for representative essays in this volume.